Revitalising Indigenous Languages

LINGUISTIC DIVERSITY AND LANGUAGE RIGHTS
Series Editor: Dr Tove Skutnabb-Kangas, *Åbo Akademi University, Finland*

Consulting Advisory Board:
François Grin, *Université de Genève, Switzerland*
Kathleen Heugh, *University of South Australia, Adelaide*
Miklós Kontra, *University of Szeged, Hungary*
Robert Phillipson, *Copenhagen Business School, Denmark*

The series seeks to promote multilingualism as a resource, the maintenance of linguistic diversity, and the development of and respect for linguistic human rights worldwide through the dissemination of theoretical and empirical research. The series encourages interdisciplinary approaches to language policy, drawing on sociolinguistics, education, sociology, economics, human rights law and political science, as well as anthropology, psychology and applied language studies.

Full details of all the books in this series and of all our other publications can be found on http://www.multilingual-matters.com, or by writing to Multilingual Matters, St Nicholas House, 31–34 High Street, Bristol BS1 2AW, UK.

Revitalising Indigenous Languages

How to Recreate a Lost Generation

Marja-Liisa Olthuis, Suvi Kivelä and Tove Skutnabb-Kangas

MULTILINGUAL MATTERS
Bristol • Buffalo • Toronto

Library of Congress Cataloging in Publication Data
Olthuis, Marja-Liisa.
Revitalising Indigenous Languages : How to Recreate a Lost Generation/Marja-Liisa Olthuis, Suvi Kivelä and Tove Skutnabb-Kangas.
Linguistic Diversity and Language Rights: 10
Includes bibliographical references.
1. Linguistic minorities. 2. Language maintenance. 3. Language policy. 4. Endangered languages. 5. Language attrition. I. Kivelä, Suvi. II. Skutnabb-Kangas, Tove. III. Title.
P119.315.O58 2013
306.44'94897–dc23 2012044137

British Library Cataloguing in Publication Data
A catalogue entry for this book is available from the British Library.

ISBN-13: 978-1-84769-888-9 (hbk)
ISBN-13: 978-1-84769-887-2 (pbk)

Multilingual Matters
UK: St Nicholas House, 31–34 High Street, Bristol BS1 2AW, UK.
USA: UTP, 2250 Military Road, Tonawanda, NY 14150, USA.
Canada: UTP, 5201 Dufferin Street, North York, Ontario M3H 5T8, Canada.

The policy of Multilingual Matters/Channel View Publications is to use papers that are natural, renewable and recyclable products, made from wood grown in sustainable forests. In the manufacturing process of our books, and to further support our policy, preference is given to printers that have FSC and PEFC Chain of Custody certification. The FSC and/or PEFC logos will appear on those books where full certification has been granted to the printer concerned.

Typeset by Techset
Printed and bound by CPI Group (UK) Ltd, Croydon, CR0 4YY

TOOVLÁŠ UÁPISOLMOOŠ

Kal tun lah ovddii náál.
Jieh tun lah ennuvgin muttum
kyevtlov ivveest.

Mut lii-uv tust
kielâ muttum?
Mon kielânsun
tuu kolgâččij tiervâttid?

SÄMMILÂŠ NÄÄLI

Kukken jo uáinám:
tuste lii sämmilâš nääli.
Tun lah mahtte
uápis olmooš,
veik jiem tieđegin
tuu noomâ.

Mut jiem mun kuittâg
eedâ tuin maiden.
Mun ervidâm:
tun jieh määti
sämikielâ.

A FORMER ACQUAINTANCE

Indeed, you are like before.
You haven't changed so much
in about twenty years.

But have you gone through
a language change?
In what language
should I greet you?

A SAAMI LOOKALIKE

From far away I already see:
you look like a Saami.
You are like
an acquaintance
even if I don't know
your name.

But I won't
say anything to you.
I guess:
you don't speak
Saami.

Matti Morottaja, in *Sápmelaš*, 1983, with the pseudonym Andârâs Roggejävri, translated by Suvi Kivelä and Marja-Liisa Olthuis, 2012

NOTHING

Nothing stays longer
in our souls
than the language we inherit.
It liberates our thoughts
unfolds our mind
and softens our life.

Paulus Utsi (born 1918), 1996: 111, translated by Roland Thorstensson

Contents

Acknowledgements

This book could never have been written without the participation of more or less the entire Aanaar Saami community, along with many other Saami and non-Saami individuals. Our special thanks go to the 17 CASLE (Complementary Aanaar Saami Language Education 2009–2010) graduates. Since the programme, they have been irreplaceable in the Aanaar Saami community, and they have played many important roles during the writing of this book. Lieggâ kijttoseh tijjân puohháid: Varpu Falck, Tuomo Huusko, Anne-Marie Kalla, Pia Kantola, Éva Kelemen, Mari-Anne Kenttämaa, Leena Kiviniemi, Tanja Kyrö, Teija Linnanmäki, Anna Morottaja, Yrjö Musta, Maijukka Pyykkö, Mervi Skopets, Terhi Rantanen, Riitta Vesala and Kaisa Vuolukka. One special graduate, Suvi Kivelä, is one of the authors of this book. *Uážus tii pargo anarâškielâ pyerrin jotkuđ kuhháá ton pyerrin, et kielâ kiävručču já siäiluččij*! May your work continue on behalf of Aanaar Saami (AS) and create new speakers to keep the language alive!

During the long writing process we have wondered whether we should name 17 or 18 CASLE participants. The 18th participant, Anja Kaarret, took part in two courses of the CASLE programme as a student – but she also played a magnificent role as a Master/teacher/leader in the cultural parts of the programme. Anja also helped us in many ways during the writing of this book. *Takkâ tunjin*, Anja!

Mij halijdep kijtteđ puoh tievâsmittemškovliittâs kielâmiäštárijd. Tii puohâi kielâsirdemmohtâ já kulttuuräššitubdâmuš lii merhâšâm ennuv ubâ projektân já uáppeid. We also thank all our Language Masters whose motivation to transmit their language and expertise has meant a lot for CASLE. All of the Masters cooperated in the documentation of the programme, as they were interviewed by CASLE graduate Anne-Marie Kalla.

Our special thanks go to our colleagues Irmeli Moilanen and Annika Pasanen, whose expertise was desperately needed during the CASLE programme. They have also generously helped us to get this book published.

We would like to thank all of the CASLE instructors for playing such important roles: Petter Morottaja, Petra Kuuva, Matti Morottaja, Taarna Valtonen and Annika Pasanen. Marja-Liisa, one of the authors of this book, also acted as an instructor. Marjo-Riitta Mattus was a great help during student selection and during the start-up and end of the programme.

We send our warmest thanks to the teachers of the culture courses: Anja Kaarret, Petter Morottaja, Aslak Saijets and Elsa Väisänen. Sadly, our thanks cannot reach the AS handicrafts Master Aili Maarit Valle in person; she is no longer with us, but we are grateful to her all the same.

We have received valuable help and information from our colleagues at the Saami Parliament, Hannu Kangasniemi and Ulla Aikio-Puoskari. We would also like to thank Katriina Morottaja, Mari Palolahti, Irja Seppänen and Pentti Tarvainen from the municipality of Aanaar for their expertise and kind cooperation during the project. Professor Lea Laitinen kindly shared the language learning experiences she had with her own Language Master in Aanaar some decades ago. Tytti Bräysy was responsible for the maps used in this book. Lee Rodgers helped with many parts of this book to get them into proper English. Ulla Isotalo, Anneli Lappalainen, Ima Aikio-Arianaick and Frode Grønmo have documented parts of the CASLE programme on many occasions. *Takkâ tijjân puohháid*!

Dr Carol Benson accepted the task of doing the final language check of the whole book, in the middle of moving across continents and all her other globetrotting. Few authors have the privilege of working with one of the world's best experts on the topic on the language check. Carol has been thorough, inspiring, and has given masses of content comments, as well as really encouraging small notes on how much she loved lots of passages and details.[1] A big hug of thanks, Carol!

We also want to thank the following people: William H. (Pila) Wilson and Kauanoe Kamanā in Hawai'i for allowing us to quote at length from their article in Info Box 12 (and Teresa McCarty who edited the journal that the article was in); Robert Phillipson for checking some of the English translations in the Info Boxes and the captions in the film *Reborn*; and Saara-Maria Salonen and Niina Siltala for the interviews concerning their personal experiences in the language nest.

We would like to thank the main organisers of CASLE: the Giellagas Institute and the Saami Education Institute. Dr Anni-Siiri Länsman, Professor Veli-Pekka Lehtola, Professor Pekka Sammallahti, university lecturer Ante Aikio, university lecturer Marjatta Jomppanen, Rector Liisa Holmberg and Associate Rector Maritta Mäenpää have been the key people in organising CASLE. Sadly, we miss the initiator of CASLE, Lassi Valkeapää, the former Rector of the Saami Education Institute, enormously. Luckily he was with us at the beginning of the CASLE programme and saw the CASLE students begin their studies in August 2009.

The whole project would not have been a success without *Anarâškielâ servi*, the Aanaar Saami Association. In particular, its two grand old men, Matti Morottaja and Ilmari Mattus, have played many important roles in the CASLE project and have meant a lot to the entire AS revitalisation movement.

The language nest staff of *Anarâškielâ servi* have given us valuable information. CASLE was designed by the project planning group of *Anarâškielâ servi*. *Lieggâ kijttoseh iššeest siärván já eromâšávt tunnui, Matti já Ilmar!*

We would like to thank all of those Saami employers that have guided the CASLE graduates in learning the language of their (new) activities: Aanaar primary school, Saami Radio, *Kielâpiervâl, Kotus* and *Anarâškielâ servi*.

We also thank our former employers: the Institute for the Languages of Finland and YLE.

CASLE as a project would not have been possible without the generous funding of *Suomen Kulttuurirahasto*, the Finnish Cultural Foundation. This funding has made dreams come true, and has also given moral support to the project in many ways. We would also like to thank the Jenny and Antti Wihuri Foundation, the Ministry of Employment and the Economy as well as the University of Tromsø Center for Advanced Study in Theoretical Linguistics and their sub-project Network for Saami Documentation and Revitalisation, funded by NordForsk.

All of us want to thank our families for their support and patience during the writing of this book.

Note from Tove: I would like to thank all of my Saami and other Indigenous friends all over the world who have taught me *so* much and who keep me informed about what is happening to them, their families, their communities and the whole planet. I would also like to thank Marja-Liisa and Suvi for their constructive, fun and efficient cooperation and engagement – you are both fantastic! Thanks for letting me have a peek into these deeply moving experiences in which you were involved.

Note from Marja-Liisa and Suvi: We are especially happy and grateful that Tove joined us in writing this book. Her advice, remarks, experience and wisdom have been invaluable. She has encouraged us and pushed us to move forward when we have really needed her support. Furthermore, she has given us a special perspective that we believe will come through to the reader. That perspective, we hope, raises our AS case to another level where it can be connected with all those thousands of other Indigenous languages and their speakers that are struggling for survival. Tove's decades of extensive, persistent and humane struggle (indeed, combat) for the rights of minority and Indigenous languages receive our deepest respect. We have never met anyone who has such wide networks and contacts reaching out to every corner of the globe. For us, Tove is a role model and a now a dear friend; she has a big heart and a strong spirit, and that combination makes it possible to move mountains.

Note from Marja-Liisa: I would like to thank Suvi for joining as a co-author. I had only a tedious planner's vision of the CASLE programme on my desk and, to be honest, I did not see myself documenting anything at all. I had no idea of how everything worked out in the classroom or in the field from the viewpoint of a student. I had only the reports of the instructors and the written student feedback from each course. I desperately needed a descriptive student view. I think Suvi as a journalist has given a very moving account and a great deal of spirit to this book. Now, after reading the parts that she wrote, I have an idea of how CASLE really worked in practice, and how the graduates experienced the programme. Suvi, *tiedâlii teevstâ čäällim oovtâst tuin lii lamaš hirmâd suotâs. Takkâ tunjin ennuv*!

Note from Suvi: I would like to thank Marja-Liisa for asking me to take part in this project. When Marja-Liisa asked me to start documenting CASLE in written form, I was terrified, but of course I was also deeply honoured by the offer. Trusting Marja-Liisa, who had trusted me, was one of the best decisions I've ever made, but it was one of the hardest too. After I started reflecting on all that I had been through during the CASLE year, it took me several months before I could write anything at all. I felt like I first needed to know everything about the history of the Saami people, as well as about language revitalisation in general. I also felt like I lacked the competence to write anything before really understanding why and how all this was happening today. Luckily Marja-Liisa was very patient, and was able to give me all the time and space that I needed for this process. Her unbelievable talent for seeing the best in people, for trusting them and the future, and for seeing the forest from the trees always helped me to carry on. She reconstructed my faith in the process every time I started to lose it. Therefore I must thank Marja-Liisa not only for her friendly encouragement and understanding but also for holding all the bits and pieces together.

We wish to donate any royalties from the sale of this book to *Anarâškielâ servi*, the Aanaar Saami Association, to contribute to the further revitalisation of the AS language and culture.

This book is dedicated to all Indigenous people in the world. Our message to you is this: revitalise your language!

Note

(1) *Note from Carol:* I am so happy that Marja-Liisa, Suvi and Tove offered me the privilege of reading and commenting on the language (and the content!) of this book, which I think is a huge contribution to the field of language revitalisation as well as generally to our understanding of how multilingual education benefits learners and communities. I am honoured to have been a small part of this process, and I have the utmost admiration and respect not only for the authors but also for all of the participants in this valiant revitalisation process. I wish you all the very best!

1 Introduction

This book has a positive message: it *is* possible to revitalise a seriously endangered language! Instead of people just stating that a language is extremely endangered and feeling sad about it, or merely working to describe and archive it, the language *can* be given new life! New first- as well as second-language speakers and new environments where the languages can be used can emerge. The degree of endangerment can be lowered, even when languages which are numerically very small will of course always remain endangered. This book tells the story of one such language, Aanaar Saami (AS), spoken only in Finland by some 350 speakers today. Others who are interested in numerically small languages may become inspired. It is hard work, though. Dedicated individuals are needed, but in fortunate circumstances even a few people can make a huge difference.

If one puts one's trust in a state to do the job – even a state such as Sweden which superficially seems to support Indigenous and minority languages through signing and ratifying international and regional human rights instruments – a language may disappear before the necessary state measures are put in place. The following quote comes from an official report by the Swedish church entitled *Våga vara minoritet. En rapport om minoritetsrättigheter i Sverige 2012* [*Dare to Be Minority. A Report on Minority Rights in Sweden 2012*]:

> Children's right to learn their minority language is, however, not guaranteed within the Swedish educational system. This poses a serious threat to the survival of the national minority languages and violates the obligations in minority conventions. If this is not corrected immediately, as the Council of Europe has repeatedly urged Sweden to do, there is a grave risk that the acutely endangered minority languages will not survive. This is particularly true for the smaller Saami varieties. (Svenska Kyrkan, 2012: 4, our translation)

Info Box 1 Criticism of Sweden's Current Minority Policies and Practices, gives some more examples of critique from the summary of this Swedish report, especially in the field of education. In Norway the educational rights situation is much better and in Finland it is somewhat better than in

Sweden. Many measures in support of Indigenous languages have been and are being taken in several Latin American countries and in Aotearoa/ New Zealand. Some practical measures to use learners' home languages in education are in place, even if haphazardly, in many countries in Africa and in some Asian countries, especially India and now also in Nepal (see, for example, articles in Skutnabb-Kangas & Heugh, 2012; Skutnabb-Kangas *et al.*, 2009; see also Kosonen, 2009; McCarty, 2012; Rubagumya, 2009; Walter & Benson, 2012). Despite these positive developments, the criticism of Sweden could be applied to more or less every country in the world. Even though most necessary measures are *not* in place in Sweden, however, the educational rights of Indigenous/tribal children as a whole are, in our estimation, better in the three Nordic countries (Finland, Norway and Sweden) than anywhere else in the world.

It is realistic to claim that Indigenous/tribal, minority and minoritised (hereafter ITM) languages are disappearing at a faster rate today than ever before in human history (see Info Box 2 Language Endangerment). *Much more attention is needed if we want the world's almost 7000 spoken languages and many sign languages (nobody knows their number) not only to survive but to develop and prosper – to become 'normalised' in the way AS may be on its way to achieving. Many people agree on this – but what *can* be done?

There are many experiments and suggestions, most of them very small scale. Some of them have been summarised in the chapters and Info Boxes in this book. The references here (and in the very large bibliography at http:// www.tove-skutnabb-kangas.org/en/Tove-Skutnabb-Kangas-Bibliography. html) give further hints. However, the kinds of measures described in this book regarding AS are new and innovative.

According to the 2009 *Ethnologue* count (see Info Box 3 The Situation of the World's Languages) 5348 of the world's 6909 languages had fewer than 100,000 speakers, and 3524 languages had fewer than 10,000 speakers. Many of these languages, especially in Africa, Asia and the Pacific, are still spoken, by both adults and children, and may be transferred to children at least for the next couple of generations. For at least half of them, however, maybe up to 90–95%, this transfer may stop before the end of this century.

Our conviction is that most ITM languages have been and are being killed. They disappear as a result of linguistic and cultural genocide (see Info Box 4 Linguistic and Cultural Genocide in Education), not as a result of any kind of 'natural' language death or as an 'inevitable' result or side-effect of what is called modernisation and/or globalisation. There are people who think that the disappearance of small languages is good. Many people think that both individuals and groups benefit from this language shift, especially economically, and that the small languages are not important, neither for the speakers and their identities, nor for the world in general (see Info Box 5 Ethnic Identity and Language). However, most ITMs who have been able to express their views seem to disagree completely with this opinion. We have collected just a few of their views in Info Box 6 Indigenous Views. Joshua Fishman's (1997) book, *In Praise of the Beloved Language. A Comparative View of Positive Ethnolinguistic Consciousness*, gives many examples. It is very clear to us, from our own experience, worldwide networks and reading, that most of those groups/peoples who are aware of the fact that their languages are endangered and may disappear *do* want to revive and revitalise their languages. They do manifestly *not* want them to disappear.

However, many groups seem to 'wake up' very late. Suddenly they realise that their children no longer speak or even understand the ancestral language. This may come as a surprise to them – somehow they have thought that their languages would of course continue to live forever; it is beyond their imagination that this might not be the case.

Starting a revival or revitalisation process presupposes that the group has enough material and psychological resources for it, including a solid knowledge base and preferably a network of contacts with other revitalisers. Revitalisers can learn from each other, even if all solutions have to be extremely context sensitive. Some basic principles can be deduced, even though there are no one-size-fits-all solutions.

Many of the revival/revitalisation experiments in 'Western' countries have been with languages that have already ceased to be spoken, or languages that have only a few elderly speakers. This will most probably be the situation for most of the endangered languages (regardless of the degree of endangerment – see UNESCO's categories in Info Box 2 Language Endangerment) before the end of this century. At the point when few or no children speak the language, language nests for children with their elders' support have been started in many places, with the Māori in Aotearoa/New Zealand and the Hawai'ians in the USA (who started only a couple of years later) being models for inspiration (see Info Box 7 Language Nests and Info Box 12 Advice From Revitalisation in Hawai'i). Similar nests using the endangered language as a day-care language will probably be started by/for many other endangered languages in the near future. Often the young caretakers in language nests are second-language speakers (i.e. not 'native' speakers) of the language; they work alongside native-speaker elders. Following the language nests, schools or classes with the ITM language as the main medium of teaching may be started (see Info Box 8 Immersion Programmes). Ideally, this could later lead to the endangered language becoming (one of) the mother tongue(s) of the next generation, not only in terms of internal identity but also in terms of at least some other criteria for identifying a mother tongue (see Info Box 9 Mother Tongue Definitions).

However, a serious question that all language revitalisation groups are facing is this: who will be the teachers, the caretakers, those who are language models? In general, where are all those (including parents) who make it possible for children, youth and adults to start or to continue using the language as a normal everyday language of communication, not only in the language nest and the immersion school but in the whole society, including at home?

What can be done if the speakers are mainly young children and elders, if one or two generations of speakers in the middle barely exist? Especially when those professionals who make it possible for new speakers to emerge and those who enable renewed use of the languages in diverse environments are missing?

This was the situation a few years ago for AS, an Indigenous language which is spoken only in Finland. Chapter 3 gives a detailed description of the development of speakers and the various estimates of how many speakers exist today. It is fair to claim that there are approximately 350 speakers of AS at present; this includes both first- and second-language speakers. Thus the language is in the group of the smallest languages in the world.

This book tells the story of what was done to reverse the language shift. How were new speakers created for the missing generations, speakers who were needed within the various professions so that the whole AS community would be able to function much more through the medium of AS?

Obviously a revitalisation process is something that the whole community, both speakers and non-speakers, should ideally participate in. There have been many debates about whether, to what extent, and how outsiders with positive attitudes could and should participate. In the AS case, the measures described in this book were based on several years of earlier mobilisation by the Aanaar Saami that included most of the community at some level. Some people and families, for example the Morottaja family (see p. 66), had already worked for this revitalisation in many capacities, doing almost more than is humanly possible for a few people. Along with Ilmari Mattus, who spoke AS to his son, these two families were for a long time the only AS families where children learned the language as their first language – and one of these children became the main language teacher in the revitalisation project described in this book. Some 'outsiders' (i.e. ethnic Finns, with Finnish as their mother tongue) also participated, and some learned the language (e.g. Annika Pasanen, who knows two Saami languages and who now speaks AS to her own children who are in a language nest; see section 4.5.2 The language nest). However, the creation of and main responsibility for the project described here rested to a large extent with one person, Marja-Liisa Olthuis. She is so far the only Aanaar Saami in the world with a doctorate; her study was about bird and mushroom species names in AS (Olthuis, 2007). Marja-Liisa lives in Rotterdam, The Netherlands, with her Dutch husband, and speaks AS only to their two daughters. She has spent much of her time during recent years in Aanaar, driving the activities described here. She is the primary author of this book.

Suvi Kivelä, a journalist, the second author of this book, is currently a researcher responsible for the Saami Archives in Finland, which were established in 2012 as part of Finland's National Archives services. Of Finnish ancestry, she was one of the 17 professionals who participated in the intensive one-year AS language education that Marja-Liisa created. Suvi's children's grandmother, Nuuvdi Ailâ (her Finnish name is Aili Koskinen), is Aanaar Saami, but she did not speak her language to her own children, meaning that the father of Suvi's children did not learn it. During the project described here, Nuuvdi Ailâ, 81 years old in 2012, started speaking her language again, and now speaks it to her two grandsons. One of them is in an AS language nest and the other attends an AS-medium school (see the video *Reborn*, at http://www.casle.fi). Suvi also now speaks AS to her children.

Tove Skutnabb-Kangas is an outsider who has worked with various Saami colleagues and friends, mainly in Norway and Finland, for some 45 years, but does not know any of the Saami languages (except for reading a little bit of North Saami if it is about her own areas of study). Marja-Liisa and Suvi requested her to write some shorter sections of the book, including this introduction.

As you will notice while reading the book, we have very different styles of writing. Suvi as a journalist writes in a way which flows and is much more fun to read than Marja-Liisa and Tove – we are more boring, with more traditional academic styles and lots of references (especially Tove). We have agreed that Suvi, in addition to providing descriptions, will also write more personal reflections. We hope that this makes the book come alive, and that our different areas of knowledge and styles complement each other.

The distribution of labour in this book has been as follows. Marja-Liisa has mainly been responsible for Chapters/Sections 2.1, 3.1, 4, 5 (Planner's view), 6 and Info Box 17. Suvi has mainly been responsible for Chapters/Sections 2.3, 3.2, 3.3, 3.4, 3.5 and 5 (Student view) and for Info Box 13. Tove has mainly been responsible for Chapter 1 and for all other Info Boxes. All of us have read all the chapters and given extensive feedback to one another, and we all have contributed to the final Chapter 7.

Back to the role of the state. Some of the other Saami languages are spoken in several countries (see p. 30). The revitalisation in Norway, with the largest Saami populations, started in a strong way, somewhat earlier than in Finland. Norwegian revitalisation has been an invaluable support, organisationally, ideologically and in terms of awareness raising. So has the support from speakers of other Saami languages, including those in Finland. Many national and regional (all-Saami) organisations have been demanding more rights for some decades, and there seems to be a breakthrough happening at present. The official Finnish revitalisation action plan from February 2012 (see Info Box 10 Visions for Saami Revitalisation, Finland) may be a really positive harbinger. Cross-border contacts and networks are flourishing – daycare, education (the only Saami-medium university is on the Norwegian side of *Sápmi*/Saamiland), family visits and marriages, and many organisations work across state borders. Still, taking back the language and bringing it forward is cumbersome even for highly motivated individuals, as Ann-Helén Laestadius' example in Info Box 11 shows.

Combs and Penfield (2012: 462) define 'language activism' as 'energetic action focused on language use in order to create, influence and change existing language policies'. Language activism may need to be noisy, with 'disrupters, campaigners and ideological pests' because if there is 'no noise, no improvement' (Todd Gitlin in *Letters to a Young Activist*, 2003, quoted in Combs & Penfield, 2012: 461). It can also be 'quiet, personal and practiced in smaller, more intimate settings' (Combs & Penfield, 2012: 463), for instance, when individuals commit to (re)learning their ancestral language. Both types of language activism are part of this book. But for a people as small as the Aanaar Saami, more or less everybody has to be an activist. Combs and Penfield state (2012: 466–467):

> We have seen remarkable changes in language policy resulting from the efforts of small groups or often single individuals who have dramatically affected policy changes for endangered or minority languages in supportive ways.

The important experiences of these individuals and groups need to be shared, both for documenting their own efforts and as part of the 'small movement [that] has arisen in several parts of the world aimed at providing targeted training in language activism', something that Combs and Penfield (2012: 471–473) mention for groups in the USA and Canada. It is happening in many parts of the world (e.g. in India and Nepal where one of us has participated) and it has long informal traditions in most parts of the Saami country. This book is an example of sharing some new experiences.

The Saami are one nation, with several languages and cultures. Just as with many other ITMs which are divided by colonial states, present-day state borders are not their borders. Cooperation and solidarity across borders and globally can give inspiration and strength to many numerically small Indigenous and tribal peoples in maintaining and revitalising their languages and cultures. We hope that this book becomes part of that inspiration. At the very least, it shows that revitalisation can be done.

2 How Did the CASLE Project Start?

2.1 Planner's View

2.1.1 The start

The basis for organising the AS complementary education (CASLE) project was created in the autumn of 2006. I (Marja-Liisa Olthuis) was taking care of the practical arrangements of defending my doctoral thesis in Aanaar. It was the first time in the history of the Faculty of Arts at the University of Oulu, Finland that the defending of a doctoral thesis would happen outside the university, among the members of the language community concerned. This was done because I am an Aanaar Saami, and because my doctoral thesis concerned the AS names of various species,[1] especially the names of birds and mushrooms. I was planning to organise my party after the defence at the Saami Education Institute, and therefore I called its principal, Lassi Valkeapää. Among other things, we also discussed the matter of how difficult it was to get qualified AS-speaking teachers. According to Lassi, the Saami Education Institute had been planning to organise AS courses but it was forced to drop the idea because of the very common reason among a great number of minority languages: a lack of teachers. He asked me whether I could do something to solve this continuing problem. I just wished I had the answer. We both knew that the municipality of Aanaar could not get qualified AS-speaking teachers, and there was no hope of enlarging the existing language nest activities because of the lack of daycare personnel. The language skills and professional skills of candidates never seemed to match. This phone call with Lassi gave me an idea for my postdoctoral research: I had to start working with urgency on AS revitalisation issues.

After defending my doctoral thesis, I got a part-time job with the Research Institute for the Languages of Finland. I had also applied for a personal grant from the Jenny and Antti Wihuri Foundation. I was very lucky to get both the job and the grant. Later, as the project progressed, I was able to convert the grant into a half-time university lectureship at the University of Oulu. I was now able to do research on AS language revitalisation issues.

At the time when I started my postdoctoral project in the autumn of 2007, there was no official language revitalisation programme for AS, but because I had been working with the language, it was easy to define my starting position. Active language revitalisation had already begun in 1997 in the language nest, which was funded by the Finnish Cultural Foundation (see Info Box 7 Language Nests and Info Box 17 *Anarâškielâ servi* [Aanaar Saami Association]). This language nest was still functioning in AS and producing new child speakers to be brought into the language community. During its entire history up to that time, the language nest had produced approximately 40 new child speakers. AS had been in use as a teaching language, that is as a medium of education (MoI), at the local primary school since the autumn of 2000, but there were only two AS-speaking teachers. Because of the lack of AS-speaking teachers, teaching in AS could not be extended at the primary level nor could it be used in the secondary school, except for the study of AS as a single subject.

The small but very active language community had been talking about the issue of how to move forward, because a language of approximately 350 speakers was not safe: it needed support and extension in many fields. Firstly, it was necessary to extend the language nest method to increase the number of child speakers to ensure a safe number of speakers for the future. Secondly, there was a need to increase the teaching of AS in primary and secondary schools, both as a subject and as a MoI, but there were no human resources available to realise this. It has been established by other experiences that the language skills of children and youth will become passive in just a few years if school teaching cannot be realised in the minority language (see also Wilson & Kamanā, 2009; Info Box 12 Advice From Revitalisation in Hawai'i). The language community was very concerned about the language development process of the language nest and how schoolchildren would continue learning. There was a dilemma: how could the community find a working method that would enlarge the youth and working generations in the language community at the same time? Time was a crucial factor in extending the language community; the enlargement had to happen rapidly before the immersed children began to lose their language skills.

My first aim was to research into what ought to be done to save the language and to create the first version of the language programme. I had three main questions in mind:

(a) How could the language skills of a young individual be brought to a level where s/he would be able to transmit AS to his/her own children in the future?
(b) Which professional adult groups should be responsible for language transmission in the AS language community?

(c)   Under which circumstances and how would it be possible to find or cultivate the desperately needed AS-speaking professionals?

I started with these questions for the following two reasons:

(1)   The main aim of language revitalisation is to guarantee language transmission to new generations.
(2)   The language learning process of an individual takes more than 20 years and correlates with his/her normal cognitive development. Therefore it is necessary to support the use of the minority language from early childhood until at least early adulthood. AS was far from this aim.

I had to put the question of lack of teachers in another way: how realistic was the hope of finding qualified professionals in the language community? There was already an AS study programme at the University of Oulu, consisting of both basic and intermediate studies. This programme was created approximately seven years earlier, and it was certainly not suffering from a lack of students, but for some reason it did not produce new AS-speaking teachers. As I examined a rough estimate of the speakers' ages, I observed that there was very little hope of cultivating enough AS-speaking, professionally qualified people in the way it 'normally' happens, by sending young people to college/university and waiting until they qualified. Since two generations had already lost the language, there were hardly any AS-speaking students among the generation aged 18–25 years. Further, this young generation had the whole world open to them in terms of choosing their future professions, so it was not realistic to hope that this handful of individuals would all want to become school teachers or kindergarten teachers, which was precisely what the AS language programme required. From this point of view, it was obvious that the native-speaker study programme was not able to strengthen the language community in the ways it needed, practically speaking. New teachers had to be found in some other way.

I reported my first observations to Lassi at the end of 2007. He advised me to discuss the matter further with the language community as well as with local employees. Especially for this purpose, we decided to organise an AS language revitalisation course for adults and to use the language as a teaching language. I prepared the course according to my own observations and searched for more information concerning the language revitalisation methods used in other parts of the world. This course was to be offered as a course by the Saami Education Institute. However, there was a new problem: no-one seemed to be interested. I called Lassi again, now for the third time, and asked for ideas of how to proceed. He was fuming:

The whole world is full of disappearing languages! Finland is full of universities and even they don't offer these courses to their students!

We could try to use your personal contacts in the academic circles and offer the course for very advanced university students!

I thought Lassi's 'marketing' idea was worth trying. I rewrote the study material in Finnish and prepared the lectures again, this time for a changed target group. I contacted my colleagues at universities, and after some time I had many potential students; more than 20 advanced students were willing to take part in the language revitalisation course. There was still one problem to be solved: these students were not able to travel to Aanaar for a single course, and an intensive course was also out of the question because we were very late with the planning and students already had their course schedules. The Saami Education Institute provided the necessary solution. It had just introduced the internet-based classroom system called LearnLinc. A new LearnLinc virtual classroom was thus created for my language revitalisation course, and the necessary codes along with practical information on how to participate in the class were emailed to the students. Finally I had the desired number of students, and the course could be taught from a distance. I was physically sitting in my home office in the Netherlands, and my students were spread around the university towns of Finland – some of them in Aanaar. One of the participants was even in Japan. The sessions were recorded, so that any student who was unable to participate in a certain session could hear it later.

This was the most interesting and also the most exhausting course I have ever given. My first intention, to offer just an ordinary course concerning the most common language revitalisation models, had to be forgotten. I had to go much deeper. When I was not teaching, I found myself reading literature concerning models for language revitalisation from the point of view of AS and writing down every piece of information that could be useful for the AS case. The further I got, the more I was convinced that it would be a long-lasting and complicated process to put all the pieces of the models together in a way that would really be of use to AS.

I was very lucky to be able to organise this course in the beginning of my postdoctoral research period. My students were advanced and they were able to think from a scientific point of view, which concretely advanced the planning of CASLE. During the course, two main ideas were born from the complexity of the status of the AS language: (1) the creation of a language consulting unit; and (2) the development of CASLE, or Complimentary Aanaar Saami Language Education.

2.1.2 Creating a language consulting unit

Concerning the matter of new child speakers, there was enough new language potential in the municipality of Aanaar. It was the idea of Taarna Valtonen, one of my students, to influence families with small children. Her suggestion was to establish a language consulting unit for parents who already had bilingual children and who intended to bring up their children bilingually.

The language consulting unit for families was taken on as a part of the language guidance service of the Research Institute for the Languages of Finland. As Taarna suggested, parents have questions and even doubts concerning the bilingual upbringing of their children, especially when the small minority language would become the second language (L2) or even third language (L3) of the family. In my experience, from speaking with families, most of the questions and worries concerning bilingualism seem to be universal and can be answered, for instance, with the help of Colin Baker's (2007) book, *A Parents' and Teachers' Guide to Bilingualism*. There also seems to be a cultural aspect to the doubts expressed: some Finnish parents have, for instance, asked whether it is possible to bring up children in AS when the family does not have (Aanaar) Saami origins. Of course, the motivation to learn a minority language does not depend on the ancestry of the children; there are also numerous other motives for learning the language. According to Annika Pasanen (2010a), the AS language community is open to new influences, so all new language speakers of all language generations, no matter the origins of the new speaker, have been very welcome.

I (Marja-Liisa) included the consulting unit in the description of my job at the Research Institute for Languages of Finland in 2008. Most people – mainly parents and colleagues working with bilingual matters – contact me via the phone or internet or just talk to me wherever I meet them. Most parents contact me at a time when they are considering the possibility of placing their children in a language nest. They often want to clarify what can be expected from participating in this period of language learning. For many parents a short conversation is enough for them to make their decision to send an application to the language nest. Some parents have invited me for home visits to discuss bi- or multilingual matters more thoroughly. Furthermore, the language nest staff, school teachers and municipal daycare management often need to discuss matters concerning the language nests, such as practical arrangements, producing materials, bi- or multilingualism and selecting children for the language nests, as well as their own individual roles as language transmitters.

In collaboration with *Anarâškielâ servi* (see Info Box 17 *Anarâškielâ servi* [Aanaar Saami Association]), I have organised open information evenings for parents who intend to bring their children to a language nest. I have cooperated with the local primary school as well, organising bilingual evenings for parents and teachers. (Tove Skutnabb-Kangas has also offered several one- or two-day seminars for parents and teachers during the last decade.) I have discussed the importance of language choices with the local counselling bureau, as their clients are also potential language nest users. The language unit services are greatly needed in the field, and operating the unit could easily become a full-time job for someone; however, there is still a shortage of AS research posts, even though there should be a few more researchers available now. My greatest fear is that it will be hard to offer these services from the university in the near future; the Research Institute for Languages of Finland closed their Department of Minority Languages, from which these services could have been offered, at the end of 2011. The tasks of the Department have been taken over by several other Finnish universities, but they seem to prefer traditional academic education. It is a real challenge for people working with language revitalisation to remain strong and trust in their own expertise. It is important that we support one another to generate new speakers, both now and in the future.

2.1.3 The challenge of CASLE: How to reclaim a lost working-age adult generation?

As mentioned above, the language nest method has produced approximately 40 new child speakers since 1997, but the crucial issue for AS revitalisation was the question of how to create the missing AS-speaking generation of professionals. The primary idea for CASLE was introduced by some of my students during the revitalisation lectures. The first idea was initiated by Irmeli Moilanen, one of the course participants, who became my colleague in this project. This was only the beginning of a long process of carrying out the project that will be described in detail throughout this book. In my personal notes, I wrote this comment: 'The idea is brilliant and surely worth considering.' Then, on second thoughts, I was not so sure:

> How about the costs? The target group shall consist of working people, probably with families and children, and they have got their households and mortgages. Probably they don't have time to study, certainly not with the high requirements the language community is placing on their shoulders.

I have also noted Irmeli's comment: 'But it is absolutely possible to arrange funding for adult students as well.' She herself was a living example of her own words; she was not a young student any more, and she was intending to graduate in the spring of 2008. She had begun her university studies in her late forties, already with a family and many years of experience working with financial issues. Later, as a colleague in the CASLE team, she proved to be a real asset in discovering the personal funding sources offered by the state of Finland. These funds were essential for the CASLE students. It was thanks to Irmeli that I finally dared to take the biggest step of all, which was to start the CASLE project.

I organised several brainstorming workshops for my students during my revitalisation course. Finally, I had a list of unanswered questions at the end of the course in November 2007. The following list will give an idea of some of the most important, yet unresolved issues at the time:

- What would happen to the children's language skills after CASLE had prepared their teachers? They would have to learn the language from CASLE graduates who are L2 speakers of AS.
- What would be the real need for AS-speaking professionals among local employers?
- What kind of language education would be best – how long, how much teaching, to whom?
- What programme should be used for teaching, and how could it be created?
- How could teachers be cultivated for this special CASLE education?
- How could the target group (students) be found from the appropriate professional fields?
- How could organisers be found, and how could the CASLE method be marketed to them?
- How could teaching be financed?
- How would the students for the programme be selected?
- How would the selected students finance their studies?
- How could it be ensured that the selected students were talented enough to complete the language programme?
- How could study materials be developed for an intensive teaching period?

The revitalisation course was too short to find the answers to all of these questions. I tried to create a sample model for setting up the CASLE method. With great help from my students, I was able to write and send a grant application to the Finnish Cultural Foundation, aware of the fact that I was asking for quite a fortune for my megalomaniac plans. To proceed, I needed a project planning team to investigate whether the CASLE method would be the most effective one to replace the lost language generations.

During the period from December 2007 to January 2008, I proceeded with my plans. Giellagas Institute at the University of Oulu was in principle ready to organise the AS studies as a complementary education, and I also got permission to modify the normal study programme. This was very positive. The programme could start in August 2009. The timing was also perfect: the preparations would take at least a year, and the study materials had to be prepared. Lassi Valkeapää from the Saami Education Institute offered his help. I was happy to have two strong organisations behind the CASLE idea. I also discussed the matter with Matti Morottaja, the chairman of *Anarâškielâ servi* (see Info Box 17 *Anarâškielâ servi* [Aanaar Saami Association]. My discussions with him helped me make the decision to stress the oral use of the language and to use common language speakers, so-called Language Masters, in the programme. Stressing the oral use of the language also meant that the theoretical study programme of Oulu had to become more practical.

I also talked to local employers to get an idea of how many AS-speaking professionals the working Saami community really needed. These employers were able to specify their needs by level, for example 'We would like to have so many extra employees of such a type'. I reached an agreement with local employers, who promised to forward the questionnaire developed by CASLE to their employees to investigate their interest in studying AS. CASLE needed to reach the appropriate target groups in the field and ensure that the questionnaire was taken seriously.

I did not have to wait very long before I received a phone call from the Finnish Cultural Foundation in February 2008. My funding application had been approved, and the AS project would become one of the major projects funded by the Finnish Cultural Foundation. I was very thankful for this opportunity but also aware of the great responsibility involved: this chance would be given only once for the whole AS language community. It was now or never! CASLE had to be carried out and it had to become a success. This funding by the Finnish Cultural Foundation gave me the opportunity to set up a planning team. I also came to the conclusion that I should not personally be an employer of the new members of the planning team. Therefore I contacted *Anarâškielâ servi* and asked if they could administer the team; this was also approved. Everything seemed to be progressing as I had hoped, but I still had one major 'what-if' question in my mind: What if everything was done for nothing? Did the programme really interest potential students in a way that the organisers could afford to implement? This question had to remain unresolved until the planning team started and studied the results of the questionnaires.

In April 2008, Irmeli Moilanen joined the team. Her main tasks were to prepare the field questionnaires, recruit students for the programme and investigate the main funding sources for the students. Two months later, Annika Pasanen joined the planning team. Her main task was to plan the practical language training part. I was to be the Project Manager of the programme. My tasks included finding cooperation partners, coordinating discussion and modifications of the study programme, finding and informing the lecturers and other teachers, and planning the contents of the courses collaboratively with the lecturers. I also had to coordinate the planning team and oversee preparation of the study material. In addition, the practical financial issues of the project had to be worked out. A very important part of my work was to start preparations for student selection and, essentially, to find professionals who were willing and able to replace the working-age generation that had suffered language loss.

As the planning team started work, it was still unclear for a few months whether the target group would be interested in the forthcoming study programme. However, finally the preparations for the CASLE programme were about to start. This book describes how the project was set up and carried out. Aware of the fact that I was only able to offer a planner's perspective of the project, I needed two fellow authors: Tove to introduce a worldwide perspective on language revitalisation matters, and Suvi Kivelä to describe a student perspective. They have written the next two sections.

2.2 An Outsider's View From Tove

I (Tove Skutnabb-Kangas) grew up with two mother tongues, Finnish and Swedish, and learned both languages up to a high native level. I identified with both Finnish speakers and Finland Swedish speakers, and was accepted by both groups. I had always experienced my (and my parents' and grandparents') bilingualism as natural (even if I was always the only bilingual in my class in school), and as beneficial. After earning my MA, I worked at Harvard University (USA) in 1967–1968 as Einar Haugen's research assistant – Einar and Uriel Weinreich were the founding fathers of bilingualism studies. I had already started collecting data for my PhD-equivalent degree (Licentiate of Philosophy) at the University of Helsinki, studying Swedish mother-tongue bilingual youngsters in a bilingual vocational school in Finland. I also taught them social studies and Swedish as a mother tongue for two years while collecting data. Their bilingualism was also a very positive feature, and their school achievement was on a par with their Finnish-medium peers.

My first experiences of dominant group members seeing bilingualism as a deficit came partly in my work with Finnish immigrant minority parents in Sweden, where the children were in Swedish-medium submersion programmes. Finns were the largest migrant group in Sweden and their/our status was extremely low. Schools failed the children completely. Full linguistic and cultural assimilation as fast as possible was the strategy; the children were often forbidden to speak their language in school and many parents were told to speak Swedish (which most of them knew very little of) at home. Many children and even parents were shy and silent, which is reflected in the book edited by Markku Peura and myself (1994) entitled *'Man kan vara tvåländare också'. Den sverigefinska minoritetens väg från tystnad till kamp* ['You Can Be Two-countrial Too'. The Road of the Sweden–Finnish Minority from Silence to Struggle]. They were made to feel ashamed of their language and culture, as was reflected in the title of an earlier volume I edited with Jim Cummins, entitled *Minority Education: From Shame to Struggle* (Skutnabb-Kangas & Cummins, 1988). They were asked to get rid of their Finnish, which was seen as a handicap. This was all exactly as Stacy Churchill later described when illustrating the typical phases for OECD (Churchill, 1985): the children, the parents and the group were supposed to suffer from L2 deficiency, social deficiency, cultural deficiency and, later, L1 deficiency (see, for example, Skutnabb-Kangas, 1981, 1984,

1990). This view on bilingualism as a handicap came as a real shock for to me (see two reports written by Pertti Toukomaa and myself for UNESCO on this: Skutnabb-Kangas & Toukomaa, 1976; Toukomaa & Skutnabb-Kangas, 1977), especially because this was at a time when Finnish parents had already started resisting the assimilation and demanded – and got – Finnish-medium classes, and later schools. I studied these aspects for my advanced doctorate (DrPhil) earned at the University of Roskilde.

At the same time, I saw the long-term consequences of a similar kind of harsh assimilation treatment with the Saami. I worked with many Saami colleagues and friends, especially on the Norwegian but later also Finnish and to some extent Swedish sides of *Sápmi*, starting in the very late 1960s. At that point, many young parents, especially North Saami speakers, still knew Saami at least to some extent, even if there were also many families where the older generation had either not spoken Saami at all to their children or had spoken both languages. At that time, the family language became Norwegian if one of the spouses was Norwegian – and the non-Saami spouse very seldom learned Saami. I was asked to speak to teachers, teacher trainers, politicians and, increasingly, parents about bilingualism. I am sure I must have spoken at various parents' evenings in Norway and Sweden close to a thousand times between 1968 and the mid-1990s. I have since met dozens of people who have told me that the one parents' evening convinced them (or in many cases their parents) about the benefits of bilingualism, with the result that they started speaking Saami to their children. There was quite a lot of resistance to what I said from dominant group authorities and politicians, especially in Sweden, but also to some extent in Norway.

Even though the Finns in Sweden started mobilising in the late 1960s, the struggle for linguistic human rights in education has been long and really hard. On paper, much has improved in Sweden (but see Info Box 1 Criticism of Sweden's Current Minority Policies and Practices). On the other hand, because of assimilationist policies, youngsters from most immigrant and autochthonous minority groups no longer know their ancestral languages, that is they are finding themselves in a situation similar to many Indigenous peoples where several generations have lost their languages and cultures (see Info Box 15 Lost or Stolen Generations). In Norway the mobilisation of the Saami started earlier. After a struggle where the state built a dam in the Alta River (the best salmon river in Europe, it was said) against strong protests from not only the Saami but also many others from around the world, things moved fast. The Saami Parliament was created in 1982 (some 10 years after Finland and 10 years before Sweden), large white papers (government policy documents) were written, and many reforms were implemented. The situation of the Saami in Norway is now arguably better than the conditions of any other Indigenous people in the world. The first chair of the United Nations Permanent Forum on Indigenous Issues was a Saami from Norway, Ole Henrik Magga.

As early as the 1960s I started to see and describe both situations (the education of both Indigenous peoples and immigrant minorities) as violations of linguistic and educational human rights and even as genocide. However, it took decades to start formulating this in stricter multidisciplinary and also legal terms (see Skutnabb-Kangas & Dunbar, 2010, for the latest one; see also Info Box 4 Linguistic and Cultural Genocide in Education and Info Box 14 Language Rights and Right to Education).

My background with my own autochthonous (Finland Swedish) minority identity positively combined with my (Finnish) linguistic majority identity (which could be considered real integration), together with my long-lasting and deep experience of having (in small ways) participated in the struggles of an Indigenous people, the Saami, in three countries, and an immigrant minority group, the Finns in Sweden, led to a life-long interest in those power relations that are decisive for the denial, or granting, of educational linguistic human rights. I have since then made many contacts and worked with ITM peoples and groups (including the Deaf) in all parts of the world. If these people had not been so generous with their friendship and knowledge, and so patient in waiting for me to grasp what they taught me, I would not know anything.

When Marja-Liisa (and Suvi) asked me to participate in this book, the idea was initially that I would just write a few compact summaries on issues that they felt they did not have enough knowledge about because these issues fell outside their core competences. These became the Info Boxes, and acknowledgement of this was supposed to be reflected by adding 'with extracts by TSK' on the first page of the book. However, somehow I was drawn more and more into the book writing process itself – reading, giving feedback and discussing issues that are important to us all. So now there are three authors, even though it is very clear that Marja-Liisa has been the main pen-holder who knew what she wanted to say. It has been an exciting journey.

2.3 A Student View From Suvi

It was just an ordinary day at the radio. I (Suvi Kivelä) was working on a news story concerning the latest turns of the Saami land ownership issue when the phone rang. The woman on the phone introduced herself and started to go on about this new and revolutionary AS language programme that targeted professional people. She wanted me to do a story on this programme, which was supposed to reclaim AS altogether. According to her, this programme was an answer to one of the biggest problems concerning the language community at the time: the lack of qualified teachers.

I listened to her and thought about my own little AS children who had been given the gift of learning their mother tongue at the AS language nest. During the past few years I had seen how their grandmother, possibly due to the language nest, had got up the courage and confidence to start speaking in her mother tongue, AS, again. Considering the fact that she had not really used her mother tongue for decades and never spoke it to her own children, I had honestly thought that everything was already fine with AS. I knew there were still some elders speaking it and now there was a new generation growing up, the eldest language nest children already being teenagers. Naively, I thought that establishing the AS language nest in 1997 had already revived the language.

However, the woman on the phone made me rethink my assumptions. I had noticed that there was a lot of talk about the general lack of teachers in the Saami language communities. Personally, I had worried about not being able to help my son with his homework, now that he had started school in the AS class. I was aware that at school there was only one teacher and, if the number of teachers did not increase, my children would have to go to a Finnish-speaking class in few years' time. This was the first time I really had to start thinking about the future of my children. Would all the hard work that had been done during the past decade be thrown away when the language nest children grew up? The reality was that we, the parents, could not expect any language support from the community, since such an AS-speaking community did not really exist. Perhaps there were some speakers but one could hardly call it a 'community' or, if that community did exist, I at least was not aware of it. Apart from my son's teacher and the couple of language nest caregivers, I did not know any AS-speaking adults.

Thus far I had mainly just listened to the enthusiastic voice of Irmeli Moilanen, one of the project coordinators. The first thing I heard myself asking was: 'How can one apply to this programme?' I tried to sound professional when I addressed a further question: 'Is this only for teachers … or can journalists, for example, also apply? I mean … there is a need for AS media also, isn't there?'

I must admit that I never managed to broadcast a story about the language programme (and I am still feeling guilty about that!), but I did get the application forms. After filling them in, I got accepted onto the course along with 17 other professionals. We all gained reasonable proficiency in the language and graduated on a beautiful sunny day in August 2009. We became a success story. The complementary studies programme became a success story. And, furthermore, AS will become a frequently used example of successful language revitalisation worldwide.

When I left my work as a news reporter to study AS, I was excited and scared. I set my goals. The first was that one day I would be broadcasting in AS. The second and perhaps even more important goal was that I was determined to make AS our family's home language.

When setting up my goals at the beginning of the course, I knew that achieving them would demand hard work. However, I had no idea how deep, on an emotional level, that year would take me. I had stepped into this community several years before, but it was only now that my eyes began to open to the culture. Although I had already learnt some North Saami language (but had to break off the course before the end because of a pregnancy), I felt that my understanding had been very superficial. AS was the key that finally explained things that had been strange to me, filled in the black holes and created real connections with these people and their land. I also started to explore some really painful past issues concerning the father of my children. He belongs to the lost generation (see Info Box 15 Lost or Stolen Generations).

I cannot even start to compare my experiences with those of my classmates who have Saami roots. I don't think I have ever seen anything as inspiring, healing and moving as someone who reclaims his or her mother tongue. And when you see people becoming whole again, when they are reconnecting with their ancestors, history and long lost heritage, you cannot but think that it must be right. It must be something that everyone belonging to a lost or stolen generation should strive for, if they are given a chance. And we, the 'others', have to do everything we can to give them this chance.

After the complementary studies programme, I went back to work to broadcast the local news – in Finnish. In other words, the first goal that I set up was not achieved. Ironically, *Anarâškielâ servi*, an association that was established to improve the state of the AS language, had already appealed to YLE (my then employer), Finland's national public service broadcasting company, to increase the number of AS radio and television staff. The resources for AS broadcasts, created 20 years ago, had not been updated even though the state of the language had changed radically from how it had been at the beginning of the 1990s; the use of the language has increased and diversified. The appeal was made in 2010, but YLE has not responded in any way up to the present. At the moment there is only one radio journalist and she works part time. She compiles a weekly programme that is one hour in length, representing only about 5% of the total broadcasting time of Saami radio. However, there is a much bigger demand now, because there is a new audience, due to the complementary studies programme and language nests. However, for young people, there is nothing available in their own language.

In the autumn of 2010 I had been back at work for a few months when the Project Manager of CASLE, Marja-Liisa, asked me to start writing a book with her. She wanted to document the education programme and its methods, and thought she would like to have a student's point of view represented. I was surprised and honoured. I knew immediately that I could not refuse the opportunity, if my employer would only grant me a year of unpaid leave. Luckily it all worked out at short notice, and my employer understood the value of this project. Next, I hope that some of the big bosses at YLE will read this book and grant more resources for AS broadcasting. I also put my hope in the Programme of Action for the Revitalisation of the Saami

Languages [*Toimenpideohjelma saamen kielen elvyttämiseksi*] (OKM, 2012b). It points out that the media play an important role in language revitalisation, and it gives concrete examples of what should be done (see also Info Box 10 Visions for Saami Revitalisation, Finland). I hope that the action programme puts pressure on YLE to increase its services in all Saami languages. After all, YLE as a public service company has a duty, legislated by law, to serve Finland's minorities as well as the majority.

As someone slightly quick tempered, I got tired of waiting for things to happen at YLE. Recently I applied for a new position in Aanaar as a researcher at the new Saami Archives, part of the National Archives Service of Finland which is to be established. I am happy to report that I launched the Saami Archives at the beginning of 2012 at the brand new Saami cultural centre known as *Sajos*.

I saw myself writing this book as a co-author for several reasons. First of all, I think every AS deserves to know why this extremely costly study programme was carried out and what the outcome of it was. In addition, I think that the other nine Saami language groups could learn from this experience. The Skolt Saami language, for example, which is also spoken in Aanaar municipality by about the same number of people as AS, is also a seriously endangered language (defined by UNESCO). In order to revive the Skolt Saami language, something needs to be done urgently. That 'something' is luckily about to happen in autumn 2012, when the first long and intensive Skolt Saami language and culture course starts at the Saami Education Institute in Aanaar. The teacher will be Tiina Sanila-Aikio, a young and phenomenal Skolt Saami language activist, a rock singer and Vice President of the Saami Parliament of Finland in 2012–2015. Expectations for the year 2012 are high.

I share my fellow authors' trust that this book can offer insight and practical advice to anyone interested in reviving or reclaiming their language. Cultures and languages are profoundly connected, and together they form a complex system that tells us about the surrounding society. It is clear that some things, such as the administrative part and funding for the study programme, cannot be taken away from this context and simply transformed into some other culture. On the other hand, some fundamental parts of the study programme can be applied and adapted in many places around the world.

After all, there is a lot to do with regard to language revitalisation. Linguists estimate that, out of the around 7000 languages spoken in the world today, 50%–95% are in danger of disappearing before the end of the next century (see Info Box 1 Criticism of Sweden's Current Minority Policies and Practices, and Info Box 2 Language Endangerment).

There are several books and studies that answer the question of why languages should be saved. We do not intend to refer much to these (except in some Info Boxes) nor to get into that discussion with any new, ground-breaking arguments. It is, however, the starting point of this book that languages should be saved, and there is no question about it. To be honest, I do not see how anyone in a democratic country can argue against it. It is sad if, for some people, diversity does not mean the richness and beauty of this universe.

According to Daniel Nettle and Suzanne Romaine, linguistic diversity is a benchmark of cultural diversity, and language death is symptomatic of cultural death – a way of life disappears with the death of a language (Nettle & Romaine, 2000: 7). As such, it is clear that, when talking about language death, we are always talking about human rights as well. This means human rights that include rights to one's own language and culture, as Tove has argued in much of her work (see above).

We are not questioning whether threatened languages can be saved. Through the example of AS, we already know that the answer is 'yes, they can'. Therefore, rather than seeking answers to these questions of why and whether it is possible, we attempt to answer and give practical examples to the question of 'how'.

Before settling in Aanaar, I studied comparative religion at Edinburgh University. I was especially interested in indigenous cultures and ended up writing my master's thesis about shamanism in Yakutia, Sakha Republic, in northeastern Russia. I spent several weeks in the city of Yakutsk and met wonderful scholars, as well as people who called themselves shamans. It was in Yakutsk that I fell in love with the Arctic.

After graduating in 2002, I decided to try and live in the Arctic region. I grew up in Southern Finland and, like the most of the people down there, I had never visited Lapland, other than some skiing centres that really don't count as Lapland. Then when I first heard (funnily enough, while I was in Yakutsk) about the Saami Education Institute in Aanaar, I knew that would be my next stop. After all those studies about the African, Asian and Siberian peoples, I wanted to learn about the Indigenous peoples in Europe – people who inhabited my homeland (or did I inhabit their homeland?). I decided to come to Aanaar for a year, take all the culture courses that were possible to take and learn the Northern Saami language.

As the reader will have guessed already, my planned one-year visit got a bit longer. You know, there are many fewer women here than men ... so it all happened very soon after my arrival. The school started in August and, well before Christmas ... I was already pregnant.

I had dreamt about postgraduate studies, but under these new circum-stances, it looked like going back to university was impossible. Instead, I would concentrate on my empirical studies of the Aanaar Saami people for a while.

I have been in Aanaar for nearly ten years now, and this is where my heart is. I thoroughly enjoy seeing how important this place, home, is for my children. And now I am not talking about the actual house we live in, but the whole entity: people, land, places, lakes, swamps, mountains, stories and – most importantly – their home language.

As far as I am concerned, I still miss city life sometimes, and the freedom that arises from feeling anonymous in a crowd. And although I think I largely understand this culture, I often intentionally nurture the fact that I will always be an outsider. As a journalist, that gave me immunity; I could criticise and point out the grievances that I noticed without caring about strong family ties. From my point of view, family is the most important thing for a Saami, which sets up a lot of norms for the behaviour of the individual.

On the other hand, even as an outsider I feel like I have a certain place in the community; I have found my way and my place on earth. My roots have slowly started to grow into this ground. Still I am acutely aware that despite how perfectly I speak the Saami language/s, it will never make me into a Saami and, unlike what some might think, I don't intend to become one. I think it is rather insulting to call someone a 'wannabe Saami', an expression I have heard many times – even if it has not referred to me personally. I am happy and proud of my strong Finnish Ostrobothnian family line that has, for example, a lot of talented and world famous artists in it. Unlike what some Saami people seem to think at the moment, when the issue of land rights is on the table again (as Finland has still not ratified the UN's ILO 169), I am not after some special rights that clearly belong to Saami people only, or anything else either. I have no hidden agenda. I just want to live a simple and peaceful life here, raise my kids and be an active member of society, and take part in discussions in any languages that I know.

My position as a co-author of this book is one of a CASLE student, a journalist and an archivist/researcher. But it is also that of a mother of two AS children, with whom I am now able to use AS at home. Marja-Liisa, besides being a great scholar, is an Aanaar Saami herself and therefore she can offer an insider's view to the subject. However, she lives in Rotterdam in The Netherlands whereas I, an outsider, live within the community under examination. I believe that our positions create a balance that is also good from the point of view of a reader.

I truly hope this book will be an inspiration to anyone who is interested in Indigenous languages and cultures and language revitalisation.

Note

(1) Species names were needed for school books, so each species had to have one specific name. The Indigenous naming of birds was often confusing: one species could have several indigenous names or the same indigenous name referred to several species. Economically important and detrimental species have been well known, but some economically less important species were not named at all (Olthuis, 2007: 5).

3 Aanaar Saami: A Small Saami Language

3.1 Facts About the Saami Languages

The Saami languages are spoken in an area stretching in an arch from Dalarna in central Sweden through northern Norway and Finland to the tip of the Kola Peninsula in Russia (Figure 3.1, p. 24). According to certain linguistic features, the Saami languages are divided into the Western and Eastern Saami. They belong to the Finno-Ugric part of the Uralic family of languages (http://www.helsinki.fi/~tasalmin/fu.html; Sammallahti, 1998: 1–2).

The Western Saami languages:

- South Saami (est. 500 speakers in Norway and Sweden)
- Ume Saami (20–30 speakers in Norway and Sweden)
- Pite Saami (20–30 speakers in Norway and Sweden)
- Lule Saami (est. 2000–3000 speakers in Norway and Sweden)
- Kemi Saami (extinct since the 19th century)
- North Saami (17,000 speakers in Finland, Norway and Sweden)

The Eastern Saami languages:

- Aanaar Saami (est. 350 speakers in Finland)
- Skolt Saami (est. 300 speakers in Finland and Russia)
- Akkala Saami (extinct since 2003; the last speaker, Maria Sergina, died in Russia)
- Kildin Saami (est. 650 speakers in Russia)
- Ter Saami (10–20 elderly speakers in Russia)

(a)

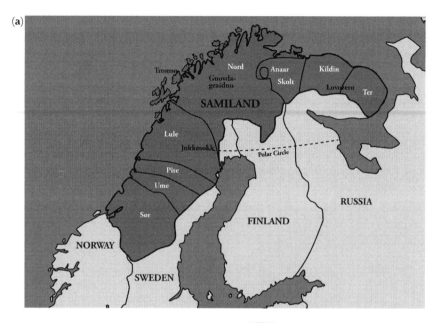

(b)

Figure 3.1 The Saami languages

3.2 Aanaar Saami in its Surroundings

The main area where AS is spoken is limited to the municipality of Aanaar/Inari. With a surface area of more than 17,000 km², it is the largest municipality of Finland.[1] Its population is about 6800, with a population density of 0.45 inhabitants per km². Aanaar is a multilingual municipality: besides Finnish and AS, North and Skolt Saami languages are also spoken. AS speakers represent about 15% of the total number of speakers of Saami languages in Finland (Carpelan *et al.*, 2003–2004).

The original AS-speaking area is mainly located in five villages around Lake Aanaar: Avveel, Aanaar, Kaamâs, Päärtih and Njellim (see p. 26; Figure 3.2, Aanaarjävri).

Nowadays Aanaar village, situated in the large municipality of Aanaar, is the area where AS is still spoken most strongly. It is the heart of AS culture: two of the three language nests, as well as the primary school, the Saami Radio and the Saami Parliament are all located in Aanaar village. Sajos, a brand new Saami cultural centre, has recently (in 2012) opened its doors there.

Avveel is the administrative centre of Aanaar municipality.[2] The area used to be inhabited by AS people but it has become a mainly monolingual Finnish-speaking area. However, after CASLE was initiated in 2010, a language nest was also established there. In addition, AS instruction is now given in Avveel at the primary school, high school and folk high school (for adult education).

The areas around the villages of Kaamâs, Päärtih and Njellim are very sparsely populated. There are only a few speakers of AS left there, that is, fewer than 50 speakers per village. The speakers are mainly elderly.

The AS community has always been very constricted: it has probably never amounted to more than 1000 speakers. At the beginning of the 19th century about 95% of the inhabitants of Aanaar were AS people. The situation changed radically in the mid-19th century with the settlement of North Saami people who came with their reindeer from Norway. The total number of Saami in the area increased but, gradually, with heavy Finnish migration particularly in the 1920s and 1930s, Saami people became a minority. By 1940 only 30% of the population of Aanaar were Saami and the rest were Finns (Nahkiaisoja, 2003a: 173, 2003b: 226). After World War II, the Skolt Saami from Pechenga also came to settle in Aanaar. In this growing multilingual and multicultural situation the AS community gradually became a minority.

A demographic study carried out by the Saami Council (Nickul, 1968: 54) stated that there were 736 AS speakers in 1910. In 1911 Professor J.E. Rosberg counted AS as one of the most vulnerable Saami languages. He therefore recommended urgent action in order to revive AS, stressing

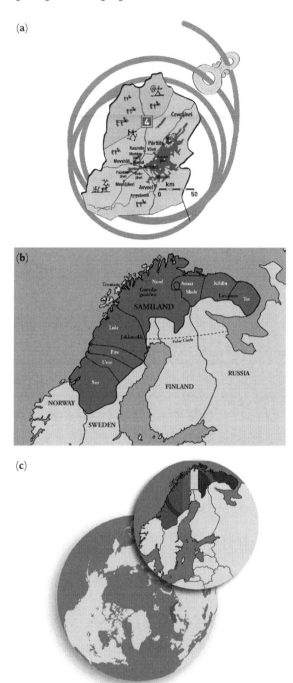

Figure 3.2 The Aanaar Saami-speaking area

the training of AS teachers for schools. He suggested that a language test be a prerequisite for hiring government or municipal officials wanting to settle in Aanaar. He furthermore stated that the Finnish state needed to fund AS literature. However, his recommendations were not taken seriously. People did not see that AS was endangered, because it was still an everyday language (even though the Saami people's knowledge of Finnish was getting better all the time) (V-P. Lehtola, 2012: 48–49). During the next 50 years the number of speakers declined by more than 200. One hundred years later, which is today, the estimated number of ethnic AS is around 900. Of these, only about 350 speak the language (V-P. Lehtola, 1997: 64). Although the group of AS speakers has always been small, its decline over the past 100 years has been substantial. The reasons for this will be explored below.

3.3 Defining the Saami and Identifying Speakers

The number of all ethnic Saami is estimated at between 75,000 and 100,000. The total number of Saami speakers is probably somewhat over 20,000, including fewer than 3000 in Finland, 1000 in Russia, 7000 in Sweden and 12,000 in Norway; all of these numbers are estimates (Sammallahti, 1998: 2). Regarding the lack of reliable data, Magga and Skutnabb-Kangas (2008: 110) formulated an explanation as follows:

> An old joke claims that a Saami family consists of a mother, a father, ten children, and an anthropologist. The Saami surely are one of the most researched groups in the world. Against this fact, it is amazing that there is serious lack of even basic data needed by the Saami themselves in order to be able to do proper language planning and implementation of strategies which lead to the maintenance of all Saami languages. 'We don't know who we are, where we are, and how many we are!' the Saami often say. The researchers were initially almost without exception outsiders, and even if much of what especially outside linguists did forms an important basis for Saami researchers today, it is clear that many of the basic data are not known. Nobody can tell, for example, how many speakers at what levels of competence each Saami language has.

The situation is not much better today. There are no statistics as to the exact number of speakers, or even the number of ethnic AS people, because there is no register where all the information about AS or the speakers of AS could be found (Kulonen et al., 2005: 5). Instead, information must be dug out of several sources, and even then they are not very reliable. The main problem is that the data do not typically differentiate between speakers of different Saami languages; instead, all Saami languages spoken in Finland are grouped together. This is the case, for example, with the voting list of the Saami Parliament. That list only shows the names of people who are over the age of 18 and are entitled to vote in Saami Parliamentary elections. That voting list includes Saami people who do not speak the language. In 2011 the election roll for the Finnish Saami Parliament had 5483 names of Saami over the age of 18. Of them, fewer than half – 2099 people – claimed Saami as their mother tongue. Of these, 1514 claimed North Saami (the largest Saami language, also spoken in Norway and Sweden), 332 claimed Skolt Saami and 253 claimed AS, both of the latter being spoken only in Finland (OKM, 2012a: 14). Most of the 253 AS speakers are elderly. The Saami Parliament Act defines a Saami as follows[3]:

> For the purpose of this Act, a Saami means a person who considers her/himself a Saami, provided:
>
> (1)   That s/he her/himself or at least one of the parents or grandparents has learnt Saami as their first language;
> (2)   That s/he is a descendent of a person who has been entered in a land, taxation or population register as a mountain, forest or fishing Lapp; or
> (3)   That at least one of her/his parents has or could have been registered as an elector for an election to the Saami Delegation or the Saami Parliament. (http://www.finlex.fi/fi/laki/ajantasa/2003/20031086? search[type]=pika&search[pika]=saamen%20kielilaki[4])

Statistics Finland shows the number of Saami language speakers who have claimed Saami as their first language.[5] In 2010 there were 1768 people,[6] out of an estimated 9000 Saami in Finland,[7] who spoke Saami as a mother tongue, representing only about 20%. However, it should be noted that in Finland one is only allowed to indicate one mother tongue on a birth certificate. According to our mother tongue definitions (see Info Box 9 Mother Tongue Definitions) one can have at least two, possibly three mother tongues (see also support from de Houwer, 2009). All Saami people who speak any of the Saami languages are either bi- or multilingual. Native AS speakers always speak Finnish, and most of them have learnt North Saami as well. The younger ones have also learnt other languages in school. AS speakers stand out among all Saami speakers in Finland in terms of their multilingualism. In 1962, 38% of AS speakers were multilingual (Nickul, 1968: 94). The corresponding percentage among North Saami speakers was only 7% and among Skolt Saami speakers 13%. Among Finnish speakers it was as small as 2%. At that time foreign languages learned in school were not included in the definition of bi- or multilingualism, because multilingualism was defined as having a very high competence in each language. Most native Swedish speakers in Finland are also minimally bilingual.

Regarding the identification of Saami as a mother tongue, it cannot be taken for granted that a Saami parent who speaks Saami to his/her child will claim it as the child's first language. In general people automatically identify the majority language, Finnish, as the first language, because they do not think or know why or how they should choose otherwise (see Aikio-Puoskari & Skutnabb-Kangas, 2007: 15–16 for the psychological reasons for this). Only Finnish or Swedish have been given as alternatives for 'first language' in the census; there is a category 'other', but because of the earlier oppression and people's image that one has to be literate in a language that one claims as the first language, Aanaar Saami have not chosen to write AS here. This is very unfortunate, because at least in the Finnish Saami area it would be important to choose a Saami language as the first language to improve the child's opportunities of getting into Saami-medium daycare. Apart from this individual benefit, in the long run it would also increase services in Saami languages. If there are very few or no Saami first-language speakers in local statistics, officials can always argue that there is no need to offer services in Saami languages because the speakers 'do not exist'.

In 2003 the Saami Language Act[8] (1086/2003) legislated that official services in the Saami area of Finland must be organised in Saami languages. This has improved the status of AS because it is mentioned separately in the Act. Nevertheless, AS has no official status outside the Saami area in Finland. This is a current issue in Saami language politics: already more than 60% of all Saami people[9] and about 70% of all Saami children in Finland live outside their homeland area (OKM, 2012a: 15).

Some sources outside the official statistics might be even more valid than the official ones in terms of accurate numbers of AS speakers. According to Ilmar Mattus, who has edited the community magazine *Anarâš* since 1987, the magazine is sent to approximately 400 households – to almost all AS speakers. In addition to these, scores of friends and supporters, as well as libraries, receive the magazine. Subscribers include both native and second-language speakers. Although the majority of Saami people live outside their homeland area, it can be argued that AS speakers are not widely spread out in the country; only 44 AS speakers (approximately 10%) who receive the magazine live outside the Saami area. These statistics, although unofficial, show that most AS speakers still live in their homeland area. These numbers are valuable for the language revitalisation process as well, as it can be argued that it is worthwhile to concentrate the revitalisation process in Aanaar municipality.

Another interesting source of information is a photo exhibition about AS speakers. Paris-based photographer Elina Juopperi took photos of all of the AS speakers that she could find through extensive research over many years. She ended up with 287 AS speakers. At the time of photographing in 2008–2010 she estimated the ages of the speakers as shown in Table 3.1.

Table 3.1 (p. 30) indicates clearly why the CASLE programme to revive AS among people of working age needed to be 'invented'. As in so many other Indigenous situations in the Western world where forced assimilation has been strong, the smallest percentage of speakers are between the ages of 20 and 39. In other words, nearly all people of working age have more or less

Table 3.1 Age range of 287 Aanaar Saami speakers (Elina Juopperi's statistics)

Age in years	<20	20–29	30–39	40–59	60>	Total
Number of speakers	46	11	20	52	158	287
Percentage of total	16%	4%	7%	18%	55%	100%

lost their language. Children and young people under 20 are now fortunately increasing among AS speakers because of the language nests, the first one of which was established in 1997. Most speakers are elders who speak the language well – but they have not transferred the language to the next generation. The age group 40–59 looks fairly good if we consider only the percentage (18%). However, speakers among this group are often so-called semi-speakers who do not use the language actively and have not transferred the language to their children. In the next section we will take a closer look at how well people in these age groups speak AS and in what kind of surroundings they use the language.

3.4 Aanaar Saami Use and Competence by Age Group

Children and young people who have learnt AS in language nests speak it mainly as a second language. The language used in the language nest is 'everyday language', meaning that it is concrete and concentrated on daily routines. However, AS culture is present in these routines, and therefore the vocabulary that children develop is closely connected to AS culture.

Before the most recent changes in the AS community, children had practically no other opportunities outside the language nest to use the language. Because of this, along with the lack of language support, children would normally use Finnish when communicating with each other. Even today, for some children, the language nest is the only place where they can hear AS. The situation is the same for primary school children. Outside school there are no leisure time activities in AS, apart from weekends once or twice a year.

The next age groups, 20–29 and 30–39 years, are the most critical. The people in these categories have lost their language – they are the lost generations. Following the Australian example, Skutnabb-Kangas calls them the stolen generations. When AS revitalisation began with the first language nest in 1997, there were only four native AS speakers under the age of 19. Other than these children who learnt AS as a first language, there were a few children who heard the language at home, since it was used every day between the older generations. However, the parents and grandparents did not transfer the language directly to the youngest generation so their language became receptive only; they understood AS but did not actively use it.

These two age groups and the next group of 40–59 were the target groups for CASLE (see also the selection criteria, p. 130). Many of these adults already had children; they had graduated and were on the labour market. They were seen as important language transmitters for the future.

The difference between the age groups 30–39 and 40–59 was that in the latter group there were already a few people who used AS at work. However, there were only five of them, and they were already drowning in work. This number was too low for language revitalisation purposes. From a language revitalisation perspective, it became obvious that there were not enough children who were learning AS, and the number of children in the language nest could not be increased if there were not enough language transmitters. This is why the idea of CASLE was born: if there were more, even a few, active language transmitters in key positions, such as in the language nest and in the school, the number of child speakers would expand and multiply over a fairly short time period.

The oldest age group, the elders, were native speakers. They formed over half of the total number of AS speakers. Not only did they represent the highest numbers, but they were also the strongest speakers. These elders used the language mainly with other elders and occasionally with younger speakers too, if they knew they could speak the language. However, most elders did not have any connection to language nest children. Further, because most of them had not transferred the language to their own offspring, they only had some older relatives or old childhood friends with whom they could use the language. Some of these elders had not used the language at all for decades. Some had even gone through a language shift from AS to Finnish in terms of usage at home with their relatives. They had given up speaking AS and accepted the requirements of what they thought was a modern Finnish-speaking Saami society. The idea of CASLE was to count on help from the elders regardless of their language competence or how much they had used AS before CASLE, through Master–Apprentice training (see p. 49).

As the statistics (Section 3.3) and the data on the language competence of AS speakers (Section 3.4) show, language loss had progressed quite far. The next section discusses the causes of this rapid language shift.

3.5 Reasons for the Decline of AS

The number of AS speakers has been rapidly declining since the beginning of the 20th century. Historically, there have been many reasons. Some AS people went through a language shift from AS to North Saami or Finnish through mixed marriages (Nickul, 1968: 55; V-P. Lehtola, 2012: 48). In 1920 the Spanish flu swept through Aanaar and killed about 10% of the population (Nahkiaisoja, 2003b: 294). This was the greatest catastrophe in the history of Aanaar and it had a strong effect on AS language and culture. One example is the loss of a great number of traditional AS songs [livđe] (Jouste, 2011: 50).

Perhaps the most significant impact on language and culture came with the Lapland War in 1944–1945. Nearly all the inhabitants of Lapland were evacuated to Ostrobothnia. According to Pekka Sammallahti, professor of Saami language and culture, the evacuation created the conditions for language shift (Sammallahti, 2011: Lecture at the Saami National Day Seminar, University of Oulu). For many Saami who came from Aanaar and the northernmost municipality of Finland, Utsjoki, the time spent in Ostrobothnia was their first long-term contact with Finnish-speaking Finland. Because many Saami became fluent in the Finnish language during this time, those who were parents thought that their Finnish had become good enough to be transmitted to their children. At that time bilingualism was viewed as a burden, and these parents saw a chance to get rid of it. According to Sammallahti, knowing and learning languages in general was thought to be a good thing, but bilingualism in Finnish and Saami was seen as harmful.

Another huge factor leading to language shift from AS to Finnish was the establishment of boarding schools. In 1927 it was decided that the migrating schools that followed Saami children would no longer receive any financial support from the state budget (T. Lehtola, 1996: 304–312). Those who were teachers in the migrating schools were catechists who usually knew either North Saami, Aanaar Saami or both languages, but in primary schools the language of instruction was mainly Finnish. AS pupils often studied the curricular content without understanding its exact meaning, instead learning it by heart (V-P. Lehtola, 2012: 284).

The municipality of Aanaar was founded in 1876, and the school system came to Aanaar around the beginning of the 1800s. Migrating schools were organised by the church, and the first catechists began teaching in Utsjoki as early as 1751. By the start of the 1920s there were still more school-aged children in migrating schools than in primary ones. The last migrating school was closed in Aanaar in 1954 (Lassila, 2001).

Primary schools were built in Aanaar around 1900, and education became compulsory in the 1920s. In the 1930s all municipalities in the Saami area had dormitories connected to the schools (Sammallahti, 2011: Lecture at the Saami National Day Seminar, University of Oulu). Until 1958 the first two grades were taught for only a few weeks in the autumn and a few weeks in the spring. Primary schooling itself lasted four years. After that, the 'kansaškovlâ' (the 'people's school') was extended to eight years. The old system of peripatetic schools ended both on paper and in practice with the Primary School Act of 1946.

In primary school, children were often punished for speaking Saami, and bilingualism was not tolerated or viewed as an advantage, neither for teachers (although assistant teachers were Saami) nor for pupils. This strict language policy was further enforced by building dormitories, where children who lived further than 5 km from the school were forced to stay. That meant that children could return home only a few times a year. The youngest children in dormitories were seven years old (V-P. Lehtola, 2012: 281).

It is only recently that some researchers have started to examine the kind of emotional effects the dormitories had on the mental health and development of the AS children (see Rasmus, 2008). It is a well-known fact that in almost all of the dormitories children were alienated and lost touch with their mother tongue (see, for example, Johannes Marainen's (1988) revealing autobiographical story about boarding schools on the Swedish side of *Sápmi*). When children finally came home for a visit, many of their parents thought they could no longer speak their mother tongue and spoke Finnish with them.

A third type of school, the most damaging in terms of language shift, was the Riutula school which was established in 1915. Riutula, unlike the two other schools in the municipality, was independent, controlled and governed by the Finns, and was therefore not under the control of Aanaar municipality (T. Lehtola, 1998: 299). When a national primary school auditor visited Riutula, he was deeply worried about the fact that most children came from either North Saami- or Aanaar Saami-speaking homes and yet the school did not promote or even tolerate their language or their culture. In his article he stated: 'Riutula kansaškovlâ does not improve the culture of Lapland, but instead seems to kill it' (T. Lehtola, 1998: 299). Many Saami children went through traumatic experiences in Finnish primary schools like Riutula, and it is only recently that these experiences have been brought to light. One touching example is a 2010 documentary film by Anja Ahola entitled *Suomi tuli Saamenmaahan [[When] Finland Came to the Saami Homeland]*.

When the number of speakers of a language goes down to a couple of hundred, the numbers have to be increased for it to survive. The AS community clearly needed a new AS-speaking generation among those of working age. In order to 'cultivate' these new speakers, the language competence of the remaining language speakers had to be put to use. For this purpose, suitable revitalisation methods needed to be specified, as discussed in the next chapter.

Notes

(1) The total area of Finland is 337,030 km^2 (130,128 square miles). Finland is the sixth largest country in Europe, for example, larger than the UK (http://en.wikipedia.org/wiki/Geography_of_Finland). The population is around 5.3 million. With an average population density of 17 inhabitants per km^2, Finland is the third most sparsely populated country in Europe, after Iceland and Norway (http://en.wikipedia.org/wiki/Population_of_Finland).

(2) The municipality of Aanaar is in the centre of the lower sector of the map of the Aanaar area (Figure 3.2).

(3) In many countries, also in Finland, and in international fora (UN Permanent Forum on Indigenous Issues (UNPFII), UN Expert Mechanism on the Rights of Indigenous Peoples (EMRIP), the UN Special Rapporteur on the Rights of Indigenous Peoples

(SRIP), UN Human Rights Council) there are discussions about the need to specify a legal definition of who is Indigenous. This question has been raised many times, initially in connection with definitions of minorities (where there is still no binding definition, despite whole books on possible definitions, e.g. Andrýsek, 1989). The most detailed definitions of who is Indigenous for the purposes of international law are still in Cobo (1987) and in ILO 169. EMRIP has recently been asked to work on the definitions, for instance by MAFUN, the Youth Association of Finno-Ugric Peoples, at EMRIP's fourth session, in Geneva, 11–15 July 2011, under Item 4, UN Declaration on the Rights of Indigenous Peoples, UNDRIP – MAFUN: 'Consider that the absence of a universal definition for "indigenous peoples" prevents States to equally fulfil their obligations' [in relation to UNDRIP] (doCip, 2012: 16). The issue is politically extremely sensitive, with implications including economic, territorial and self-determination for many areas (e.g. land rights). Discussions about possible changes in definitions are often emotional; unfortunately they are sometimes also less than well informed. Finland is here no exception. Relative linguistic competence and the fact that forced assimilation has for some Indigenous people(s) removed knowledge of their ancestral languages already some generations ago is one point of contention. We will not touch upon this issue in in this book – it would require an in-depth analysis that there is no space for here.

(4) The Finnish and Saami languages have only one gender-neutral third person singular personal pronoun, denoting both genders. The translator of the law has made the English language sexist, using only 'he'. We have corrected this.

(5) http://www.stat.fi/til/vaerak/2010/vaerak_2010_2011-03-18_kuv_002_fi.html

(6) That is 0.03% of the population of Finland (*Statistics Finland*).

(7) The total number of Saami people in Finland is estimated by the Saami Parliament at http://www.samediggi.fi.

(8) http://www.finlex.fi/fi/laki/alkup/2003/20031086?search%5Btype%5D=pika&search%5Bpika%5D=saamen%20kielilaki.

(9) http://www.samediggi.fi/index.php?option=com_content&task=blogcategory&id=105&Itemid=167.

4 The CASLE Revitalisation Method

4.1 Background for the CASLE Model

The complementary Aanaar Saami language education programme introduces some new aspects to the latest theory-based revitalisation models. It builds on methods previously created and introduced but adds a new perspective to them, 'creating' new speakers in the age group 26–54, through a very intensive one-year teaching process. The CASLE method represents a new model specifically planned for professional adults. It adopts suitable parts from common revitalisation models, with the hope of achieving the benefits they have generated in other linguistic communities. It also takes suitable parts from an existing university language study programme, modifying them while maintaining their intensity. These aspects, along with the generous funding (which enabled the intensity) and good planning, were unique to this programme.

The programme approach treats the local Indigenous language as a second language (L2) or 'foreign' language. Most CASLE students were L2 speakers of AS or, as it were, L3, L4 or even L5 or L6 speakers; in other words, all of them already knew other languages when they started.

The following revitalisation and language learning models (summarised by Grenoble & Whaley, 2006: 50–68) were used and adapted to create the content of the CASLE curriculum and its practical training environment:

- the local language as a second, 'foreign' language (Baker, 2006; Grenoble & Whaley, 2006: 56–58);
- California's Master–Apprentice (M-A) programme where young people learn from elders (Grenoble & Whaley, 2006: 60–63; Hinton, 2002);
- total immersion programmes (especially the language nest method) previously used for children, including very small children (see Info Box 7

Language Nests; Grenoble & Whaley, 2006: 51–55); here they were adapted for adults;

- partial immersion and bilingual education (Baker, 2006; Grenoble & Whaley, 2006; see Info Box 8 Immersion Programmes);
- community-based programmes (Grenoble & Whaley, 2006: 58–60); and, finally
- a language documentation model (Grenoble & Whaley, 2006: 68), which was added in order to film and record the most unique parts of the programme.

All of these models and approaches, along with the adaptations we developed for CASLE, are discussed in more detail in this chapter.

4.2 The Local Indigenous Language as a Second or 'Foreign' Language

4.2.1 Choosing to teach the local language as a second or 'foreign' language

The revitalisation approach to teaching the local language as a second or 'foreign' language was the most important basis for the CASLE curriculum. Adopting this approach linked CASLE automatically to literacy programmes and foreign language learning processes, especially those in school teaching and academic education. Choosing this approach represented a fascinating experiment which was also very contradictory, raising at least as many questions as it solved. However, since the programme was designed to teach AS to adults who had little or no background in the language, it seemed to be the only possible approach. It was not possible to wait for the young native speaker students from the language nests and lower primary grades to grow up and join relevant professions, since the fluent AS-speaking elders would no longer have existed as language models. New language transmitters had to be found among L2 speakers. The really haunting worry was that this model did not offer any certain results. No one knew for sure whether these adult students could learn the language well enough in a period of one year to be able to transfer the language to younger generations. No-one knew how the new language transmitters would eventually react in their new roles, either: would they be completely happy and satisfied, or would they mistrust their language skills in the same way that L2 English teachers worldwide tend to do? Research on non-native teachers of English has shown that some lack familiarity with the local culture (e.g. Liu, 2006: 172). This would not be the case with CASLE students, since they could be selected from among people who were committed to Saami languages and society. According to Llurda (2006: xi), many non-native teachers of English know that they need to struggle with the language and overcome threats to their self-confidence posed by a perceived inferiority relative to native-speaking teachers. This could, of course, happen to CASLE students as well, and therefore it was important to select students who were willing and motivated to put serious effort into learning the target language.

Another reason for using the second or 'foreign' language approach was that CASLE was designed for adults. According to Grenoble and Whaley (2006: 57–58), there are two ways of thinking about target groups. One is to begin language revitalisation with adults in the middle generation, relying on elders to provide the linguistic knowledge for the curriculum; this is the approach favoured by UNESCO. The other way is to begin creating a new speaker generation with the youngest, often starting with preschool or language nest programmes.

The recommendation to start with adults (Grenoble & Whaley, 2006: 57–58), in this phase where there was already a small new child speaker generation, was prioritised for several reasons. Firstly, since August 2000 when the first participants in the language nest reached school age, AS had an official status at school as a teaching language in the municipality of Aanaar. Secondly, the language nest was still producing new child speakers, so a small generation of AS-speaking young children already existed. The problem here was two-fold: (1) there were not enough school teachers, and (2) the number of child speakers had to be urgently increased to guarantee the survival of the language. An approach was needed to address both these problems at the same time. The problem of having a limited number of speakers in the youngest generation could only be solved through expansion of the language nests, which would entail training more staff and establishing new language nests. Because two generations had already lost the language, there were no young speakers of secondary school age or working age, so there was a gap between the generations speaking AS. Thus AS had to be taught to the middle generation first. After careful investigation, it seemed to be possible to produce a new working-age generation for the AS community by using a L2/foreign language approach.

4.2.2 Models for educating L2-speaking professionals as language transmitters

When planning for CASLE began, there was a lack of experience about revitalisation programmes for teachers or language nest workers, and little knowledge of their language learning processes. As Grenoble and Whaley (2006) point out, a lack of trained teachers is a common difficulty for revitalisation programmes. One possibility is to take a stepwise approach, using qualified speakers in combination with trained teachers who are not speakers. This usually happens through the pairing of teachers with elders, who often serve as classroom assistants, until younger teachers can be trained to use the target language. This has to be a temporary solution, because the fluent speakers are, from an administrative point of view, only able to take on the role of 'informal' teachers. Some communities may prefer to bring in outside language experts like trained linguists to help with the initial instruction and training of teachers. A critical component of the revitalisation programme is to train teachers who are language leaders (Grenoble & Whaley, 2006: 177–178). Andrea Bear Nicholas (2009), a Maliseet scholar from Canada, has described the immense difficulties of getting a teacher training programme going in order to create language nests and school immersion programmes in Canada. In addition, she sums up the challenges and details prerequisites for success, in order to share lessons learned with other Indigenous peoples struggling in similar situations.

Many Saami people seem to have an idealised notion of the middle generation as the only possible transmitters of the language, that is, they expect the middle generation, fluent parents, preschool and school teachers, to raise the children speaking Saami. However, if this middle generation has few or no native speakers, how can this 'lost generation' be recuperated? Yet there are options, according to the research literature. As Grenoble and Whaley (2006) point out, apart from the native speakers, the community often has at least some highly proficient speakers, semi-proficient speakers and even non-speakers who are all in some way committed to the language community. They continue: 'It is not particularly fruitful to divide the potential speech community into four distinct categories, but rather to recognize the shifting nature of communicative competence' (Grenoble & Whaley, 2006: 163).

Acquisition planning that recognises all of the shifting levels of communicative competence has been a fundamental idea of CASLE, where less fluent speakers can improve their language skills and even non-speakers can become active speakers through appropriate language education. This requires motivation on the part of the participants and coordination on the part of the staff. CASLE used as an example a few highly proficient L2 speakers of AS who had learned the language as adults and now speak it to their own children, who are growing up fully bilingual. These talented L2 speakers thus play crucial and multiple roles in the community in transmitting the language to younger generations.

As there was little relevant information available concerning the design of teacher training in revitalisation programmes (see Bear Nicholas, 2009 for similar problems), it seemed logical to look for answers in the research on non-native teachers of dominant world languages. Non-native language teachers are in the majority in language arts classrooms. School subjects other than the languages themselves are also taught most often by teachers who are not native speakers. This is, for instance, still the most common situation in African classrooms, especially after the first three years.[1] The teaching of the CASLE curriculum has been strongly influenced by worldwide research conducted on L2 English teachers (see Llurda, 2006; http://www.tesol.org).

The greatest difference between AS and English is that AS speakers number only around 350 while English is the most widely spoken foreign language throughout Europe. For example, 38% of EU citizens state that they have sufficient skills in English to hold a conversation (e.g. European Commission, 2006[2]). However, since L2 English teachers mainly teach English as a school subject, their role is different from that of teachers in the ambitious CASLE programme, which aimed to prepare L2 speakers at working age to be almost wholly responsible for the whole language transmission process. Finnish teacher training and also the training of teachers of foreign languages such as English is generally at a high level; this is one of the causal factors in Finland's high placement in PISA results (see OECD, 2010). The Finnish universities' experience in teacher training in a modified form influenced CASLE pedagogies more than TESOL-type approaches.

4.3 The CASLE Model of L2 Learning and Teaching

An implicit goal of second or foreign language teaching has traditionally been to gain skills that are as close to the 'native speaker' as possible, since the native speaker is seen as having the only acceptable form of language. For the past two decades or more, this goal has been seriously questioned, as has the whole concept of a native speaker (see, for example, Annamalai, 1998; Coulmas, 1981; Dasgupta, 1998; Davies, 1991; Faez, 2011; Graddol, 2003; Kandiah, 1998; Li, 2009; Phillipson, 1992a; Rampton, 1990). Rather than expecting native-speaker proficiency, a more useful and achievable goal is to become a successful L2 (or L3, etc.) user. The aim is thus to be able to use the new language appropriately for different purposes in different situations (Cook, 2006: 53, 55; see also Hymes, 1972 for the concept of 'communicative competence' – as opposed to a narrow Chomskyan 'linguistic competence' – which has since created a massive literature).

Replacing the lost generation through teaching the language to qualified professional adults fitted into this basic frame. A few Saami professionals argued that other school subjects in addition to AS language arts could be taught by non-native teachers using AS as a medium, if methods could be developed to bring their AS proficiency up to adequate levels. The language nests had already been seen to work by pairing a native speaker with proficient L2 speakers. Useful teaching and learning methods like this were thus needed for CASLE.

Most professionals needed communicative language skills at work, so communicative teaching had an important role to play. We found Vivian Cook's *Second Language Learning and Language Teaching* (1996) especially useful, since it presented L2 research along with language teaching methods in a manner that was useful in achieving the goals of CASLE. For example, the book introduces basic language learning and teaching styles. An *academic teaching and learning style*, which is characterised by grammar explanation and translation (Cook, 1996: 176–177), became an important part of CASLE because the AS university programme was used as a basis. An *audio-lingual style*, which stresses dialogue (Cook, 2006: 179–180), was partially used in creating CASLE study materials. *Social communicative and information communicative styles* are also part of the curriculum, designed to encourage students to interact with other people in the L2 (Cook, 2006: 185–187, 191). Regarding this latter point, having a conversation requires someone to talk to and also something to talk about. Since the main purpose of CASLE was to teach students to communicate in their L2 with native speakers and be able to teach the language to younger generations in everyday situations, the use of AS both for relationships between people and for the exchange of ideas fitted well, and was the main approach used in CASLE study materials.

4.4 Learning the Target Language From Elderly Masters

From the point of view of language learning, elders have a great deal to offer to students, but they are not likely to offer the use of their language skills without prompting and coordination. CASLE used two models where the language could be learned from elder speakers: California's M-A programme and the AS M-A training.

4.4.1 The Master–Apprentice programme of California

The original M-A programme was developed in California in 1992 by a Native-run organization called the Advocates for Indigenous California Language Survival (AICLS); in order to revive Indigenous languages with extremely low numbers of speakers. California used to be home to a large number of Indigenous languages, estimated to have numbered approximately 100 in the 18th century. Due to a range of political and historical circumstances, their numbers diminished rapidly, so that by the start of this century only some 50 languages remained, and only four of them had more than 100 speakers. The rest were very near extinction: 12 languages had 10–60 speakers, 13 only 6–10, and 21 languages had fewer than five speakers (Grenoble & Whaley, 2006: 60; Hinton, 2001: 217).

AICLS's programme is a total language immersion programme for adults. It pairs language learners with 'Master' speakers, that is, elders who speak the language, so as to form a language-learning team. The aim of the programme is to produce apprentice graduates who are conversationally proficient in the target language and are prepared to teach it to others. The Masters are often tribal elders who may not have actively used the language for many years, so they spend some time in training sessions, getting used to speaking the language again. Training sessions for elders also devote time to introducing the principles of language immersion, building and practising the vocabulary, and enforcing the importance of repetition, revision and patience in language learning (Hinton, 2002: 8–10).

The theory is that adults can learn a language informally in much the same way as children learn their first language. This happens through listening, speaking and eliciting language from a native speaker, mainly by doing activities together in an environment where the language is being used. One of the challenges has been finding a way for learners to get regular exposure to the target language every week, especially in situations where a language community does not exist. This is why specific immersion situations were created by the organiser (Hinton, 2002: 7, 9). The AS society has had the same need to create coordinated authentic immersion situations for the Masters and Apprentices, even though AS is still spoken by community members.

The programme in California followed a set of principles (see Hinton, 2002: 10–19) considered essential for successful language learning. These principles are as follows, including some modifications that we made for the CASLE programme.

(1) According to Hinton, the use of the dominant language (English in that case) is not permitted in M-A interactions; everything should be done and discussed in the heritage language. CASLE followed the same principle, that is, that Masters and Apprentices should not use Finnish. To ensure the cooperation of both Masters and Apprentices, the Apprentices were not sent into the field until their language skills were good enough for everyday conversation.

(2) Both Masters and Apprentices must be able to make themselves understood with non-verbal communication. This is essential in situations where there are unknown words in the target language. Even though both Masters and Apprentices in CASLE were told not to use Finnish in conversation, in practice Finnish was used occasionally, mainly in searching for a certain AS word.

(3) Use of full sentences is encouraged. Even though the speakers are often focusing on specific words, the real lesson comes by embedding the words in sentences and conversations in the target language. This principle was not followed in AS conversations in CASLE, because it is very common in all natural discussions to answer with one word, for example: *Kuás tun puádáh?* [When are you coming?] – *Onne* [Today].

(4) The aim should be for real communication in the heritage language. Everything should be discussed and done in the target language. This was also emphasised in CASLE.

(5) Language is also culture. Hinton points out that a great deal of vocabulary is embedded in traditional ways of life, like participating in ceremonies, traditional food gathering, and making or using objects such as

traditional houses, tools, weapons and cooking utensils. For CASLE, the traditional ways of life could not be taught in the classroom; the Masters were examples of real lived tradition.

(6)   The focus of the programme is on listening and speaking. Hinton argues that it is unnecessary to focus on writing and grammar in order to learn to speak the language. This principle was not as relevant in CASLE because the basic knowledge of the language was taught using written materials. However, language should be taught through activities, and the M-A activities should be seen as normal patterns of everyday life. For CASLE, this principle was very close to principle (5): the daily activities of the Masters brought the students closer to Saami culture and traditional ways of life.

(7)   The use of audio- and video-taping is valuable during the M-A programme. It can be seen as a record of the language as it is spoken by elders. It also makes the recording of (unique) gestures and actions possible. The students are able to use the tapes for studying later. The CASLE planning team discussed the principle thoroughly and advised students not to use pen and paper during the sessions. The students were equipped with digital audio recorders and told to record particularly interesting or difficult parts of conversations. They familiarised themselves with their recorders in the classroom before the M-A sessions.

(8)   The Apprentice needs to be an active learner. The Masters are language experts but often the Apprentices know more about teaching methods. Apprentices should feel free to guide their own learning processes by asking the Masters questions about the language, by suggesting activities, by setting up role plays or by asking the Masters to tell them about the things they have been doing. This principle was not strictly followed by CASLE: the Masters and Apprentices were free to choose their activities.

(9)   Masters and Apprentices need to be sensitive to each other's needs. The success of the M-A programme depends on the team members developing a warm, friendly and trusting relationship with each other. In CASLE the students could choose where to go for their M-A sessions. Some students wished to see as many Masters as possible in order to enlarge their knowledge of vocabulary and Saami cultures and language varieties, while some of them wished to work only with a couple of Masters in order to learn a particular variety thoroughly.

Hinton's book *How to Keep Your Language Alive* (2002) gives numerous hints on what aspects should be taken into account when setting up a community-based M-A programme. There are many factors: how many speakers are there? How many adults are willing to learn the language? Will the Apprentices be teaching the language themselves, perhaps in a school? Who will run the programme? Is there a need for grants and other funding? Will the M-A programme be a component of a broader programme or does it stand alone? The book introduces two variants of the programme: one intertribal and one college based. The main reason for choosing an intertribal programme, which might encompass different languages or varieties, is that some groups are too small to have a community programme, or lack the personnel for grant writing and administration. The college-based programme can be conducted as a course during the school year, as a summer course or as a college-based M-A programme. One example is the native elder apprenticeship at the University of Alaska, where both Apprentices and elders participate in an orientation workshop of 10 hours and in all local workshops organised for their language study. Students also meet for 10 hours per week for language instruction and maintain regular, independent contact (half an hour per week) with the course instructor (Hinton, 2002: 91–105). The CASLE programme used the principles of the college-based programme.

In the California programme the goals and expectations for each M-A year of participation are defined by the organisers. By the end of the first year, Apprentices should be able to ask and answer simple questions about themselves, describe pictures and use some culture-specific language. They also have to recite a short speech which they have prepared with the help of the Masters. This basic repertoire is expanded in the second year, with the goal of being able to speak in simple grammatical sentences, carry on extended conversations, have increased comprehension, converse about most topics and give short speeches. Finally, by the end of the third year, Apprentices should be able to converse at length, use long and more complicated sentences and develop plans for teaching the language to others. It should be remembered that Apprentices are not expected to acquire native-level proficiency. The programme does not attempt to revitalise speaker bases nor to make the target language a fully used system of communication in all aspects. Instead, it is a realistic, practical approach in situations of severe language attrition where it is most probably impossible to build a new speaker community (Grenoble & Whaley, 2006: 62–63; Hinton, 2002: 21–83). In CASLE there were no expectations of correct grammar during the M-A sessions. The most important aim was for learners to hear more of the target language than they got from the teachers in the classroom, and to learn the cultural vocabulary that belongs to the Saami way of life.

4.4.2 Documenting earlier individual AS Master–Apprentice 'training' experiences

During the last few centuries in particular and even until quite recently, linguists, ethnographers, anthropologists, missionaries and priests needed to learn the Indigenous languages of the peoples that they worked with 'on the job'. This was also true for those working with Aanaar Saami people in the

19th and 20th centuries. Individual researchers and priests used mainly local AS-speaking people as Masters. Most linguists documented the language at the same time through recordings and notes. Some did research for their own academic degrees. In the 20th century, Professor Erkki Itkonen cooperated with a great number of Masters in Aanaar. His closest Master was a local fisherman named Uula Morottaja, who accommodated Itkonen for a few summer periods so that Itkonen could be closely involved in the daily routines of his Master. During his field periods, Itkonen collected data for his AS dictionary known as *Inarilappisches Wörterbuch* (1986–1990) and for AS phonology research. He also collected stories that were published in his book entitled *Inarinsaamelaisia kielennäytteitä – Aanaarkiela čájttuzeh* [*Samples of AS*] (E. Itkonen, 1992).[3]

Because this earlier M-A 'training' in AS was for the needs of individual researchers, no organised programmes were developed. There is no documentation on the learning processes and goals, or about the practical realisation of these M-A sessions. To generate a basis for comparison, CASLE organisers interviewed Lea Laitinen, who studied AS using this individual method from 1973 to 1976, at a time when the language was starting to disappear.[4] The following description is based on two interviews with her, one in 2007 and one in 2010.

Lea had her first contacts with AS as a student in the late 1960s when she was researching place names in Sodankylä, her mother's home village. She was encountering Saami names and needed more knowledge of the language. After her graduation, she started collecting place names in Aanaar, where she also familiarised herself with AS. She started cooperating with Elsa Valle (née Kuuva) in August 1973 in Njellim. Lea found Elsa via Professor Itkonen, who considered Elsa the best possible Master for 27-year-old Lea because of Elsa's age (then 51), residence and language skills (she spoke AS at home). Lea spent one month in Njellim in 1973, and another month in 1974. In 1975 she could not travel to the north because of her baby son, but with a small grant she was able to invite Elsa to her home in Southern Finland. In 1976 Lea returned again to Aanaar for one month.

Lea did not know any AS before this training. She had studied Itkonen's publications, especially his phonetic transcription for AS, and read old AS folklore and vocabulary from *Inarinlappalaista kansantietoutta* [*AS Folklore*]. Itkonen had also given her some word inflections. Studying AS was challenging because there was hardly any written material. There was also a strong movement against earlier research about the Saami by 'outsiders', so she had to keep a low profile. During her fieldwork Lea observed that most people in Njellim used Finnish with each other, even if they were capable of discussing everything in AS. This happened often when Finnish-speaking people were present. Many informants even had difficulties in using AS. Language shift had clearly begun, and the assimilationist trend of the time was for Indigenous peoples to use the majority language wherever possible. Elsa

Valle's own children spoke only Finnish, but their receptive AS knowledge was excellent.

Lea remembers Elsa as an intelligent and talented Master whose language skills were outstanding and who tried to avoid the use of Finnish in teaching. Their sessions took one to two hours every weekday, as Elsa also had her daily tasks to perform. In the afternoons Lea worked unassisted, mostly rehearsing the day's recordings and going through her notes. Sometimes Lea joined Elsa in fishing or baking. For example, Elsa showed Lea how to roast thin barley bread outside using hot stones.

Elsa was often accompanied by her friend Elsa Saijets (née Mattus), also a mother tongue speaker of AS. They discussed everyday matters, including topics based on the stories of *Inarinlappalaista kansantietoutta*. With these familiar themes, it was easier for Lea to follow the discussion. The two Elsas even improvised a 'radio play' where the protagonists went fishing and picking berries. (This is consistent with Hinton's principle (9), as discussed above.) Lea's main learning method was to listen and try to understand the discussions, and to take notes. When her language skills improved, she also took part in discussions.

During her first journey she recorded as much AS as possible. She recorded Elsa's reading and word inflections as she read from *Inarinlappalaista kansanti-etoutta*. Lea followed the text from the book. Lea and Elsa were often accompanied by Elsa's husband, Heikki-Tuomas, along with Elsa Saijets. Together they visited and interviewed local AS speakers. The interviews were done by Lea's companions; this enabled them to use AS without switching into Finnish.

Later, as Lea's language skills improved, she transcribed her recordings together with her Master as exactly as possible. As the AS orthography was still unstable, people wrote the language in their own ways. However, Elsa had practiced AS writing with the Aanaar congregation's Vicar Antero Niva, by translating ecclesiastical texts into AS. Erkki Itkonen's orthography was developed later.

In Lea's view, the time she was able to spend with her Master was too short to learn spoken AS. Later she felt sorry that she did not spend longer periods in the Aanaar area. She relates:

> I discussed the matter with my husband recently. At that time, this pos-sibility did not come to our minds because we were building our home. I also could not see a future as a researcher: only men were researchers and women worked as research assistants.

She used M-A training in the early stages of her language learning pro-cess just as described in Hinton's programme. Her view now is that easy learning exercises should be prioritised at the beginning. She recommends inviting native speakers with good phonetic competence to discuss topics that are arranged in advance. The conversations can be recorded or filmed.

The Master can, for example, read texts aloud as the Apprentice follows them. The Apprentice can advance to a more advanced level by transcribing the recorded discussion word by word, together with the Master, and analysing the written forms of each word, as well as the declinations. At the beginning of the training, this can be done by offering the trainee a summary of the content of a whole text that is read aloud or by giving the text to the student before the listening comprehension exercise. The Master can also freely talk about topics discussed previously; this will make following the discussion easier. The use of recordings can be helpful, especially in cases where the Apprentice lives far away from the Master. In this case it is perhaps possible to organise weekend sessions or other types of periodic teaching in the language-speaking area.

Citing the positive aspects of her training, Lea emphasises that her teachers were talented and that the experience gave her the opportunity to learn the language intensively in real-life situations. A negative point was the short learning periods, realised only once a year. However, Lea developed a lifelong friendship with Elsa Valle that continued until Elsa's death in 2006. Lea also continued her language studies as a research assistant while editing *Inarilappisches Wörterbuch*. With her 'one month per year' method Lea attained the language skills she needed for her work, and now she understands everything she reads and hears in AS. She also knows the structure of the language thoroughly, but her active speaking is still slow. In her own assessment: 'If I had been able to spend a whole year in the Aanaar area, I would have learned to speak the language actively.'

4.4.3 Comparing Master–Apprentice methods: AICLS, Laitinen and CASLE

The three M-A programmes (AICLS, Laitinen and CASLE) described in the above three sections have very much in common, but they also differ in important ways. The main differences of the methods are described in Table 4.1.

4.5 Total Immersion Programmes

As stated in Info Box 8 Immersion Programmes, there are two basic types of immersion programme: one mainly for linguistic majority/dominant groups, and the other for Indigenous peoples or minority group members. In this section we concentrate on the latter type, drawing on what is known about dominant group immersion programmes only where needed. The models presented by Grenoble and Whaley (2006: 51–52, 86) are, like most immersion programmes, based on the assumption that daycare centres, schools and formal education are the main learning sites for the language,

Table 4.1 Goals addressed/achieved by three different Master–Apprentice programmes

Goals of M-A programmes	Hinton	Laitinen	CASLE
Goals for individual language proficiency and usage			
Full native-like proficiency	–	–	–
Understanding everyday spoken language	++	++	+++
Ability to speak fluently about everyday issues	++	+	+++
Ability to read	–/+	+++	+++
Ability to write fluently	–	+	++
Ability to analyse the structure of the language at a high level	–	+++	+
Ability to participate in community life	–/?+	+	+++
Knowledge about culture and traditions	++	+	++
Goals for community language usage Recreate the linguistic community	+	–	++
Provide human resources for language transfer/revitalisation	–	–	+++
Provide human resources for linguistic research	++	+	–
Create new language domains or revive old ones	++	–	+++

Notes: +++, The trait is present and the goal is reached extremely well; ++, the goal is reached well; +, the goal is reached to some extent; –, the trait is not present/the goal is not reached.

since it is not learned at home, and may not be used (or even heard much) in the environment of the learner. CASLE functioned as total immersion during the last nine and a half months of the study year, mainly because of its intensive nature. However, it was also influenced by the immersion programmes discussed next.

4.5.1 Informal short-term community-based non-school programmes

Community-based programmes are well suited for informal learning styles. They focus on language use rather than language instruction per se; at the same time, they automatically create a domain for use of the local language. Typical examples would be summer immersion camps or after-school activities. The AS community has organised language camps, AS evenings, art performances for children, music activities for youth, musical tours and religious events (*Anarâškielâ servi*'s Annual Reports, 2009–2011; see also Grenoble & Whaley, 2006: 59–60). These activities can be organised based on different kinds of minor grants. Because the programmes vary, they are often time consuming to plan. However, these events should become a permanent feature in language communities because they offer excellent domains to use the language. They are necessary for native speakers to maintain their language skills and for non-natives to learn the language in an informal, authentic way. Many AS speakers have experienced these events as unifying, healing and empowering because the speakers can act and discuss their experiences together.

4.5.2 The language nest

The language nest has been the backbone of AS revitalisation since the first one was founded in 1997. It offers daycare services through AS with total language immersion, that is, the language nest staff speak only AS to each other and to the children. The idea is to engage families with small children for a long period of their lives in the language revitalisation process. The AS language nest method is a copy of the Māori programme Kōhanga Reo (see Info Box 7 Language Nests; Info Box 8 Immersion Programmes; Info Box 12 Advice From Revitalisation in Hawai'i).

The Finnish Ministry of Education and Culture has based language nest funding for 2011 on the following definition (by Professor Pirkko Nuolijärvi, Research Institute for the Languages of Finland):

Language nest is included as a headword in the dictionary *Kielitoimiston sanakirja* [*Language Office's Dictionary*] (2006) where its meaning is defined in the following way: 'A crèche where the language immersion method is used in an attempt to revive an endangered language.' As an example, the dictionary gives the AS language nest. Nuolijärvi also quotes Annika Pasanen's[5] definition (2003: 1): 'Language nest is a crèche for children belonging to language minorities or indigenous people. In the language nest, all interaction happens in the minority language although the children don't speak it in the beginning.'

Our definition in Info Box 7 Language Nests states:

Language nests are early childhood daycare/nursery/pre-school/kindergarten/crèche arrangements for children from birth to school age. They are used by Indigenous peoples to revive or revitalise their languages, culture and values. They are based on total immersion in the language, that is, only the Indigenous language is spoken. Fluent elders support the staff who are not necessarily fluent in the language; many of them are second-language speakers. They can likewise be used (and are being used, e.g. in Catalunya and elsewhere) for non-Indigenous children, who are later going to attend immersion programmes.

The language nest programme has had a strong influence on CASLE planning. One of CASLE's primary target groups is that of childcare experts who will be essential in increasing the youngest generation of speakers through the AS language nests in the near future. This method is essential for school teachers as well, because by now practically all AS-speaking schoolchildren have attended the language nest programme. A practical reason for CASLE to highlight this method is that the language nest in Aanaar offered excellent language training facilities for students. Even though CASLE was designed to educate adults as opposed to children, the model of total immersion in the nests was a valuable one to consider for the CASLE approach.

At present, that is, immediately following the CASLE programme, the AS community has three language nests, two in Aanaar and one in Avveel, with eight employees. The aim of the language nest organisers has been to pair new L2-speaking staff with native speakers to strengthen the language skills of the L2 speakers.

4.5.2.1 Aanaar: Piervâl [literally, a bird's nest] and Piäju [literally, a fox and bear cave]

The first AS language nest known as *Kielâpiervâl* (now *Piervâl*) opened its doors in the autumn of 1997. In the 15 years leading up to CASLE, it produced approximately 40 new AS-speaking children. This number of young speakers was clearly higher than the number that would have grown up before the language nest activities, when the AS community had only four school-age speakers. *Kielâpiervâl* was widely seen by the AS community as a successful solution to the problem of language loss. However, 40 speakers in 15 years meant that fewer than three new speakers were cultivated per year. This did not guarantee a safe future for AS. The decision was thus made to enlarge the language nest activities, which caused astonishment in Saami society. The necessity of tripling the number of nests had to be explained to both authorities and funders.

The second nest, *Piäju*, which opened in Aanaar in March 2011, was a concrete product of the CASLE programme. Before opening *Piäju*, organisers discussed the experiences and results of *Kielâpiervâl* during the preceding 15 years. Quite a few children had already left the language nest and gone on to an AS class in primary school. According to *Kielâpiervâl* staff, the care of small children was time consuming, which reduced staff time with older children. Meanwhile, primary school teachers observed that language nest children seemed to have difficulties with AS vocabulary and some morphological and syntactic structures. Therefore it was necessary to revise the working methods of the language nest. After thorough discussions, it was decided that children up to two and a half to three years old would be located in *Piervâl* and older children in *Piäju*. This way *Piäju* staff would not need to work with bottles and nappies and would be able to pay more attention to older children's language skills.

During the year of the CASLE programme there was still scepticism as to whether or not there would be a demand for these new language nests. This fear seemed to be unfounded, as the nursery places of *Piäju* were very soon filled and there was still a queue for the AS language nests. It seems that the positive activities in the AS community have also increased the popularity of the nests.

The language nests in Aanaar offer full-time daycare, mainly during work hours, but there is also the possibility of offering early morning care and late afternoon care if necessary. Weekend care is not offered because of limited human resources.

4.5.2.2 The AS language nest in Avveel

The history of language nest operation in Avveel differs from that in Aanaar. Although Avveel is the centre of the municipality and has more language potential than Aanaar, there was a period of 10 years when there were no language nest activities.

According to notes by Katriina Morottaja, the former head of the education and culture department of Aanaar municipality, the first language nest was set up in Avveel in 1997. This language nest functioned in cooperation with *Kieláapierváal* in Aanaar until 2001. There were enough children to continue the language nest operation, but funding was unstable. During this period, the Saami Parliament received a grant from the European Social Fund for the organisation of intergenerational interaction in all three Saami languages. Several Language and Cultural Hamlets (LCH) were set up in the Saami area, including one for AS purposes in Avveel. Because the intention was to continue daycare services in the new LCH, the normal language nest funding was discontinued. This change was not in itself an issue, but the idea of replacing the language nest with a short-term project aimed at all ages had not been thoroughly considered. Eventual difficulties with funding allowed language loss among children in Avveel to resume. Every Saami language community had to plan LCH activities taking the specific needs of the language into account. Organising daily activities in the LCHs was the task of the LCH leaders, but their hands were tied because of funding issues, specifically that the LCH could not be used for children's language learning or daycare purposes. According to Kerttu Paltto, the former leader of the AS LCH, the regular users of LCH services were adults, mainly 30–80-year-old women who were interested in handicrafts. The leader was present full time and people visited for short conversations or for short courses organised by the LCH (Interview with Kerttu Paltto, December 2010). Funding for LCH activities was guaranteed only for a period of three years (2001–2003). The Saami Parliament applied, unsuccessfully, for follow-up funding. Although the LCH managed to activate elderly speakers to use AS, it certainly did not produce new young speakers in the same way as the language nest did (Olthuis, 2003: 576).

After the LCH programme, there was a period of two years when municipal AS daycare was organised for two AS-speaking children, since the Finnish municipalities have a commitment to organise instruction for all children in their native language. There was one family who wanted AS daycare for their children because AS was spoken at home. After this period, there was no AS daycare in Avveel until October 2010 when the AS language nest *Kuáti* was opened. *Kuáti* was a copy of the old *Kielâpiervâl* in Aanaar. It will take at least a few years for Avveel to create the same kind of language revitalisation pattern as in Aanaar, where the language nest produces AS-speaking children. As new AS classes are needed in the future, there is still a need to educate at least a few AS-speaking teachers there.

4.5.3 Some remarks concerning Saami language nest activities

In the Saami experience, language nests are a good method for language revival in districts where there are enough children and where the families are motivated to participate in language revival. In the Saami area, people's willingness to bring children to the nests seems to depend on the daycare needs of the children. That is, if the family has no need for daycare, it is usually not interested in using language nest services. One reason for this seems to be the municipal daycare fee[6] for parents that also has an impact on language nest activities.

The Skolt Saami community has revived its heritage language with the language nest method in Avveel and in Čevetjävri (Sevettijärvi). Although Čevetjävri is still the main speaking area of Skolt Saami, it seems to be extremely challenging to keep a language nest running there. One reason is that most families with small children have left the area because of a lack of career possibilities. Another is that the few families that have stayed do not have a need for nursery services. A third reason is that in Finland parents receive a child home care allowance if their children under the age of three are not in municipal daycare. This child home care allowance is in many cases the only regular income in Čevetjävri, and the family will miss it if the child goes into municipal daycare. Considering these facts, it can be argued that the language nest method may not succeed in all areas, especially where there are too few children or in cases where there is no need for daycare.

AS language nest activities are restricted to the municipality of Aanaar. Unfortunately they do not cover the whole Saami area nor the whole country, even if Saami Parliament statistics state that about 70% of Saami children under the age of 10 live outside the Saami administrative area. For successful revitalisation, it would seem to be necessary to bring the language nests into other cities and towns where Saami people live.

The language nest method, through total immersion, can support the language learning process for adults as well. However, research and experience suggest that the L1 of adult students should be used in order to support the learning of advanced vocabulary and skills in the target language. For appropriate methods, we turn to bilingual programmes.

4.6 Partial Immersion and Bilingual Programmes

The first two and a half months of the CASLE curriculum were taught bilingually, beginning mainly in Finnish and increasingly stressing AS until the students were fully able to follow tuition in AS. A separate teaching model for this part of the programme was needed. The main idea of the bilingual period was to use Finnish as little as possible, even at the start and even if the students felt unable to express themselves in AS, because they had to get ready for the forthcoming total immersion part of CASLE.

The notorious submersion education model in Finnish only was in use in Saami boarding schools until the 1970s (see p. 41). This meant that language minority students were thrown in at the deep end and expected to learn to swim as quickly as possible in Finnish without swimming lessons or floats. Students could either sink, or struggle and learn to swim (see Baker, 2006: 216–219; Cook, 1996: 195–207; Skutnabb-Kangas, 1984: 114–120). In our case, CASLE students were not minority students who needed (and were forced to learn) a dominant language, as in this type of submersion. Regardless of whether or not CASLE students had AS (= Indigenous) or Finnish (= majority) backgrounds, they had chosen to learn a non-dominant Indigenous language, and their command of the dominant language was excellent. They thus needed immersion.

Since the usual beginner level of the university AS study programme was too high for CASLE students, a kind of transitional bilingual education needed to be used in the initial period. Here the transition was in the opposite direction from that used in ordinary transitional models, which begin with a short period of non-dominant mother tongue-medium teaching and transfer to a dominant language. CASLE transitioned learners from a dominant language to an Indigenous non-dominant one (see Info Box 8 Immersion Programmes; see also Skutnabb-Kangas & McCarty, 2008 for more definitions). Transitional models are mostly categorised as a weak form of bilingual education, but in this case because of the direction from dominant to non-dominant it was a strong alternative. CASLE students had to learn a minority language and become insiders in the local community as soon and as deeply as possible (see also Baker, 2006: 214). We were able to document this process to some extent.

4.7 Language Documentation

Language documentation often has a nasty sound in a language research-er's ears; except for traditional missionary activity, it is most often started during the late stages of a language loss situation (see a critique of this 'archivism' in Skutnabb-Kangas, 2000: 237–238, and points 3 and 4 in Table 5.3, p. 79; UNESCO has also at times tended too much towards archivism). However, it is arguably important to document a language when it is reduced to a few speakers, as their linguistic and cultural knowledge must be preserved. This can be seen as a basis for future language revitalisation efforts (Hinton, 2001: 413). Fieldworkers should collect a wide range of information, including pragmatic and paralinguistic information, to give future generations an idea of how the language was used (Grenoble & Whaley, 2006: 68). It is, however, extremely important to note that documentation does not happen *instead* of language revitalisation efforts, but *in addition* to them.

AS has been documented for the forthcoming generations in dictionaries, in grammars, in numerous texts and in the archives of the Saami Radio. In addition, the Saami Archives have plans to develop documentation activities in the near future. There should be enough linguistic data to save AS, as no-one doubts what kind of language it is or how it sounds.

The CASLE planning team used two methods to document AS. Firstly, the students recorded their Masters, mainly in order to do research on AS dialects. These recordings were archived by the University of Oulu. The Masters spoke mainly about their own lives as Saami and about their ways of life. Some students managed to record vanishing information about AS traditions, for example, the healing effects of local plants.

Secondly, some field courses/situations were filmed by Anneli Lappalainen, a North Saami broadcaster who has acted as a director of Saami films. She filmed CASLE Apprentices along with their Masters and other teachers. The purpose of these recordings was to produce short films as study material on traditional ways of Saami life. Anneli filmed entire processes of sewing traditional costumes, making shoes from reindeer skin, preparing traditional meals such as reindeer sausages and blood pudding, and fishing. Reindeer roundups were also filmed to show where foodstuffs come from. Only two M-A sessions were filmed, mainly because the students wished to keep these sessions as private learning moments. In our view, these were all areas where old traditional vocabulary fitted together with traditional tasks.

Initially Anneli faced a conflict between film making and CASLE. Normally she strictly directed the 'crew and cast' during the film-making process, but this time she decided to play the role of an outsider/guest behind the camera, working among people who were just beginning to revitalise their language. Anneli decided to be extremely sensitive and let the language and everyday activities guide the work. According to her, the traditional film maker's view, that is, directing 'the cast' by asking for silence and filming the same shot again and again, would certainly have disturbed the authenticity of the moments between the Masters and Apprentices. She filmed what she could, and if she missed important pieces concerning the plot and process, she completed the material later with extra shots. Anneli stated: 'I did not film every little detail in the sewing process. The filming can be used as additional study materials but it does not replace a teacher.'

The only thing Anneli asked as a director was for her 'cast' to arrive and leave as a group in the filming. In real life, almost everyone had arrived alone. She tried to follow the same students as much as possible during the CASLE programme year in order to place them easily in different kinds of places and language situations.

Apprentices and Masters reacted differently; some of them were shy when they were filmed and found it disturbing, but others acted normally in the presence of Anneli's camera. All in all, we see that it is important to film language revitalisation programmes like CASLE, to document both the programme and the learning processes. However, one has to consider the authenticity of the programme, the film maker's requirements and the feelings of the 'cast'. Anneli's two CASLE films on shoemaking and traditional cooking were shown at the *Skabmagovat* Film Festival in 2011. During the writing of this book, Anneli is continuing her work on the filmed materials in order to make a documentary about the CASLE programme.

This book can be seen as part of the efforts to document the CASLE programme, representing our commitment to describe our revitalisation efforts for worldwide use.

Notes

(1) For a summary, see Alidou *et al.*, 2006. This document has been re-edited into Ouane and Glanz (2011).
(2) http://ec.europa.eu/languages/documents/2006-special-eurobarometer-survey-64.3-europeans-and-languages-summary_en.pdf
(3) According to Lea Laitinen.
(4) From 1979 to 1990 Lea Laitinen worked with Itkonen on the AS dictionary *Inarilappisches Wörterbuch*, published in 1986–1990. Earlier, she had edited the second edition of *Inarinlappalaista kansantietoutta [AS Folklore]* (Koskimies & Itkonen, 1978). After the dictionary project, Lea edited the book *Inarinsaamelaisia kielennäytteitä – Aanaarkiela čäjttuzeh* (Itkonen, 1992), based on Erkki Itkonen's field recordings from the 1950s. In 2011 Lea retired from her Chair in Finnish at Helsinki University.
(5) Annika Pasanen is a language sociologist who has learnt AS as an adult and speaks it now to her two children, who have become bilingual since early childhood.
(6) This is the obligatory municipal daycare fee for everybody; only households with very low income can apply for the fee to be waived.

5　The CASLE Year

5.1　The CASLE Study Programme 2009–2010

First a reminder: all the students were speakers of Finnish; some had heard or knew North Saami; a few had heard (some) Aanaar Saami. Finnish and all Saami languages are related Finno-Ugric languages. They are all agglutinating, which would make understanding the principles of the morphology easier for these students than for people with no exposure to such morphology. However, the languages are not mutually comprehensible, even if some vocabulary may be similar. For practical purposes, and for people with no training in linguistics, the benefits from any linguistic proximity of the languages would be marginal, at least initially. On the other hand, all of the students had learned several languages already, so their multilingual skills and metalinguistic awareness would be an asset.

The AS study programme at the University of Oulu was the best available programme prior to the creation of CASLE (see p. 66). However, because its starting level was too high and because it was too theoretical for revitalisation purposes, the programme needed to be modified to create CASLE (see p. 66).

As mentioned in the introduction, the CASLE study programme consisted of two parts: courses that were taught in the classroom and courses that were taught outside the classroom, the latter in cooperation with the AS community. Both of these parts are discussed in this chapter.

5.2　Language Lessons Building on the University AS Study Programme

5.2.1　Classroom teaching: Planner's view

Because the CASLE programme had to be more practical than a 'normal' academic-style programme, the AS instructors (see p. 71) needed to prioritise the learning of everyday language, as well as language related to the domains in which students would work after CASLE (see p. 20). The language lessons thus stressed daily language skills, especially oral productive skills and writing.

Most of the classroom-taught parts of the programme built on the university AS study programme. The exceptions were the Beginning course and the Continuing course, each added for CASLE purposes. These courses, as shown in Table 5.1 (p. 57–59), were managed and funded mainly by the University of Oulu.

The classroom-based teaching listed in Table 5.1 consisted of lessons, practical exercises and independent student work. In the original programme, each study point represented approximately 13 hours of contact lessons and 14 hours of independent study. Because the aim of CASLE was to teach the students to speak AS competently as early as possible, the workload was temporarily raised to 16.5 hours of contact lessons per study point. CASLE thus offered 90 extra contact hours during the first three courses: 30 extra hours spread out over the Beginning and Continuing courses, and 60 hours spread out over the courses in Phonetics and morphology. During the Beginning and Continuing courses the students had four full days of work outside the classroom during which they were supposed to do homework and study for the exams. As many of them drove about 80 km a day to the study centre in Aanaar, such flexibility in the programme was greatly appreciated, and students generally liked homework days very much.

The writing course also demanded extra attention because students asked for individual guidance concerning their texts. The extra time meant that grammar, errors and expressions could be analysed thoroughly. Student style could be commented upon as well, indicating the extra time people put into learning AS (see also p. 132).

The students' high level of motivation was appreciable. When there was a teaching-free learning week scheduled, originally meant for independent student work, the students wished to learn professional vocabulary for their respective areas and more grammar. In response, the instructors organised several workshops during that week on authentic situations (in the language nest, at school and at church) and on grammar, writing and special AS domains such as mathematics and biology.

As noted in Table 5.1, Finnish was used as a teaching language during the first three courses, mainly during the Beginning course and remarkably less during the Continuing course. In Phonetics and morphology Finnish was only used to explain difficult aspects of grammar. After these first three courses, AS became the teaching language and Finnish was used only occasionally, for example to explain the meaning of single words or some difficult grammatical points. From the fourth course, CASLE continued as a total immersion programme with AS as the only teaching language. It was expected by then that the language skills of the students would already have progressed to a reasonably competent level. This had to happen because the

Table 5.1 Classroom-based courses

Course	Study points	Expected learning outcomes related to content	Teaching languages[a]
Beginning course	5	The student knows the basics of AS grammar and pronunciation as well as the most essential vocabulary related to everyday life. S/he is able to carry out simple conversations and read elementary texts.	Finnish–AS
Continuing course	4	The student demonstrates deepened knowledge of AS grammar, pronunciation and vocabulary. S/he is able to discuss more complicated matters related to everyday life and can write elementary texts about familiar topics.	AS–Finnish
Phonetics and morphology	9	The student demonstrates familiarity with the following specific features of AS phonetics: half-long consonants, stretched vowels, regular vowel changes in the 1st and 2nd syllables, length of diphthongs and consonant changes beyond the 2nd syllable. The student can apply systematic AS consonant gradation and shortenings/lengthenings of consonants and vowels related to consonant gradation. The student demonstrates an understanding of AS morphology by correctly inflecting common nouns and verbs.	AS (Finnish)
Introduction to AS research	2	The student demonstrates familiarity with AS researchers and can describe the most important AS linguistic research. S/he can describe AS usage, using linguistic terms, especially AS linguistic terminology.	AS

(*continued*)

Table 5.1 (*Continued*) Classroom-based courses

Course	Study points	Expected learning outcomes related to content	Teaching languages[a]
Development of literary language	2	The student can describe the history of AS as a literary language and its development from the first written texts in the 19th century until present, with particular focus on the 19th and 20th centuries.	AS
Syntax	6	The student can parse AS by analysing the syntactic and semantic roles of the constituents. S/he can identify the morphosyntactic differences between Finnish and AS.	AS
AS texts and modern literature	3	The student demonstrates familiarity with modern written AS and with narrative traditions (oral and written), and can describe the development of the written literary language.	AS
Writing	3	The student writes AS correctly, observing orthographic conventions, using appropriate sentence structure and employing a variety of text types. S/he can produce linguistically and stylistically highly proficient texts.	AS
Word formation	4	The student applies appropriate rules of word formation in her/his oral and written AS, with attention to compounding, derivating and loaning words.	AS
Translation	5	The student is able to describe the translation process thoroughly, solve basic translating problems, attend to the outcomes of the translation process, i.e. produce a proper translation from Finnish to AS, and critically analyse completed translations.	AS

Table 5.1 (*Continued*) Classroom-based courses

Course	Study points	Expected learning outcomes related to content	Teaching languages[a]
Language planning	4	The student is able to provide advice in AS. S/he is able to answer questions with regard to terminology and to address other issues concerning the language planning of a minority language.	AS
AS dialects	2	The student can apply methods and findings of (regional) dialect research in AS to plan, carry out and report on an investigation in this area.	AS
Independent study week	1	The student expands her/his familiarity with AS terminology in his/her own profession.	AS
Study weeks in total	49		

[a]Order reveals relative amount of use, e.g. Finnish–AS means that Finnish is used more than AS, and (Finnish) means that Finnish is used only as needed.
Notes: The courses are in sequence, i.e. each builds on the one before it.
Source: http://www.oulu.fi/hutk/opiskelu/opwas/Opas_11_13/Saamen%20kieli.pdf

students would soon be sent into the field where they were supposed to use only AS.

5.2.2 Classroom teaching: Suvi's student view

5.2.2.1 Getting started – with a psychologist's help!

CASLE started in mid-August 2009 with a day of orientation for the programme itself and AS language and culture. Through a few interesting presentations we students were given a general overview of the present state of the language community: the AS language association (see Info Box 17 *Anarâškielâ servi* [Aanaar Saami Association]), instruction in schools, the language nests and the key people involved in AS revitalisation. From the viewpoint of a student it was all very inspiring and gave us a better picture of what we were getting into.

On the second day we had a team coaching day with psychologist Marjo-Riitta Mattus. She had already been involved in the process of student selection (see p. 130), and now she had been asked to spend the second day with us in the classroom. In the project planning team there had been some serious discussion and diverse views about the necessity of team coaching for academic adults. When the project planning team agreed that it was necessary in a special programme like this, the team members still had to convince the University of Oulu to grant the funding for it.

The idea of adults playing games and getting to know each other under external guidance may have seemed too strange for the world of Finnish academics, but for us, the students, team coaching proved to be one of the most memorable days of the whole year. Marjo-Riitta encouraged us to talk about our hopes and wishes for the coming year, as well as about our personal motivations for joining CASLE.

For some of us, especially for those who had AS roots, CASLE was a lifelong dream come true. Here are my translations of what my fellow students said in the student feedback; the answers are anonymous[1]:

Answer 1: My father's first language was AS but he did not speak it to us – to his children. As a little girl I wanted to learn AS at school but it was not possible. It was such a relief to actually realise that that was about to change. It was healing to cry together for all those lost possibilities that I, and many of us, had had in our lives before.

Answer 2: AS was the language of my grandmother but she couldn't speak it to us. I had been dreaming of becoming a part of language revitalisation and giving my own children a chance to learn it.

For some of us, CASLE offered a concrete chance to return to our roots:

Answer 3: I liked my job but I never felt at home in the capital city. I missed my home, family and friends all the time more and more. When I read about this programme in the newspaper I thought that learning AS would take me back to my roots and to my Saami identity.

For others, especially for those of us of Finnish background who had moved to the Saami region later in life, our goals for participating in CASLE were more of a practical kind. Perhaps this language would be the key to cultural understanding, and offer students a better chance to stay in the region in the future, in terms of career[2] and salary.[3]

Answer 4: I was planning to move to Aanaar but I had no idea about getting a job. The employment situation, in my field, did not look good either. I thought that perhaps knowing AS would become useful someday. Learning that the language was endangered gave me extra motivation.

Answer 5: I work as a teacher in the field of social and health services. I have seen the benefits of nursing patients in their own language.[4]

As for me, I thought that I could perhaps help to improve the somewhat lousy situation of the AS electronic media (see Info Box 13 Saami Media in

Finland). I also dreamt of helping my AS children with their school home-work. At that point, I did not dare to even imagine that AS would become our home language one day (as it later did!).

On the team coaching day I remember sobbing, saying that it should have been the father of my children there instead of me. He was the one whose mother tongue had been lost, not me. I was weeping not only for him but for the whole lost/stolen generation (see Info Box 15 Lost or Stolen Generations). It made me so sad to think that there were so many people like him in this village, in this country and in this world who shared the same story. Only a very few of them would ever have a chance to reclaim their language (see Info Box 11 Ann-Helén Laestadius: A Personal Example From Northern Sweden). It was painful to realise that, because of my fortunate background and the opportunities that I had been offered previously, I was privileged again, in this case to join CASLE. As a non-Saami I also felt a bit guilty for that, and knew that I would have to face some critique, as not everyone would appreciate my decision to learn the language.

As seen from the examples above, for some of us that connection to AS and AS culture was tighter and more emotional than for others. It was touch-ing and certainly also rather confusing to hear and share all those different stories right at the beginning when we hardly knew each other. I do not know if it was due to the skills of the psychologist in the classroom or what exactly happened, but certainly no-one could have described us as 'stiff, quiet and shy', as Finns are often characterised.

All those tears and laughs that we shared shaped us into a group. We realised that we shared a common goal – the goal of reviving an endangered language. We knew that each and every one of us would play an extremely important role in doing this. We were the representatives of the lost genera-tion. We realised that we could improve the present language situation, that we were active doers, and that in the future it was our own responsibility to transmit AS to new speakers. At least for me, realising the importance of our part in the language-speaking community and in its future was really empowering and motivational.

I think that the strong team spirit we developed from the start made each of us try a little harder every time it all seemed impossible and our tar-gets seemed far too idealistic, unreal and out of reach. Out of solidarity with each other we tried to hang in there until the end of the programme.

5.2.2.2 Becoming inspired by a great head teacher and other instructors

A year before the start of the CASLE programme, Marja-Liisa Olthuis as Project Manager had already mapped out possible teachers who could take responsibility for the Beginning and Continuing courses (see p. 128). Basically there were two possible teachers. One was Petra Kuuva,[5] an AS herself, who reclaimed her mother tongue as an adult. However, Petra was expecting a baby and lived more than 600 km away from Aanaar where the course was to be held. At that time, it seemed impossible for her to take on such a great responsibility, considering her situation. As Petra had to be excluded, there was only one option left. Luckily, that option happened to be perfect.

Petter Jori Andaras Morottaja (born in 1982) had already taught AS, for example at the Saami Education Institute in Aanaar and at Helsinki University. He thoroughly understood what the demands of CASLE would be because he had worked on the study materials team (see p. 128). Because of their positive experiences and intense cooperation, Marja-Liisa trusted Petter and his ability to cope with the great challenge he was to be given. As she said, 'Petter is, by nature, a person whom you can easily cooperate with. He is also a real all-round person who has the capacity to see things from many viewpoints.'

When Petter first stepped into the classroom, we saw a relaxed, quiet and humorous young man. It was also funny how much he reminded us of his father, Matti Morottaja, the well-known AS teacher and initiator of the AS revitalisation movement.[6] Of course it was an advantage for Petter that we all knew about his father's reputation and his relentless work. We had also learnt that in 1986 there were only four children under school age who spoke AS as their mother tongue. One of them was Petter; the others were his two brothers, Mikkâl and Saammâl, and Anssi Mattus, the son of Ilmari Mattus, the former secretary of Anarâškielâ servi (see Info Box 13 Saami media in Finland; Info Box 17 *Anarâškielâ servi* [Aanaar Saami Association]). We realised we were very lucky to get a native AS speaker as our head teacher.

As most of us were older than Petter and many of our group were teachers themselves, it could be expected that Petter would experience at least a little stress when he started teaching us. However, he denies there was any:

Already at the early stage I had to admit to the students and to myself that I did not know the answers to all the questions. When I admitted that, it was a lot easier to get on with the teaching. In general, the group was easy to teach, because everyone wanted to learn. Of course they challenged me. But no, I felt no pressure.

I think it was partly Petter's humour, humility and down-to-earth appearance that won us all over and charmed us. Petter received very positive feedback from all of us students, right from the beginning of CASLE and until the end of it.

Petter knows the language well but he does not hesitate to admit when he does not know the answer. He seems balanced and he treats everyone in a pertinent manner, equally. He does not bring his ego through in a disturbing way. (From the summary of student feedback for the Beginning and Continuing courses.)

Petter was also capable of creating an environment where everyone could relax and practise the language without feeling ashamed of making mistakes.

> One of the best things throughout CASLE was the fact that we had such great teachers, especially Petter. That benefited our language learning. If I had felt uncomfortable in the classroom I would not have learnt the language as well as I did. (From the summary of student feedback for the Beginning and Continuing courses)

From the beginning, Petter's way of teaching was conversational, although theoretical as well. We students liked his style of teaching. We worked a lot in pairs and in groups of three when we tried to repeat and use some common phrases. Every Friday we had a short written exam to give and get feedback on what we had learned during the week. Petter also gave us regular written vocabulary tests.

One prerequisite for all CASLE students was that we had studied and also learnt languages before. Some of us knew even five or six languages. Even so, the starting level among us students varied a great deal (see Info Box 16 Third Language Learning). Despite this, most students thought that Petter managed to keep up a tempo that enabled everyone to follow and did not allow anyone to get bored. He was always ready to offer extra practice for those who had already learnt the basics of the language or were otherwise really quick learners.

Asked about the greatest challenge of classroom teaching, Petter replied that it was the language itself. In particular, the course on Phonetics and morphology took the students deep into the peculiarities of AS and apparently also challenged him as a teacher. He states:

> One of the difficulties I experienced was that AS is a difficult language. It is a difficult language to learn, but also to teach. For example, conjugating verbs is very difficult. Teaching that properly would have also needed more materials,[7] and the materials we had should have been there well before the start of the course. (See p. 128)

According to most students, the language bath (or immersion) started at a good stage, when we were ready to stop using Finnish. Petter himself thinks he could have used more AS right from the beginning and that the immersion could have started even earlier. The students who already knew the North Saami language would have liked to switch to immersion earlier, even during the Beginning course. In fact, out of 17 students, only a few did not know North Saami at all. Some knew North Saami very well, some fairly well and some had taken at least a beginners' course. Even though North and Aanaar Saami are different languages altogether, they do have a lot of similarities in terms of grammar and vocabulary, and therefore knowing North Saami was a great advantage, at least at the start of the course. However, all of us students, regardless of earlier Saami language background, enjoyed starting the immersion phase of the programme. The following quotes are from the summary of anonymous student feedback for the Beginning and Continuing courses:

Answer 1: I for once had already been hoping for some immersion. To me, learning a new language by listening is crucial. My weakest link in language learning is the grammar. North Saami language I had already learnt – mostly by listening to the Saami Radio. Changing the teaching language into AS helped me to start thinking in AS in the classroom. Speaking followed soon after that. If the teaching language had not changed I don't think that studying would have remained as reasonable as it did.

Answer 2: I hadn't learnt any North Saami before, and therefore I panicked about the language shift in the classroom even from the beginning. However, when the instructional language changed and I got over the first shock, I realised that I actually understood something. It was just perfect timing – I think the threshold [stopping us from speaking] would have become even greater if the language shift had not happened by then. My goal was to get practical, everyday language skills but my biggest fear was to speak to people. However, bringing AS into the classroom in this way, and in this way only, made it possible to speak.

Petter acted as a head teacher most of the time. As described, he was responsible for the Beginning and Continuing courses as well as for Phonology and morphology, Writing, AS texts and Modern literature as well as the independent study week. Because the programme was very demanding, additional instructors were needed. Marja-Liisa taught Word formation and translation, which were her specialities from her doctoral thesis (Olthuis, 2007). She also taught Writing together with Petter. Matti Morottaja, Petter's father, was very experienced in AS language planning, so it was natural to ask him to teach this course. Petra Kuuva, who was not able to take responsibility for teaching at the beginning of the CASLE programme, was later able teach two courses, Development of literary language and AS dialects. Taarna Valtonen, a Finnish linguist who learned AS as an adult, taught AS syntax, as she wished to teach the more theoretical parts of CASLE. Taarna lives in Helsinki (the capital of Finland), so she travelled to Aanaar a number of times to conduct her teaching periods. It was CASLE's speciality to teach through strict teamwork, and every instructor had his/her own specialities that could be exploited in productive ways by the programme.

5.2.2.3 Getting lost in linguistics

Once we had warmed up and felt as though language learning was proceeding quickly (you know that euphoric early stage of language learning!) there were still hundreds of complicated grammatical things to learn and hundreds of lessons to sit through. I had never studied linguistics or any language at university level before. When it was time to move on from the Beginning and Continuing courses to more theoretical subjects like syntax, I knew I could expect some trouble. Unfortunately, I was right about myself.

I trusted our teacher, and tried to follow the lessons carefully and do everything that I was told to. However, I kept constantly drifting off the subject, asking myself (and sometimes the teacher): 'What the heck do I need this for?' During those 60 hours of sitting in the classroom and 100 hours of independent work required by the Syntax course, I am not sure if I ever got an answer to that question. I think that was exactly the problem; I could not find the connection between the theory and the everyday language.

According to Marja-Liisa, it was known that the Syntax course would be CASLE's most theoretical course. Knowing the learning aims of the group, she had already taken out the heaviest parts of the Syntax course that had been constructed along the lines of the programme at the University of Oulu. The focus in syntax was especially in parsing; this was what we would need the most.

We all had our own interests that affected our motivation, but one thing that I only thought about later was that perhaps some of the difficulties that I in particular experienced during the syntax course were caused by the fact that my language skills at that point in mid-January were not yet good enough to study entirely through AS. We had already started the immersion so we were kind of used to not understanding everything. However, perhaps my frustration at the time was at least to some extent caused by the fact that I missed too much information because of the language barrier. Since all the study materials were also in AS I think we spent far too much time and energy trying to understand things that would have been complicated enough even if they had been taught in Finnish.

Luckily we could always find the study materials on the internet after the lessons. Our teachers used to save all the material from the classes there, using a special University of Oulu site, and this was a lifeline that saved us many times. It was of course also crucial when one had to be absent from lessons.

In order to learn proper language skills, we also had to struggle. Later I realised that another reason I sometimes got so tired of grammar was that I was simultaneously making a language shift at home with my kids. I remember that once my elder son, who was five years old at the time, shouted at me: '*Mun jiem haalijd kuldâlid tuu, ko tun sáárnuh nuuvt hitásávt!*' [I don't want to listen to you because you talk so slowly!]. Ironically, it was his first whole sentence in AS that was directed to me. Getting this kind of not very encouraging feedback from my kids and wrestling with grammar during the lessons was sometimes rough, especially because of the timing – it was in the middle of the long polar night. In the spring, when the sun finally showed itself after one and a half months, things started to get easier. Slowly my son also got used to me speaking (slowly), and slowly my language skills got better and I was able to speak faster and make fewer mistakes. . . .

Today, when I look at the number of hours we spent in the classroom, I smile and admire myself and all the others who passed that year and learnt the language. After all, learning a language and being able to communicate, write and read in it within a year, as an adult, is a little miracle (see student selection criteria, p. 130). And of course to achieve such a goal, one has to be prepared to struggle a bit.

Although at times AS grammar seemed to me just like a complicated bunch of exceptions without any logic, most of the courses that were taught in the classroom were really interesting. I especially enjoyed the courses in AS research history and the Development of literary language. I think it was nice to learn about the people who had contributed to all of this. Different teachers also brought variation to our routine.

At the end of the programme, after seeing the outcome of the course and reading both teacher and student feedback, I can see that a new kind of curriculum that approaches AS from the angle of language revitalisation and a foreign language has been developed. Today, as an outcome of the CASLE programme and Marja-Liisa's work, it is possible to take AS as a major at the University of Oulu (see p. 154). This programme uses a curriculum modified from CASLE.

5.2.2.4 Getting creative during independent study time

On top of the 12 courses mentioned in Table 5.1 (p. 57), we had an optional independent study week with various themes where we could learn things that were useful from the point of view of our professions. For example, during that week I finished my documentary film project *Reborn*.[8] Some other course participants collected kindergarten vocabulary or translated religious texts, hymns and prayers.

The number of independent study hours was quite impressive too. Throughout the year we had 340 independent study hours, the equivalent of more than two full months of eight-hour study days. There were some independent study hours every day, but sometimes we had whole days or even a week.

In general, we students seemed to be very active doing our independent study hours. One student (quoted from the summary of anonymous student feedback for the Beginning and Continuing courses) described them like this:

I am very happy with myself in this course. I edited some poems in AS. The work was explicit and goal-directed because it was a part of an overall study unit that was promised to the primary school. According to my count, there are 96 independent study hours included in this course, and they equal 72 lessons that are each 45 minutes long. I have kept a diary of my independent study hours and so far I have come up to 69 hours. Working independently has been rewarding and fun. I have learned a lot.

The independent study hours gave us a chance to do things that we were fascinated by. We could plan the content of these hours by ourselves and improve those specific sectors of language learning that we were interested in and where we needed the most practice. Some of us wrote stories and poems and some of us dug into the old AS audio archives at the radio station.

Normally I spent the independent study hours with four other class-mates, singing in the basement. While others were working upstairs, doing their homework, translating, gathering a vocabulary list relating to their pro-fession, or on other activities, we were busy translating new songs, transcrib-ing and rehearsing them. Thanks to all these independent study hours, a band called *Koškepuško* [Dried Pike[9]] was founded. We had started to sing and translate Finnish folk and popular songs into AS on a fishing trip in October 2009 (see p. 82). It was so much fun that we just could not stop it, and soon we realised how well all the words stuck in our heads when we sang them all over again, with a melody, in AS (see http://www.casle.fi).

5.2.2.5 Reflection

As mentioned, the study materials team began planning the study materi-als a year and a half before CASLE started. Their work resulted in a massive pile of printouts consisting of reading chapters and discussion and writing and listening exercises. Because of funding issues and since there were two sepa-rate timetables for two separate study material projects, we never managed to have proper books.[10] This was also what received most negative feedback from the students. However, we managed well with our heavy paper piles and files; we students understood the circumstances very well. Somehow the lack of a proper study book also demonstrated the reality of the conditions of AS study in general: too few materials. My son, who started his first class at school in 2010, received a brand new ABC book in AS at the beginning of the term (see also p. 152, *karvakenkälähetystö*). It could be stated that there was no rush in the marketplace: nearly 150 years had gone since Pastor Edward Wilhelm Borg had written his *Sämi kiela aapis kirje* (1857).

We students also required theme glossaries and conjugation lists. Some of us also thought that we could have used more time on pronunciation exercises and that a language lab would have been useful. Some of us would also have liked to have started Master–Apprentice (M-A) training (see p. 49) during the Beginning and Continuing courses instead of waiting until later in the learning process.

At the end of every course and every element of practical training, we students filled out a feedback form. Some of the suggestions for improvement that we made were very detailed and addressed a particular teacher and subject. However, some general notes and rough lines concerning the classroom teaching were made at the end. In general, we students liked, for instance, the team work, presentations, independent working hours, listening exercises (both new and archive tapes), transcribing, conversation practice in pairs, discussions, analysing problematic grammatical issues together in a group, translating texts in small groups and the opportunity to find all the exercises and study materials on the internet later. Students also often mentioned that they liked how teachers had given us the chance to influence the content and methods of the course.

I was not too interested in my grades but obviously some students were, because Marja-Liisa mentioned that we could raise our grades if we were not happy with them. According to her, we all passed with better than average grades. Both the classroom teaching and participating in the AS study programme of the University of Oulu in general were definitely hard and challenging but absolutely worthwhile. Our results, in other words our ASL skills, would not be at the level they are today without this theoretical part of the CASLE programme.

5.3 Cultural Group Activities: Students in the Field

5.3.1 Planner's view

The requirements set by CASLE for high language competence among the students necessitated the inclusion of a strong communicative part of the programme. The most theoretical courses from the original university programme, which had targeted future linguistics researchers, were therefore replaced by new courses that particularly stressed the oral use of the language. The aim was to bring students in contact with everyday language and help them integrate into the AS community. These extra communicative goals were realised by organising cultural group activities and practical language training through personal guidance.

Students participated in the cultural activities (see Table 5.2) as a group. They were able to become familiar with the cultural surroundings where the language has been preserved and transmitted from generation to generation. They also learned in practice something of the traditional ways of Saami living – knowledge that could not be learned in the classroom.

During the net fishing and media courses the whole group was together. During the burbot[11] fishing, winter fishing and cooking courses, the learning-by-doing method required smaller groups so that each individual student could act. Therefore the students were divided into two groups. All three fishing courses and the cooking course emphasised the

Table 5.2 Practical language training through cultural group activities

Course	Contact hours	Content
Fishing I	24	Net fishing (two days + one night with the whole group; evening programme)
Fishing II	15	Burbot fishing (two days)
Fishing III	14	Winter fishing (two days)
Preparing traditional meals	27 + optional one-day programme	Preparing traditional Saami meals; optional day of reindeer roundup (8–10 hours), to learn where the traditional foodstuffs and raw materials for clothing come from
Media course	53	Editing the community newspapers *Anarâš* and *Kierâš*; writing AS documents
Compulsory courses	*133*	*5 study points in total*

traditional ways of Saami living. The media course was the opposite of tradition: it concentrated on the present-day issues of AS people.

The teachers of the traditional cultural activities were local fisher-people, reindeer herders and cooking specialists, with two exceptions. The AS broadcaster Anja Kaarret was present as a language guide and cultural expert during all three fishing courses, the cooking course and the reindeer roundup (see also Info Box 13 Saami Media in Finland). The teacher of the media course was CASLE's head teacher Petter Morottaja. All of these courses were given in AS. The CASLE team planned the courses, and the teaching was funded and organised by the Saami Education Institute.

All of the cultural group activities were organised especially for CASLE students. Only the voluntary cartoon course was also open to other AS speakers. This course was actually a 'relic' from the early stages of CASLE when funding of the M-A programme was not yet secured and we needed some alternatives for variation in the programme. Only a few CASLE students participated in this course.

During the cultural group activities, each individual student was, of course, an active watcher and listener, but these activities did not offer as many opportunities for discussion as personal contact would. Therefore another kind of practical training, M-A training, was needed.

5.3.2 Diving into the culture: Student view

From a student's point of view,[12] the culture courses really balanced those theoretical courses in a classroom. The skills and things we learned about AS culture were more familiar to some of us than to others, but even those who had grown up in the AS cultural environment found that the traditional ways of life were given a new meaning by recuperating the once-lost mother tongue.

One of my classmates, an AS herself, said that one of the most amazing things in reclaiming her language was that all of the common places that she had always known suddenly took on new meaning: 'The whole environment came alive when I understood the connection between names and places.' I assume that her experience with doing the same old things like fishing or cooking – but now in the once-lost mother tongue – might have made the difference for her. The words in AS were like keys that opened the door to a deeper understanding of her culture.

The culture courses represented the learning-by-doing method at its best. I often noticed how words stuck in my head better when I was actually holding and touching an object, the unfamiliar AS name of which I was supposed to remember. Likewise with verbs, I found it easier to remember the name for the activity when I was actually simultaneously performing it myself. Compare this with Nils Jernsletten's description of how cultural knowledge was – and to some extent still is – learned in traditional Saami culture (see Info Box 18 The Saami Language and Traditional Knowledge).

Some of the words that I learned during the culture courses are so specific, old and connected to a certain activity that it is hard to find a Finnish counterpart for them or to translate them into any other language. Quite often it also happened that I did not even understand the Finnish name if I found it in the dictionary. Somebody might wonder what was the use of learning these traditions and vocabulary related to them. I also sometimes wondered why I should know dozens of different AS names for a reindeer. Would it not be okay to call every reindeer a *puásui* [reindeer], no matter what kind of antlers it had or how old it was? Everyone would know what I meant anyway. Or would they? Both Jernsletten (above) and Ole Henrik Magga explain not only the enormous richness of this vocabulary but in particular its meaning for the maintenance of Saami life (see Info Box 18 The Saami Language and Traditional Knowledge).

Some Saami people are in fact really worried that the wide range of reindeer vocabulary will vanish along with the livelihood that is struggling for its existence. Some might think that reindeer herding is reindeer herding or fishing is fishing, regardless of the language used, but some of the old traditions and wisdom encoded in these ways of life will vanish if the language is no longer preserved.[13] Without culture there is no language and without language there is no culture. The culture is alive only when the language is alive.

While it is important to create new vocabulary that arises from the needs of today's society, it is equally important to preserve the old traditions. By learning AS cultural traditions we also revived some of those old words that were going out of use. Through our actions those words suddenly became current and totally up to date. I cannot say whether it was the words that created the need for action, or action that created the need for words, but at least in my family, where a language shift from Finnish to AS took place during the CASLE programme, these various fishing and cooking traditions started to become more predominant features of our everyday life. I found myself in the kitchen with my children's grandmother every now and then, and the whole spring was about fishing. This went on to such an extent that my three-year-old son even refused to go to *Kielâpiervâl* [language nest] without a fishing rod! Luckily the caregivers were very understanding and knew how to deal with his fishing mania. In the winter the language nest children had their own fishing nets in Lake Aanaar just in front of the nursery school, so we could avoid those little battles in the morning.

5.3.3 Fish as highest in a holy trinity

To the AS people, who have always lived around Lake Aanaar, fish have been the basic prerequisite for life. It has been said that fish, deer (later reindeer) and berries form a 'holy trinity' for AS people. Unlike the North Saami people, who are often known as the 'reindeer Saami', the AS people have placed fish at the top of this trinity and the two other elements have complemented them.

AS people have fished throughout the year, throughout all the seasons. Since ancient times they have used several different fishing tools and techniques. This was the reason why we had three fishing courses in CASLE, each lasting two days. The first, the net fishing course in October, was for the whole group. The other two were burbot fishing in February and winter net fishing in March, and here the group was split in two smaller groups so that the teacher could instruct the members of the group more individually.

The first net fishing course was only a few months after our studies had begun. It was perhaps the most successful course of the three, at least from the viewpoint of team spirit. We had been studying hard all autumn in the classroom and were really looking forward to getting away to this little cabin for a couple of days to spend some time together and go fishing.

In terms of catching fish, though, those days were a bit of a disaster. It was horrendously cold, the lake was already freezing and we caught only a few whitefish. We learnt a phrase: *'Ain kyeli čääsist, jis ij ain väärpist'* [There are always fish in the water if not in the net], and luckily we had other food with us. The cabin was warm and cosy. By the fireplace, instructed by Annika Pasanen, we went through some fishing-related texts, listened to some old fishing stories on tape and collected fish and fishing vocabulary.

Anja Kaarret, the teacher of the course, also showed us how to repair fishing nets. We cast the nets, a few of us at a time, and checked them again the next morning. Although it is a little embarrassing to admit, I cleaned a fish for the first time in my life. Up to that time I had always got someone else to do it. I also learned to make a proper knot to tie down two nets. In fact, that was one of the most useful things I learned in the whole year.

In the evening, after the sauna, some of us wanted to sing, but there were no AS songs, only Finnish ones. So we translated, or Annika Pasanen did, a popular Finnish song. We noticed that some of us actually knew how to sing and enjoy it too, so on the way back on the bus we joked about establishing a band. We were eating slices of dried pike, *koškepuško*, and thought that would make a great name for our band. So the net fishing days produced not only some fish but also a singing group. Later during that year of the CASLE programme *Koškepuško* took a little community singing tour to the AS villages of Avveel, Kaamâs and Njellim (see Figure 3.2, p. 26).[14]

Most importantly, those few days of the fishing trip represented a turning point in our language use. Before going to the cabin we had decided that we would only use AS. For many of us, including me, this was the first time that we really used AS for communicating, without any formal exercises or situations that were kind of set up. For the rest of my life I will remember the first AS sentence I spoke in front of everybody. I was pouring drinking water into a bucket and asked: '*Leškiistâm-uvks mun lase?*' [Should I pour more?] I had just learned that from one of the chapters we had in the reading materials. I remember the delighted face of our teacher Anja as she understood me. This still motivates me. After the net fishing course we really started to use AS in the classroom too.

The secret of the positive experiences in reversing language shift at this point of CASLE was based on the right timing, good briefing for the activities and our motivation. After about two months of study, we had some basic knowledge and vocabulary that we could use in order to produce simple sentences and communicate.

I think it was also important for the improvement of our language skills that we students had been given an explanation of the net fishing course in detail beforehand. It must have had a psychological effect. No-one wanted to be the one to break the promise of only using AS by speaking Finnish. I remember feeling embarrassed every time I used Finnish, not only at the cabin but throughout the whole year. Any Finnish words normally came out in whispers. We were loyal to each other and if anyone even tried to speak AS others showed their support by using the same language in turn. One of the students said:

There was always a bit of a competition going on as well. It was a good kind of competition. Everyone just wanted to show off what they had learned. That encouraged the others to try again a bit harder.

Besides the right timing, proper briefing and motivation, I think it was important that throughout the whole course we were surrounded by many fluent AS speakers. As well as our teachers, we had AS visitors who kept the conversation up and running, and we had a chance to practise our language skills with many different people outside the classroom.

The only critique from us students about that course concerned the actual fishing. Because we were there, the whole big group together, some students felt like they did not get to fish enough, even though everyone did have his/her turn. That only shows how highly motivated we were!

The next culture course we had was the burbot fishing in February. Unlike net fishing, the method we used for catching burbot was not at all familiar to any of us. By that time the sun was shining brightly after a long, dark winter. We went to Anja's house in *Päärtih* (Partakko) (see Figure 3.2, p. 26), Eastern Aanaar. On the first day we learned how to make a trap out of a stick, fishing line and hook, baited with a minnow. Then we drilled holes in the ice and put the traps down close to the bottom of the lake where the burbot stay in wintertime. The traps were left in the water for the whole night.

The next day we drove back to *Päärtih* and checked the traps. We were surprised that we had caught so many burbot! I had sometimes seen one or two burbot getting caught in a fishing net, but I did not remember how ugly and big they were. I am not the most sensitive person but for some reason I was unable to skin those snake-like things. However, the soup was delicious. While I was eating I decided that, if I was able to eat it, I must also be able to prepare it. The next day at home, without anyone around me (such as the cameraman who was filming us at Anja's house; see p. 64), I succeeded in skinning a burbot. I remembered the AS phrase Anja had taught us when she cut its head off: *Njäähi ij huškongin jäämi* [A burbot won't die from being hit]. I nearly cried, but again I felt like I had grown inside. Afterwards I was so excited that I started to plan to dry and tan the burbot skins in a way that could be used in handicrafts. I had seen beautiful little bags and purses and even trousers made of burbot skin. Well, my handicraft project never really happened; in fact I found some rotten skins in a plastic bag outside under my terrace later, but the idea and the challenge had inspired me.

Again the only negative feedback given about the course concerned the practical issues and organisation. Some active students would have liked to do more. Some of us also thought, as did our teacher Anja, that we could have stayed overnight somewhere near the fishing site. Since the course was organised over two days, some of us had to spend about three hours each day driving back and forth between our homes and the fishing site. But as always, opinions varied. One student mentioned how much s/he especially enjoyed those moments in the car. S/he writes:

> That time I spent in the car, as well as in Anja's living room, chatting with some students while others were cooking, were very rewarding.

Those moments had a great effect on the improvement of my ability to think in AS.

That again shows how we all experienced things differently and how things that were perhaps annoying to one person were especially important to someone else. As individuals we were also different kinds of learners. Some of us more actively took part in activities, whereas others preferred to watch activities from a distance, learning by watching and listening.

The next fishing course was in March. This time the goal was to put winter fishing nets under the ice, near the place where we had been catching burbot. Anja was again in charge and her uncle, our Master Aslak Saijets, accompanied us. The sun shone brightly and the catch was generous. The feedback from those days was extremely positive. Students were happy about the arrangements and wrote things like: 'Everyone got to do this equally', 'The instructions worked and no-one had to stay in the background', 'I learned some new tricks', 'I enjoyed understanding' and 'It was great to meet a new speaker of AS'. We students were indeed happy to meet Aslak, who is a great character and has been a professional fisherman since the age of 12. Undeniably, he knew all the tricks and his lake like he knew 'his own pockets', as we say in Finnish.

Just as always in real life, there were some blunders too. I laughed at one little incident and still do, knowing that it was not necessarily too funny at the time. A day of winter net fishing was about to end and it was time to go back to our base, Anja's house. Aslak and his snowmobile were responsible for our transportation. Four women got on the sledge behind Aslak's snowmobile. Aslak started the snowmobile and enjoyed the drive. He was driving quite fast, and when going under a bridge that was close to our destination the sledge fell over, sending all four women flying. One of them recalls:

> I flew in the air and fell down on top of my classmate. Although everything happened quickly it felt like it was a film in slow-motion. While in the air I had time to think that I have to land like stuntwomen do in films, and that is what I did. We were lying in the snow and Aslak continued driving. He noticed only on arrival that something was wrong. After we had checked that everybody was just fine, we laughed our heads off. Luckily we had hats on and we just had some bruises.

So we have memories that we will always keep with us, and experiences that strengthened our team spirit even more. I thought these trips were like awards for milestones that we had achieved. It was always nice to look at our schedule and realise there was a culture course coming up in a while. There was always something to look forward to, a little break with fresh air in the middle of our theoretical studies in the classroom.

5.3.4 Hoof soup and sausages

The traditional cooking course was organised in late spring but it had actually already started in the late autumn with a visit to a reindeer roundup at the *Čivtjuuhâ* corral. *Čivtjuuhâ*, the old corral of the *Muddusjävri* reindeer herding area, was built in the late 19th century, although its name indicates even older use (T.I. Itkonen, 1984; Länsman, 2000). That visit was tied to the traditional cooking course.

The visit to the roundup was not compulsory but most of us participated. There were surprisingly many among us who had never attended a roundup before. I had, a few times, just watching and following, but never before had I separated intestines from a reindeer that had been butchered around the corner a minute before. We let the reindeer blood run into buckets where it was whisked to prevent it from clotting, and we separated the intestines that were going to be used for making sausages.

The best part about the day was that one of our Masters, Eeva Seurujärvi, who is a reindeer herder from the area, spent the day with us. That day we did not see much action because the herders were gathering the reindeer into herds in the surrounding forests. However, Eeva was able to bring the place to life with her colourful stories from the past. While we walked around the area she told us about the history of the corral. In the past, roundups used to attract lots of people from all over, even from neighbouring countries. Eeva told us stories about market traders selling different kinds of goods and how there was a school and a bank and dances late into the night. Today, as times have radically changed (roads, transportation, electricity, etc.), roundups are not as important social events and gatherings as they used to be. When we left the corral, thanks to Eeva, we had great stories and a picture of the past to take with us, as well as ingredients for the cooking course. Intestines that would be used for sausages were rinsed and put in the freezer, along with some blood, to wait for the cooking course in April.

The cooking course took place in Avveel, in a house that had been rented for CASLE purposes. We had already taken a handicraft workshop there with the Masters, and the house had been used for accommodating CASLE teachers. The place itself was perfect for the traditional cooking course. It had a big kitchen with lots of light and all the utensils we would need in order to cook. Our group was divided into two, which was good: we all got to prepare and do things and no-one could stay in the background.

Our main teacher was Marja-Liisa's mother, Elsa Väisänen, who had already been a Master for some of us before. Elsa had planned four days of traditional AS menus for us to prepare. During that week we prepared traditional Saami dishes: reindeer sausages and pudding cakes (see Figure 5.1), boiled whitefish and potatoes, sautéed reindeer and a soup made of reindeer hooves.

As supplementary materials for the course we had an *Anarâš* calendar (see Info Box 13 Saami Media in Finland; Info Box 17 *Anarâškielâ servi*

```
1 kg reindeer meat
0.5 litre reindeer blood
0.3–0.5 litre reindeer fat
0.5 kg potatoes
0.8–1 kg rye flour
handful of oats
½ teaspoon ground white pepper
Salt

Take a saucepan, the bigger the better. Add about a kilogram of chopped reindeer meat and pour water until the
pieces are fully covered. Add salt, about 1.5 tablespoons. Let boil and skim the froth from the top. Mix reindeer fat,
salt, white pepper and rye flour into the blood. Let this dough rise for about an hour. Take lumps from the dough with a
tablespoon and drop them into the saucepan. Let boil for about an hour. When the soup has boiled for about 40
minutes, add potatoes. Add a handful of oatmeal and let boil until tender.

Traditionally people used to separate meat chunks, blood pudding cakes and potatoes into a separate bowl and drink
the broth from another cup.
```

Figure 5.1 Blood pudding cakes boiled in meat soup

[Aanaar Saami Association]). It was a themed calendar about traditional dishes, presenting one traditional meal with a photo and a recipe for every month. Before the course we were supposed to go through the calendar and translate it. We students thought it was a good thing to do, because we got to recognise the cooking vocabulary before doing the cooking activity. Once we were in an actual cooking situation, it was then easier to ask questions and follow the instructions. I had not done my homework very well and I remember regretting that. As for the nouns, e.g. kitchen utensils, I could always show and ask what this or that was called, but all those verbs! All Saami languages are said to be 'verb languages', because they concentrate on action. And to me it seemed like the language was very active in the kitchen.

The course was successful and the student feedback very positive. The main reason was that the students adored Elsa. She was able to create a relaxed and peaceful, homelike atmosphere. We kept asking her questions and Elsa never got tired of giving us answers. At the same time she told us stories and cooked.

While cooking we learned a lot about the history and how the AS used to travel to northern Norway to exchange reindeer meat and cheese, furs, cloudberries and willow grouses for flour, sugar, salt, coffee and margarine. We also learned about the various ways of preserving foods before the time of freezers and fridges – how people used to freeze reindeer blood and milk in a reindeer stomach, for example. We realised that many of these traditional means of livelihood connected to food (such as gathering waterfowls' eggs and preserving little fish in barrels full of salt, making cakes out reindeer brains, etc.) had already been lost.

Although the group was big and some thought that it could have been smaller, everyone got to participate. Besides cooking there were lots of other things to do in the kitchen: washing the dishes, setting the table, and we cannot forget the best part – eating together around a huge kitchen table every day! While enjoying the meal we also learned useful everyday vocabulary and phrases. I could immediately put these into practice at home with my children: 'Please can you pass me . . .¿' 'Would you like some more¿' 'This is delicious!' These kinds of sayings really found their way to our dinner table.

All in all, the cooking course opened up new horizons for us in the world of AS foods. Ingredients that are used in the traditional AS kitchen are very simple and vegetables are rare: only potatoes and turnips. The Saami kitchen is really not a good choice for a vegetarian (which I used to be when I moved to Northern Finland!). But what I really like the most about the Saami (kitchen) philosophy is that that everything is used and nothing is wasted. Fish heads and fish intestines are the best parts of the fish for many, and from a slaughtered reindeer one can use the meat, stomach, tongue, hoofs, brain, bone marrow, blood and intestines. Any of the rest that cannot be eaten such as skin, bones, antlers and sinew are used for making clothes, utensils and handicrafts.

Both the kitchen course and the chance to get to know elderly AS people made me think about how important it is to keep traditional livelihoods, reindeer herding, fishing and berry-gathering alive. Every single one of our Masters (see p. 92, Master–Apprentice training) that I visited offered a meal that one would call 'traditional'. I realised that food is also important for one's identity; we want to know where the things on our plates come from. This is especially true today, I think, if we really are what we eat, as they say. At first I thought it was not very polite for my three-year-old son to ask every time he came to the dinner table: 'Who has killed this¿'[15] instead of 'What is this¿'. Now I think that in fact it was a quite reasonable question. It was not so long ago that everything the AS people ate had to be hunted, caught, grown, gathered and prepared themselves. And today I am quite happy to be able to answer my son's question surprisingly often.

Familiar flavours also bring back memories. One of my fellow CASLE students spent all her adult life fantasising about *koškepuško*, dried pike, which her AS grandmother used to prepare hot especially for her. It was a flavour from her childhood, a significant mark of her AS identity. Once I saw a documentary film in which a little Indigenous girl from the tundra somewhere in Siberia (Russia) almost vomited when she was forced to eat buckwheat at school. She ran away from the dorms to go fishing for her own food. As a culture course, I think traditional cooking was a great choice. Food is culture.

5.3.5 Films and magazines

The third course, media, was selected because it is one of the main forms of modern AS culture. The organisers wanted people to take an active part in writing and producing stories and films in AS. The course was carried out in two sections in June and July. Our teacher was Petter, a real jack-of-all-trades, who had also taken some media studies before and, for example, established an AS online magazine called *Kierâš* (see Info Box 13 Saami Media in Finland).

The course took place in the media classroom of the Saami Education Institute. The Institute has a long tradition of organising media studies so it had all the proper equipment: computers, video cameras and computer programmes for editing video material, doing layout and so on.

The idea of the course was to introduce the wide scale of AS media to all of us students so that we would get an overview of both magazine- and film-making. After an introduction, we were divided into pairs. Each pair concentrated on their own project. One pair wrote, edited and compiled that week's *Kierâš*, and one created an issue of the *Anârâš* magazine (see Info Box 13 Saami Media in Finland). The *Koškepuško* group made a music video of one of their songs, and the rest of us made short documentary films.

One of the short films was about our Master, Aili Maarit Valle,[16] a great *tuáijár*, or Saami artisan. In the film she showed and instructed us as to how the traditional AS costume must be worn. At the end, when she had carefully dressed herself in her *mááccuh* [traditional ladies' dress], *poovij* [belt], *sovskammuuh* [winter shoes made of the skins of reindeer legs], *vuodduuh* [bindings wrapped around the shoes] and *kappeer* [bonnet] she laughed heartily and said that now she was ready to leave. None of us could have imagined that a year later we would be watching the film at her funeral. It was sad but also comforting to see that, even though she was a woman with no children, she had passed on her precious knowledge – her native language and the skill of making beautiful traditional costumes – to so many of us (see http://www.casle.fi).

Another two short films were both made about another Language Master, my sons' grandmother Aili Koskinen (her Saami name is *Nuuvdi Ailâ*). In one of the films she spoke about some traditional knowledge and beliefs associated with the weather.[17] I directed the other one, a 10-minute documentary film *Uddâsist šoddâm* [*Reborn*]. In *Reborn*, Nuuvdi Ailâ tells how and why she stopped speaking AS many decades ago and how she later decided to reclaim the language when her grandchildren started going to the language nest. The premier for the film was at *Skábmagovat* in 2011, the Indigenous peoples' Film Festival organised in Aanaar every January.

As a former journalist, I think this media course was very important. 'Culture' cannot be viewed as merely something traditional. The AS media have played a great role in advancing and promoting the AS language revival. I think the course could have been longer and broader, and one teacher for the course was not enough. The original plan had in fact been to have two teachers, but when the assistant teacher suddenly cancelled,

Petter had to cope on his own. Anyhow, he coped fine and did not lose his temper like some students did when they had to wait for a long time before it was their turn to get some help. After all, somehow we all managed to finish our media projects successfully, and some CASLE students have even continued to produce stories for *Kierâš* and *Anarâš*. The course also inspired some of us to document the language and its few native speakers while it is still possible.

5.4 Personal Language Guidance: Master–Apprentice Training and Practical Training at AS Workplaces

5.4.1 Introduction

We students became more active conversationalists through personal language guidance. This way of practising brought us individually or in pairs in contact with AS-speaking people. The two specific methods that were used included the M-A programme and practical training at AS workplaces (see Table 5.3). The intention was to connect us students both vocationally and privately with local people.

The main difference between these two ways of learning was the fact that the workplace training approached the language from a professional point of view, whereas the M-A programme was more informal, benefitting from the language skills of the whole AS community.

There was also a period of one week that we students had to plan by ourselves. This week produced, for instance, lots of translations, including a liturgical service for the closing ceremony of the CASLE year and new study materials. We also put our professional skills into practice at the language nest and school, on the radio and as managers of the *Koškepuško* band, among other activities. Films were also produced.

Table 5.3 Practical language training through personal language guidance

Course	Study points	Aim/content
Language training at workplaces	5	To learn AS as a professional language. The primary focus was to master the vocabulary of each student's own profession
Master–Apprentice programme	5	To learn AS and AS ways of life informally through listening, speaking and eliciting language from a native (elder) speaker, by doing activities together in AS

5.4.2 Master–Apprentice training

Student feedback showed clearly that M-A training was experienced as the most beloved part of CASLE. The elderly Masters, recruited to work as language teachers in the field, were the real specialists in the AS language because they had learnt it as their first language. They were also masters of their own professions in Saami society, so they were able to bring us students to our own specific language domains and show us glimpses of traditional ways of Saami life. Marja-Liisa experienced them as very modest people who never offered their services spontaneously in their mother tongue but, with some encouragement, they were happy to serve their own language community.

CASLE had altogether 23 Masters who were specifically recruited to transfer their language and culture to us students. The idea was simple: Masters were supposed to spend time with their Apprentices, talking and doing ordinary everyday things, just as in the original M-A programme created by AICLS (1994; Hinton, 2002). The training took place mostly in the homes of the Masters where we students were invited. The most typical, most wanted and easiest-to-organise model was to have a combination of one Master and two students (Apprentices). There was no planned programme for the meetings between Masters and Apprentices. We were allowed to plan and spend the day with our Masters in any way we wanted. Our first step towards using AS had been taken already, before the first training day, when we phoned our Masters to arrange in advance matters such as meals.

Every one of us students spent at least 70 hours, equalling 10 days, in M-A training. On top of these meetings there were 'feedback and reflection days', some for Apprentices only and some for Apprentices and Masters together. The programme also included days when we students were supposed to work independently, planning for the next training, extracting tapes and transcribing what we had recorded or learnt from our Masters. In total, 142 hours of this training were filmed for the purpose of documenting the language and culture.

5.4.2.1 Background to the training and its targets

In Section 4.4 Learning the Target Language From Elderly Masters, Marja-Liisa described two specific models that both gave inspiration to the M-A training that was tailored to the particular needs of CASLE. The first model is AICLS's Master–Apprentice Language Learning programme (p. 46) and the second is the linguistic/anthropological model (p. 49) used widely with Indigenous languages, including AS, which started in the 19th century. However, these models could not be adopted as such for CASLE because their requirements were different. For example, CASLE was not supposed to be based entirely on the M-A programme; M-A training would start only when students had gained a basic knowledge of the language. The targets set for the M-A training were as follows (Pasanen, 2010a).

- The Apprentice gets a chance to use AS actively.
- The Apprentice gets used to spontaneous interaction in AS.
- The Apprentice gets to hear AS in different kinds of environments, used for different kinds of topics with different people (as compared to the classroom).
- The Apprentice gets to know the AS community.
- The Apprentice gets to know modern AS culture and, through Masters' stories, to become more aware of the past.
- The Apprentice learns to interview and transcribe.
- The CASLE project succeeds in documenting and recording the lives and language of AS people (see Section 4.7 Language Documentation).
- The M-A revitalisation method can be tested and documented.
- The M-A training gives Masters the opportunity to transmit their language and culture. They feel important in the process of language transmission.

5.4.2.2 Planning and organising

About a year before the beginning of the CASLE programme year, the project planning team started to work on the M-A training. According to Pasanen (2010a), the team had to solve the following issues:

- find suitable Masters;
- think about the substance of the meetings between Masters and Apprentices;
- plan how to familiarise Masters with their work and carry out their briefing;
- organise and plan the hands-on logistics such as transportation and meals;
- find funding for the training, and determine how much to pay the Masters for their contributions and on what basis this could be done; and
- plan for the compositions of meetings (individual students, pairs or bigger teams).

As stated before, one of the starting points of the project planning team was to keep meetings between Masters and Apprentices mainly unscheduled and unplanned. This freedom, however, brought some stress into the planning. The team would take care of running errands, and the rest would be up to Masters and Apprentices.

In practice, the project planning team started off consulting with Matti Morottaja and Anja Kaarret. The task was to find all the AS elders living in the Aanaar area who spoke AS as their 'first language'. Elders also had to be healthy and in relatively good condition; the oldest ones were not even asked because it would have been a burden. Another criterion was that Masters would have to stick to the language, not shift easily between AS and Finnish, even if the Apprentices did so.

Marja-Liisa had her own rating system for Masters' language skills. She scored AS speakers from one to five along these lines. Only AS speakers from the fourth and fifth category were accepted as Masters. The project planning team naturally never told the Masters that these categories even existed.

- **1 point**: A person with a passive knowledge of AS. S/he has heard the language from childhood but does not use it any longer.
- **2 points**: A person who knows some phrases in AS but cannot lead a proper conversation in the language.
- **3 points**: S/he speaks AS but shifts easily into Finnish.
- **4 points**: S/he can speak AS but sometimes feels insecure in terms of his/her language skills.
- **5 points**: S/he can speak fluent AS and does not easily switch languages even if the other person does.

Annika Pasanen, who was responsible for organising the M-A training, asked 31 AS elders to work as Masters. Seven of them declined the offer for various reasons. Annika reported that some of them just did not feel it was for them; some others simply did not want strangers in their houses. Some thought they did not speak AS well enough. Some also said that they were too old and weak for this kind of activity and commitment. Finally, some elders did not give any reason.

The remaining 23 accepted Annika's request. Some who said they would be interested did not, at the end of the day, work as Masters; on the other hand, some who were doubtful at first changed their minds! When the CASLE year started in August it was clear that there would be enough Masters. The team wanted to recruit them according to need and not end up with too many and not enough work for everyone interested. Strict timetables for meetings between Masters and Apprentices were not made, either, because these were elderly, mainly retired people who did not live according to a calendar or watch. The team trusted that they would be available closer to the point in time when they would be needed. This was a good decision; there were very few situations where someone had to start phoning to find a Master, or where there was a sudden change of plans. This of course was also something that the team had already prepared for.

Once all the Masters had been chosen, they were invited to a briefing and familiarisation session. The project planning team told them about their future roles, and the Masters asked what was expected of them. This meeting was important because the Masters, who largely knew each other from before, got a chance to exchange thoughts and gain support from each other. This also happened during the M-A period, because they discussed their roles with one another quite often and exchanged thoughts.

5.4.2.3 Short profile of CASLE's Masters

The average age of the 23 Masters was 66 years. There were 13 women and 10 men. Most of them were native speakers but there was even one second-language speaker. Six Masters were language activists who have contributed a lot to the AS language revival. The 17 'ordinary' speakers were recruited into language revitalisation by the CASLE programme. Most of the Masters had lived in Aanaar all their lives. For most, AS had been a language that they used only with a few people in an otherwise Finnish-speaking environment. Many said that they had lost a lot of words from their vocabularies and that their language was stiffer than it used be in childhood. A few Masters also told of how they had not used the language for years, sometimes even many decades. Often they had already gone through a language shift with their siblings in their youth, and therefore had not had the courage to use AS as adults.

The 'professional' Masters worked as teachers, reporters, translators, interpreters, writers and artists. The 'ordinary' Masters worked in more traditional livelihoods like fishing and reindeer herding, as well as professions of a 'Finnicised' society, like care and catering, forestry and construction.

Although all the Masters had spoken AS at home as children, as adults with families their home language had mostly been Finnish. AS was the home language of only a few families. Only seven Masters had transmitted AS to their children. The rest either did not transmit it or they had no children. Four Masters who did not transmit their language to their own children started later to use the language with some of their grandchildren, basically due to activities of the language nests, schools and parents.

5.4.2.4 Student reflections

The CASLE year started in August, and already after a couple of months of intensive language learning in the classroom, we students had the first meeting with our Masters-to-be. All the Masters were invited to an informal meeting in our classroom where we drank coffee, got to know each other and sang together. Of course, the project leaders also introduced themselves and briefed us about the theoretical and practical parts of the training.

Despite the fact that not all the Masters could make it to the first meeting, it was an important and exciting event. After all, for many of us it was one of the very first times that we had to introduce ourselves in AS, and to more than just one person at a time. I remember how my voice trembled when I explained about my background and family. But I also remember those faces on the other side of the table, some moved, some slightly shocked. Everyone was silent and listened carefully, almost as if they could not believe their ears. A couple of months later, when we had had our first training days, I heard an anecdote from my course mate. For some reason this memory of hers reminds me of the Masters' expressions that I remember from the first meeting and conversations.

I was with a Master at his home in northern Aanaar. He was happy and cheerful and told stories of his past in his own smooth way. Suddenly in the middle of a story he changed the subject, took a break and said: It is so nice and almost like a miracle to speak my mother tongue with a young lady and not always with the same old fellows.

All of we students could communicate in AS already after about four months of studying, but naturally the level of language skill varied a great deal between us.

My first training experience was a day that I spent with Unto Aikio. Unto was born in 1939 in Jolnivuono, on the shores of Lake Aanaar. We had a family connection (my children's grandmother had been married to his elder brother) and we had even met a couple of times before, so it was easy to go to his home, which was already familiar to me. Still I was terrified at first, knowing that I – a verbally oriented and talkative person – could not use Finnish, in which I was used to communicating, but only AS. Luckily I had a classmate with me who seemed to be a language genius from the start. I knew I could call upon her when I was lost in the conversation. For me, like for most of the other CASLE students, going to a Master's house in pairs worked best, because it relieved some of the pressure of finding the words all the time. About 60–70% of training days were carried out in teams like that.

Anyway, when we arrived at Unto's, all my fears were quickly forgotten. As soon as we stepped inside, the atmosphere was cosy and warm. It was also so nice to see him taking such good care of his old mother (who sadly passed away the year after CASLE ended). I just remember a quiet and lazy feeling in their tidy house, which was full of blooming flowers. A clock was ticking on the wall and two beautiful Lapponian herding dogs came to my feet, begging to be scratched.

As a young man, Unto had worked as a reindeer herder, but later he had sold his reindeer and become a baker. For Unto, food was a 'matter of heart' and the meal he prepared for us confirmed that. We ate, and enjoyed the atmosphere. Words were secondary. Still Unto was so excited about us saying even one word aloud in AS. He kept saying: 'I feel like I have known you forever. Could it be the language? It must be the language.'

I think it was very touching how Unto associated AS with his own people who were close to him, his family. The language brought back memories from his childhood when all his family was still around. Since his father and brother had passed away, he had not used AS in his everyday life, not even with his AS mother or his neighbour who was also one of our Language Masters.

Unto kept apologising about how his language skills had become so rusty over the years because of his scarce use of AS. In general, the other Masters seemed to like the respectful nomination 'Language Master', but Unto felt it was an exaggeration and it was rather embarrassing for him. In an interview that was done after the CASLE year, he said: 'They [students] are more Masters than we are. They speak so well and I hear words that I have never even heard before' (Kalla, 2010).

In fact many Masters said they were constantly learning new words from us students. Clearly, language learning between Masters and Apprentices worked in both directions. We learnt so much about the old ways, the traditional AS ways of life, and we absorbed the vocabulary and idioms simultaneously. Hundreds of new words, even word-grouped by certain themes,[18] have been created in the language only recently, mainly because of the demands of AS school books (see Olthuis, 2007). As we had studied those words through texts in the classroom, we then transmitted some of those words to the elders. However, some Masters thought it was important to preserve the old vocabulary and to 'clean away' the new, especially loanwords from Finnish. Other Masters were more open and pleased to have a chance to adopt new words into their vocabularies. Some Masters mentioned that they got the courage from the students to use the language. They wondered how we had the guts to give interviews on the radio in AS right from the beginning, even when our language skills were so imperfect. Some also remarked how their own language skills improved during the CASLE year and how they now, for example, use fewer and fewer Finnish words in the middle of sentences.

Altogether, I had five Masters. They were all such characters, and very different from each other. After having visited Unto, I spent a day with Aslak Saijets at his home in Päärtih (Partakko), Aanaar (see Figure 3.2, p. 26). It came to me as a tiny shock that I understood so little of his language. I still do not know why that was, exactly, but again I was lucky to have my language genius classmate with me. Perhaps my ear was already used to listening to the dialect my children's grandmother speaks, and Unto's dialect was close to hers. Perhaps Aslak's way of speaking was just a little original? I do not know, but I quickly came to understand that there is a great variety of dialect in AS.

Later I learnt that it was not a mere dialect, or the rhythm and accent, but the fact that there are a bunch of completely different words for the same thing, depending on the area where the language is spoken. This is why most of us thought that having more than just one or two Masters during the year was a good idea.

Even though I hardly understood anything of what Aslak was saying, it was not a problem. We looked at old family photos and Aslak showed us trophies that he had won at trolling competitions. We drove on snowmobiles to check the winter fishnets at the lake and even caught some fine whitefish and trout. Who needs perfect language skills to be able to do and follow these activities? At least I didn't. I was enjoying bathing in the language, the rhythm and every sound of it. And I trusted that at least some of it would somehow penetrate into my brain and come out again later. I went with the flow and tried to remember that only a tiny percentage of communication between people is actually based on words.

What proved to be useful, at least for me, was recording the Masters. Normally most Masters felt comfortable in recording their stories and our conversations, but some of them were more shy. We always carried a tape recorder with us and asked politely if we could record conversations. Some students felt uncomfortable with recording but for me, as a radio journalist, it was understandably the most natural thing to do. I found it very useful to listen to the tapes after meetings. Often I only understood at home what we had been talking about and laughed aloud by myself. Some students wrote in their final reports that they regretted that they had not recorded enough or any of their Masters' stories. They regretted being too shy or too polite, thinking it would have disturbed the Masters or affected the situation negatively. There were only one or two Masters who did not want their stories to be recorded. In these cases it was clear that the recorder would stay in the handbag. In most cases the Masters did not mind, but rather they liked the idea that their stories would be recorded. I remember one Master sighing a bit sadly, just before starting her story about being evacuated in the 1940s, saying that 'after a while there will be nobody to tell these stories'. One Master even suggested to an Apprentice that they should write his biography together.[19] In other words, most Masters had the will and the urge both to speak AS and to tell their many stories.

Some of the training was organised as handicraft workshops, which meant that there were several of us students who stayed with Language Masters Elsa and Aili Maarit in a house for a week at a time; they instructed us in the making of traditional Saami handicrafts. Even I, all thumbs, took part in one of these workshops, perhaps because I wanted to learn how to knit woollen socks, but also because I knew that Marja-Liisa's lovely mother Elsa was coming to teach us. I had met her briefly before and I had instantly liked her calm appearance. I also thought I could learn some handicraft vocabulary from her. And, sure enough, she knew the handicraft terminology and all the tricks associated with knitting beautiful AS mittens and socks.

But Elsa knew so many other things too. I sat next to her the whole week, knitting, laughing and listening to her. She spoke about the past, and I could never get tired of her stories. My knitting was full of mistakes, but Elsa was tireless in instructing and showing me what I was supposed to do, over and over again. I burst into tears when she told me her life story. She had lost both her husband and father to the lake when she was only a young woman. I listened to her calm voice, telling me how she struggled to survive during the harsh winters, alone in the house with her little daughter Marja-Liisa and her mother whom she was also taking care of.

I don't want to sound naïve, but as someone who grew up in a city, born to a middle-class family, and who never really had to fight to make a living, and never having experienced a real loss … these stories really touched my heart. I imagined how different Elsa's life was when she was at my age, how lucky I was, how wise and strong she was, how much we had to learn from the elders.

I also think the M-A training really built bridges between the generations. In today's world, we working-age people do not often have time to sit down and listen to the elders, even if we want to. Saami society, from my point of view, is still quite family based, but for many reasons associated with modernisation, ties with family and relatives are no longer as strong as they used to be. I think M-A training somehow healed the community in this sense. Many of our Masters did not have children of their own and, even if they did, the language they had transmitted to their children had mainly been Finnish. As one of the Masters described it, they finally had a chance to tell these stories in the 'language of their heart'. That brought to my mind Nelson Mandela's words: 'If you talk to a man in a language he understands, that goes to his head. If you talk to him in his language, that goes to his heart.' These stories that our Masters shared with us came from the bottom of their hearts. And, as a result, they also went straight to our hearts.

Storytelling has always played a large role in the lives of Indigenous peoples, and this is equally true for AS people. It is very common that when AS people meet each other they start remembering and telling stories of past times. It is not so often that they speak about themselves or the people who are present.

I was often amazed at the memory of many of our Masters and the skill and mastery with which they would tell stories, describing places, animals, people and events. They had the urge and a strong will to keep their stories alive by telling them to us. We students, the Apprentices, were hungry to hear them.

For me, those stories told about my sons' family background, their roots. In an odd way, they made me feel more connected to my children and to their ancestors' land. I am happy to be able to help preserve these stories now, and I realise that, even though I am not a Saami myself, I have the right and perhaps even the duty to pass these stories on to my children, and perhaps one day to my children's children. I believe they will value this heritage that I was given by our Masters.

To about half of us students, those who were AS themselves, those stories they heard from the elders were even more personal. It is estimated that there have never been more than a thousand AS people. In other words, those with Saami roots often learnt about their family history only when they visited the Masters. I had not realised before reading students' reports on the M-A training that many CASLE students had in fact found lost or missing pieces from their family histories during the CASLE year. As one student said: 'Visiting AS elders was like putting together a puzzle of my past. I was constantly constructing and exploring my Saami identity through their stories.'

Perhaps the most common activity that the Masters and Apprentices did during training days was looking at old photos. Nearly every student mentioned having done this with at least one of their Masters. Looking at old photos certainly worked as an important basis for conversation but, looking at these family relations, it was remarkable how many family members and relatives CASLE students found in these photos. Some of these students went really deeply into finding their roots and genealogy, and even gave presentations with slide shows for the rest of us about their explorations. I could only listen and try to imagine what kind of a journey they were making. Those little pieces of information that helped these people of the lost generation reconstruct their identity were sometimes small and almost impossible for us others to see – yet they were important, both to the individuals and to the entire process of revitalisation.

There were four of us students who did not have any AS connections in their family. These people had come into the Saami area for one reason or another and then become interested in AS and culture. Three of them had already lived in the north for several years. All of them, except for one who had moved to Aanaar because of the CASLE programme, had been working, setting up families and learning the North Saami language. Even these Finnish people, who obviously had not heard stories about their ancestors growing up, thought the M-A training was superb. One of them writes in the report:

> I am not the only one who says that the M-A training was the most important section in the whole study year. It was not only because of the language but also because of the culture and emotions. I felt that I was taken into the AS community. I also came to understand their life much better.

Regardless of our different backgrounds and relationship to the AS people and language, we were all equally happy about the M-A training. We were impressed by the fact that these elders took us as strangers into their homes, opened their hearts and shared their stories and skills, sometimes even their secrets, with us. And they did it with such warmth.

From the point of view of language learning, it is interesting to think about the different approaches the Masters took in teaching us. Most of them did not care or dare to correct our mistakes at all, but rather would support our speaking delicately by giving the right word, form of a word or idiom in their own reply. Some were more precise than others and some of them found taking a Master's role very challenging.

> One has to think carefully how to teach, when there is no previous experience from teaching. The first day did not go well because I didn't know how to teach. At first I was too pedantic and corrected every word, but then I understood that this is not what I should do. Nobody can deal with it if somebody corrects every word. (Master, male)

In general, the Masters were very encouraging. They gave us truly positive feedback and they were amazed at our progress. This is what one Master thought after the whole programme was over:

> It was like a miracle, when I followed your [students'] progress over the year. Some people dared to speak right from the first days. Some did not, but then in the autumn everyone was speaking, people even gave interviews to the radio. It was like a miracle. Was it a coincidence that it

succeeded this well? No-one even dropped out. ... If the results were so good, would it not make sense to organise the same thing every year or every second year? It must have been hard work for the organisers, and for students too. It must be, if students learn a foreign language in a year so well. (Master, male)

Sometimes the Masters gave this positive feedback straight to their Apprentices. One student writes in her report that appraisals had great meaning for her self-esteem and language learning:

One Language Master said that I spoke like I was a real Saami. I am so insecure and sometimes even desperate about my language skills, so I really took this praise with great joy and wanted to believe that I had made a lot of progress.

M-A training served us all, but I think it was especially important for those students who learn by doing, rather than in the classroom. The same student continued:

I have been so thin-skinned about negative feedback. You know I don't always get the best grades. In many ways I am not the most patient student when it comes to grammar. ... Anyway, when I get unsatisfactory grades I feel that I am a lousy student. That is why I felt especially good when I got positive feedback from a Master.

Our Masters did not differentiate between CASLE students with AS roots and those without. For our Masters everyone was equal, and with open arms they welcomed all of us new speakers. I especially remember how one of the Masters once asked me why someone who is not a Saami him-/herself would bother to learn the language. I tried to give him the answers that felt right for me at the time. After a little silence he looked straight into my eyes and replied: 'I respect that. Hard-working people. For me it is an honour to be your Master.' After that I felt like I was adopted by the AS language community. Since then I have never hesitated to speak the language. I know I have the support of the elders and they respect me for my attempts to transfer their language. The meaning of that is huge.

5.4.2.5 Evaluation

In general, the M-A training was a success. All of the targets (see p. 103) were achieved, but there were some little things that could have worked better. This evaluation is based on student feedback and interviews with the Masters by my fellow CASLE student Anne-Marie Kalla, my own experiences and a report by Annika Pasanen about the practical training part of CASLE.

One of the targets of the M-A training was to create an environment where the student could be totally immersed in AS and use AS only. This succeeded rather well. Communication between Masters and Apprentices was primarily in AS, but sometimes when there were distractions from outside, Finnish was also used. For example, some Masters had Finnish or North Saami spouses who were around at least part of the time. When sitting around a dinner table, for example, it was difficult to carry on speaking AS if someone who did not understand the language was present. Some Apprentices were more aware of the 'danger of language shift' in these situations and were brave and stubborn enough to carry on speaking AS with their Masters. I admit I normally switched to Finnish because I did not want to exclude anyone from the conversation.

Normally the spouses were very considerate, however, and let us spend time with our Masters without disturbing us. Sometimes, if the language switched into Finnish because of a third party, my strategy was simply to get away from the situation, along with my Master. Using Finnish with Masters was a mistake because to get back on track in speaking hesitant AS after expressing myself in fluent Finnish was always painful. From this viewpoint I think it is very important to pay attention to the environment where the meetings between an Apprentice and a Master take place. Any distraction that prevents Masters and Apprentices from using the target language should be eliminated. Also the spouses and family members of the Masters should be informed about the training and its targets.

Furthermore, in terms of the environment, I never visited any other places with my Masters except their homes and home grounds. I was actually quite surprised to hear that some students had travelled with their Masters even to Norway or to the nearest city of Rovaniemi (about 350 km away from Aanaar). I thought everyone had spent their time just drinking coffee and chatting with their Masters like me! Well, in fact these trips were exceptions, although people did engage in several everyday activities like fishing, making handicrafts, cooking and even reindeer herding with their Masters. This was the best part of the training; when there were no solid plans one could never really know what to expect of that day. For both Apprentices and Masters these unscheduled meetings were good, but this is perhaps something that is bound to local culture.

The second target of the training was to get to know about AS culture. I do not think anyone could deny that this target was fully accomplished by this part of CASLE.

The Masters were told that they could also make us do some work. Some Apprentices, for example, did some work in the garden, but only because they had insisted on that themselves. Normally the Masters treated us like venerable guests, as one of our Masters described:

They said we could make students work. I made one student bake doughnuts in the beginning but then I no longer wanted to make others (work). They were like guests. I realised that if I make them work, there is no time for talking. It is better that we sit at the table and talk.

Although none of the Masters commented on the pay they got from their job, which was €10 per hour, I think that the pay itself had an effect on their commitment and motivation. Some of them really took their job seriously. My children's grandmother, for example, said that she used to warn her friends and relatives not to disturb her on the day that a student or students were coming to her place. The pay that each Master earned was not very high considering the fact that not so many hours were spent per Master. No-one got rich from the job but, as most of the Masters were retired, I suppose any extra income was welcomed with humble respect.

The third target was to strengthen the students' language skills. All of us students felt that the M-A training improved our language skills and especially our readiness to speak. Only a few months after we had started our studies, we were sent into the 'field', where we got that important experience of trying to make ourselves understood in a foreign language. That motivated us a great deal and provided the needed self-esteem to use the language even more. Because we had already learnt AS intensively for a few months before M-A training, the training worked, especially towards the spring when our language skills had improved, as a means of language planning rather than as total language immersion.

The Masters had been asked about the idea of taking on students who had no prior knowledge of the language. Some of them were more open to the idea than others but most Masters were doubtful. They realised that the full immersion method would have meant a lot more M-A days. Since most of the Masters were rather old, this would have been too demanding and heavy a commitment. The timing to start the training was perfect. Every one of us knew the basics already. We understood a lot and could carry on at least simple conversations, but our vocabularies were still very narrow and our grammar was horrible – at least mine was.

The M-A training widened our vocabulary and helped us to find the right verbs and grammatical cases more often. Sometimes we gathered some special vocabulary inspired by a certain surrounding. I remember sitting in a sauna (a cold one and with clothes on!) with a Master and another Apprentice and asking for sauna vocabulary. We kept looking around, asking for words and repeating them. Luckily my classmate had a cell phone and she could record all these words. The same Master told us that with another Apprentice, while walking in the forest, he had given all the possible words related to hunting elk and bear.

M-A training also helped us to get the right pronunciation. Getting the chance to listen to different native speakers slowly gave us the rhythm and the sound. Now that it has been nearly two years since our graduation, I listen to some of us who use the language every day and I cannot but wonder at how well we have done (see also Section 7.8 CASLE Graduates at Work in the AS Community). Of course I am not the best person to judge, and surely even the most talented of us make mistakes, but still we have accomplished a lot. Those idioms and phrases that people use, for example, did not come from our study materials. Those came from our Masters, and it is sometimes funny to recognise from whom exactly. The richness of different dialects can also be heard. Some people spent more time in the Eastern Aanaar village of Njellim (see Figure 3.2, p. 26), where the dialect is rather different from that of the Northern Aanaar. It is nice to recognise the variety of dialects, which we normally do in the context of using certain words that are characteristic for the area, in some of our language.

Most students and Masters thought it was a good idea that all the Apprentices had more than just one or two Masters. Besides being a nice change, it was good to hear different dialects and to get to know people. This served the fourth target: students were supposed to get to know the language community.

According to some people, we would have learnt the language better if each of us had had just one personal Master. One ('professional') Master who suggested this said that it would enable a method where all the students could follow a personal study plan, tailored only for them. Perhaps that is true; it is hard to say. But if I had had only one Master I would have missed out on so many beautiful people, places and experiences around the shores of Lake Aanaar. If each one of us had had only one Master we would have perhaps made one really close friend. This way we made many – so many that we can already feel we are part of the AS language community. This seems to be a choice well made.

Before the training started we students filled in a questionnaire about the upcoming training. I think it was a good idea to have us map out our wishes for the training. These were taken well into account. The questionnaire contained questions such as: What do you expect from M-A training? What kind of a Master would you like to have in terms of gender, age, profession, birthplace, etc.? What kinds of things are you interested in? What would you like to learn? Do you wish to go to the Master on your own or in pairs or in small groups? Do you have a car at your disposal? Is there something that you are afraid of, concerning the training? Are you able to spend weekends away? Can you stay overnight at your Masters' places, etc.?

I remember naming some Masters who I really wanted to meet, knowing that they were going to be involved in the programme. Some CASLE students were very enthusiastic about *tyeji* (traditional handicrafts), and it was easy for the CASLE team to partner them with the Masters who were *tyeji* specialists. From the point of view of logistics and moving around in the geographically vast Aanaar municipality, it was also good to know about practical issues such as whether one owns a car or not. Generally, coming and going to different places worked well. We students were also paid for mileage driven, and given compensation for petrol. Because the distances were sometimes long and timetables were hard to plan ahead, it was important to know whether we could spend nights or weekends at our Masters' places. I know some people stayed overnight and they had good experiences.

As mentioned before, for me and most other Apprentices it was both comfortable and useful to go to a Master with another study mate. However, those students who went to a Master on their own for the very first time were very happy with that decision too. Students say it was good, when the language skills were still quite inadequate, to be with their Master alone. That enabled them to receive all the Master's attention and they did not have to be ashamed of their imperfect language in front of other students (according to student feedback). However, what worked for one did not necessarily work for another. Some people were afraid of going to a Master's place on their own, so it was good that we were given the option of going with another student. We are aware of the fact that this can be a budget question: with a narrow budget, small groups or pairs are often the only possibility.

Sometimes there were three students with one Master. In general, these combinations worked quite well. However, it was typical in a situation with lots of people that those who were shyer than others remained silent and did not get to practise their spoken language skills as much as they could have. Sometimes curious visitors or neighbours came around to see the visiting students. Students seemed to think these days were really interesting from a social angle, but thinking about the language, they were not too productive because the topics for talking were more superficial and in general they could not speak as much as they would have if there had been fewer people.

The length of the training days was normally from five to seven hours. Both Apprentices and Masters alike thought that this length was good. Many had the sensation of 'time flying' and although some Masters were elderly, they did not admit that they were too tired. I think the days were heavier for us Apprentices because we had to think so hard in order to be able to communicate. Most students said they were knackered after those days.

The weekly structure of the training, which consisted of two training days, two independent working days and a feedback day, worked well. Some students would have wanted to have more days in a row with a Master, but in general two days a week was seen as enough and appropriate, because of organising the coming and going for different places.

After the training days we had a couple of days of independent study. I have already mentioned that during those days we were supposed to deal with the material we had recorded or written at the beginning of the week.

I admit I could have worked more on those days. Perhaps if someone had asked for a little presentation about the training in the classroom later in the following week, it would have motivated me to get more out of these days. Overall, we did not have to do anything but a final report of the M-A training. Perhaps there could have been some exercises or little challenges for us to do on those independent study days. One student, for example, suggested that everyone should have had something concrete to bring to the feedback session later. Perhaps we could have asked every Master to a song, tell a short story, share a recipe or create a theme list of words – anything that we could have used as a material for transcribing on the independent study days.

The feedback and reflection sessions that we had with the CASLE team in the classroom on Fridays, at the end of each M-A week, served their purposes too. We students were able to share our experiences with each other, and the organisers got to hear our news from the field and could adapt future planning on the basis of the feedback.

There were also sessions like this with Masters involved. Every couple or group of students and a Master were supposed to speak freely about their training day. These days were nice and comfortable. Students prepared food and also some programme like singing for the Masters. However, these meetings also received some critique. Students found it difficult to 'talk about talking', if that was the way they had spent the day. Most Masters could not make it to the meetings either, as many of them did not have cars. According to Marja-Liisa, these days were not planned by all the CASLE team members or other partners. In general that phenomenon could be seen directly in the student feedback: if a certain section was planned by many people and reflected upon before it was carried out, the feedback was brilliant. If a section was more or less one person's responsibility, the implementation was weaker. This refers overall to the whole CASLE programme, not only to M-A training – CASLE and the success of it were based on teamwork.

As an outcome of CASLE, the Saami Education Institute started to run a one-year AS language and culture course in 2011–2012 (see Section 7.5 Aanaar Saami at the Saami Education Institute), which also contained M-A training. Now that we have had this experience it is easier for everybody – organisers, Masters and Apprentices alike – to get the full potential out of the training. A lot of new Masters have been activated, meaning the active AS-speaking community has continued to grow. I have to admit that I am almost jealous of those students who still have all these amazing experiences ahead of them. Then again, I do not have to be jealous. All the Masters I had, and many more that I met on different occasions during the CASLE year, said that their doors would always be open to CASLE students. The connection is there. M-A created it and now it is mine and the other CASLE students' responsibility to keep it alive.

5.5 Aanaar Saami at their Workplaces

5.5.1 Planning and organising

Every student spent four weeks (equalling 5 study points), spread out during the CASLE year, doing practical training at AS workplaces. This training was a very central part of CASLE. By being introduced to and taking part in the routines of the AS workplaces, we students got a realistic picture of our futures-to-be, or different possibilities and challenges in our working lives.

The following goals were set for the practical training: the trainee gets a chance to speak and write (secondary goal) AS actively; s/he gets to know the people and tasks in the workplaces where AS is being used; s/he can help ease the routine of a working place; and the training combines the theoretical and the everyday language use of CASLE.

There were only three workplaces where AS could be used continuously: the Aanaar school (two classes), the language nest and the Saami Radio station. One workplace, the Research Institute for the Languages of Finland (KOTUS), made some adaptations specifically for CASLE: Marja-Liisa was working there part-time, so practical training was planned around her KOTUS job in AS research and language planning. The editorial offices of *Kierâš* online weekly (see Info Box 13 Saami Media in Finland) were also offered as an option, as well as the Education office at the Saami Parliament. Organising the last training week (in May) was each student's own responsibility; this gave us a chance to explore something completely new, or concentrate on something we already knew was of interest.

The choice of training places depended on our careers, future plans and interests, but the main principle was that each of us students could have at least one training period at either the language nest or the school. Teachers, or those who were studying to become teachers or were interested in teaching, were prioritised to train at the primary school; likewise those who worked with children, or who could think of working with them in the future, were prioritised to train at the language nest. Most of us got to practise twice at the workplace of our first choice.

Organising timetables with students and different workplaces was a real challenge for the project planning team. After all, workplaces had their own preconditions too. Because it was impossible to find a training place for all 17 of us at the same time, the CASLE group was split into two. While one group was getting work experience, others took part in M-A training (see p. 92) or the traditional cooking course (see p. 86) that was part of the culture courses. Only the last training week (which we could plan ourselves) was at the same time for everybody.

5.5.2 The Aanaar primary school

The CASLE students joined two AS teachers in their classrooms at the Aanaar school. Guidelines for the training had been negotiated with the Aanaar municipality, and the starting point was that the trainees should not disturb the daily routine of the school too much. Those routines varied a lot, as did the tasks of our students. In the multi-grade classroom (from preschool to second grade), students often took one of these classes as their responsibility. They adapted easily to the role of an assistant teacher.

Answer 1: I checked pupils' homework, helped with exercises and listened when the pupils were reading texts aloud. I also prepared some exercises: a sort of a book with multiplication table from one to six.

Answer 2: I had several minor tasks in the classroom. I asked questions concerning the story children had to read, translated a few pages from a book, made Valentine's day cards and helped the children with their modelling clay animation.

Answer 3: I sat behind a school desk and listened to what was going on in the classroom. I followed carefully how pupils reacted and behaved, and what the communication was like between them and the teacher. All the time I was reflecting and thinking how I would cope with children. This was a great chance to reflect about myself as a teacher and review my future working options.

Both of the cooperating teachers also gave a chance for the CASLE trainees to teach classes on their own. Some students who were already comfortable and fairly fluent in AS happily took this opportunity to teach. The students taught AS as a mother tongue as well as a second language. Some students also taught arts and theoretical subjects (biology and maths) using AS as the teaching language.

Answer 4: I taught some music classes, as well as environmental education. Environmental education went really well because the theme was universal and pupils were very interested in it. We had a long and profound discussion about the universe and my pupils had thought about it at home too, so they asked me extra questions the next day. The music lesson did not go so well, although I had planned it very carefully. It was hard to get the children to participate.

Sometimes our expectations were so high that disappointments could not be avoided. The main reason for that was poor guidance. The teachers, who had their own routines, did not always know what kind of help they could ask for from a trainee. The CASLE team, knowing that teachers are overloaded with work already, had not asked the teachers to make any special preparations for the week when a trainee would be sharing their classroom.

Students often ended up translating chapters or exercises from Finnish textbooks if they could not help in other ways. Producing material in AS was more than useful; nearly everyone mentioned the lack of AS schoolbooks. That was also one of the main reasons why the teachers' work in general was seen as so challenging, even difficult.

From the perspective of language learning, the primary school might have been the best training place. One of the CASLE students joked that certain grammar rules were learnt especially well: 'The school offered an excellent place for learning the language, especially imperatives, and negative verbs.' It was also rewarding for the students when pupils understood what they were trying to say.

> **Answer 5**: The children were very nice. They accepted my language mistakes. It was perhaps the most important thing that they trusted me and asked me questions if there was something they did not understand.

The practical training certainly improved our language skills. Despite that, we were still painfully aware how much we still had to learn before actually starting to work in AS. However, we were professionals and luckily the language did not change that.

> **Answer 6**: It was good to notice that my teaching skills did not disappear because of the language shift. Nevertheless, at that point I could not be 100% sure of any conjugation. I still have a lot of work to do before I start working as an AS teacher, but now I at least have the confidence that I will get along. Anyway, a dictionary and a grammar book are going to be my dear friends for a long time.

For me, the practical training at school was an eye-opener. It was in a way good to see how poor, in general, the primary school children's language skills were. I realised that the children who had learnt the language mainly or only at the language nest would need to hear the language outside the school environment as well. Furthermore, that motivated me to make a language shift at home. Today, nearly two years after CASLE, I am really happy to get positive feedback from my son's teacher. She thinks there is a clear connection; my son's language skills are strong because the language is spoken at home.

5.5.3 Kielâpiervâl: The language nest

The practical training at the language nest was not planned ahead in detail, because the project planning team expected that the trainees would have enough to do while taking part in the daily routines of the kindergarten. According to student experiences, the team seemed to be right.

> **Answer 1**: This week at the language nest was the hardest for me. There was so much work to do! I also had to think all the time about how to say this or that in AS in a way that the children would understand. On the other hand this was also the nicest week because the children were so sweet.

In terms of learning the language, *Kielâpiervâl* was an excellent training place because language learning is based on an immersion, and uses a method in which action is accompanied by explanations to the children in a simple and very concrete manner: 'Now let's take this piece of paper and wipe your nose … good … and then you can wash your hands … see this is how you open the tap …'. Observing and engaging in this kind of communication between the caregivers and the children offered a great chance for total language immersion at a level we could easily understand. In addition, everyday child-related vocabulary including clothes, colours, weather, food, animals and other concrete and visible things became familiar.

> **Answer 2**: During the training week I learnt some new words. For example the word *käniores* [rooster], which I had never heard before. And I learnt some new verbs like *touhustid* [hustle and bustle around] that I could not even find in the dictionary. There were many words that found their way into my vocabulary after that week.

Through working with children, the negative verbs became especially familiar. Still, some trainees mentioned that their poor language skills were connected with being more authoritative. For example, they found it hard to explain to the children why something should or should not be done. Maybe they became more authoritative because of this?

> **Answer 3a**: At the end of the week (in December) my speaking was already more fluent, but I still felt like an elephant in a porcelain store. I still heard new words all the time, but in the evenings I felt like I could not remember any of them. Part of the work does not even exist when you can only speak about simple things. I felt like my thinking stopped and I was like I was 30 years ago when I was first practising in this field. For example, playing games was very difficult when I could not help or teach the game.

About six months later, the same person felt s/he could manage a bit better; s/he could instruct the children and have a proper conversation with the school children who came to *Kielâpiervâl* for an after-school programme.

Answer 3b: Discussion topics with the children were for example Chernobyl, mining gold, can a man die and rot while standing like a tree and then falling down. ... I tried to give my best answers to these questions of life and death, but I did still have a headache with my poor vocabulary.

Many trainees mention that, although the children, especially the small ones, did not necessarily speak AS that much, they were eager to correct the language mistakes trainees made. The CASLE team had also instructed the language nest staff to correct (in a sensitive manner) the trainees' oral language. And so they did. It seemed to be natural for them because they did that all the time with the children anyway. Most of us students liked that and thought it was helpful. In general we students thought that the language nest was a gentle environment for language learning; with children we did not have to stress about making mistakes.[20]

5.5.4 Saami Radio

The Saami Radio station (see Info Box 13 Saami Media in Finland) was one of the most popular places for practical training; there were no daily routines that we students could interrupt, so it was easy to place many of us there at once. Every one of us CASLE students got a chance to broadcast in AS. Anja Kaarret, the one and only broadcaster of the AS radio programme *Anarâš saavah*, was our instructor.

Answer 1: Anja took time to instruct us even though she had her own work to do as well. She told us about her work and let us do several things: figure out the topics, do the interviews, edit the stories and choose the music. She also took us around to different places with her.

We trainees did many interviews, news reports and stories about all kinds of topics. One student remembers how she was supposed to do a report about how Anja herself went with a CASLE student and others for a winter swim through a hole in the ice. Since it was this student's first interview she had prepared well and thought about the questions, written them down and searched for information about the famous Finnish hobby of Arctic swimming.

Answer 2: I started to ask questions and record answers already in the dressing room. The girls acted like they had ants in their swimsuits. The whole place was full of energy and good spirits. I tried to stick to the point and be a convincing journalist. Then it was time to go. Happy yelling echoed when they ran in their bare feet on the snow down to the shore and I kept on running after them. While they took a dip in the freezing water I continued to ask them questions. Later back at the radio station I started to edit the story. At first, listening to my own voice (high-pitched, nervous and squeaky) and the language mistakes I made was painful. But it was also useful. I ended up deleting nearly half of the interview because I was ashamed of my own language mistakes. Nevertheless, the story was broadcast.

Most students struggled with embarrassment and self-criticism when they heard their own voices at first, but later gave up and simply communicated.

> **Answer 3**: At this point (of the CASLE programme) I thought there was no point in being too critical of myself. I thought it was better to be foolhardy – to speak and try my best in everything, stick my neck out and take all the risks. Perhaps otherwise this kind of crazy attempt to save a minority language would not even succeed.

Besides doing interviews and making reports, many students also had the opportunity to learn more about their roots. This was possible because of the huge number of radio archives at the Saami Radio station. Those old studio tapes, some of them dating back to the 1950s and 1960s, offered some students a chance to listen to their ancestors' voices.

> **Answer 4**: I knew that I should be able to find interviews of my grandmother and father. I found those, more than 20 interviews of them. Those recordings were so old that I had to digitise them first. That was easy and then I had a chance to listen to them. It was very important to me to hear these recordings and not just because of the language. My grandmother died when I was a small child; my grandfather died only five years ago (but I did not hear him speak AS after my grandmother died] – so I do not remember how they spoke AS. Listening to them brought back memories. It was one of the most important experiences I had during the whole year.

Listening to the radio archives also proved to be important from the viewpoint of language learning.

> **Answer 5**: By listening to old stories one can learn a lot of new words and phrases. Besides, one learns 'correct language'. I am not saying that what we learned was not correct, but the spoken language is somehow different. And I don't always bother to study grammar; for me it is easier to listen to the native speakers and learn from them. I don't have to sit and read and read and read.

For me, radio work was of course familiar. My office was in the same building as the Saami Radio station and, in practice, although we were working in different languages, I had been cooperating with the Saami Radio staff almost daily. It was therefore only natural that, since I was familiar with the station, its staff and equipment, I could start working straight away and could take some students with me to guide into radio work. Anyway, I think there was the need for another instructor; Anja was alone and sometimes she had as many as seven trainees at once. That was, in fact, one of the only things that students criticised about the training at the radio station.

I was used to delivering news and other reports about issues that would be of interest to the inhabitants of Lapland and even the whole of Finland. Now, since the target group and audience were more restricted – the Saami people in Finland – I had to find a new approach, a more relaxed one, to my topics and stories. The goals compared to my previous job were so different; there was no need for strict news criteria or breaking news. The main thing was to make the language heard. Any event or occasion that arose from the community, no matter how small or insignificant it would seem in the eyes of the outside world, would be of interest and carefully listened to by nearly all the AS people, and not only them but also by the North Saami.

Soon I realised that it was only my imagination that set the limits for choosing topics for stories. Since such a big percentage of the AS speakers I knew were children and they were easy to reach, it was natural to choose stories where children were the focus. The foremost challenge was exactly that: where to find new people to interview (if no dubbing was done)? Anja once laughed that she had already interviewed every one of those 350 speakers, at least twice. Also for her, CASLE brought new people to interview and new issues to broadcast about.

5.5.5 Kotus: Institute for the Languages of Finland

One workplace was especially appropriate for CASLE students because of Marja-Liisa's part-time position as a researcher at Kotus, the Institute for the languages of Finland. The students who were getting work experience at Marja-Liisa's workplace ended up preparing grammar materials and creating new words for first aid, lichens and butterflies.

Answer 1: At first I thought that it was a mission impossible; I knew nothing about lichens and at that time I did not know AS as well as I do now. It was a surprise that it went so well: I just needed some time and it was even fun! I just had to let my imagination fly.

One group made more than 150 suggestions for butterfly names during one training week. Later Marja-Liisa brought them to the AS Language planning group, *Kielâravvimjuákku*, which evaluated whether these word creations could be put into use.

> **Answer 2**: Translating butterfly names from Finnish into AS was quite difficult. When the Finnish equivalent was not clear to us we had to find out why it had been given that name. Often the reason was in the habitat, nutrition or appearance of the butterfly. One butterfly, the Speckled Wood butterfly, for example, had received its name in Finnish *(täpläpapurikko), Appaloosa,* from a horse that has a lot of spots. The Saami people were not so used to having horses that we could have found these colour terms useful . . .

The students who trained with Marja-Liisa viewed these sessions as especially good for their language use. They gave very positive feedback on this practical training, and Marja-Liisa received extra points for preparing the weeks' work so well beforehand.

> **Answer 3**: If I compare this practical training place to the others where I was, this was the best when it comes to language learning. The reason was that Marja-Liisa was with us all the time. I liked this week the best. Marja-Liisa had planned everything so well and she could instruct and help us all the time.

In January 2011 the Saami research done by Kotus was transferred to the University of Oulu, with the result that the practical research done by Kotus does not fit very well into the frame of theoretical research at the university. It is urgent that this language planning be extended, but there are still no plans for expansion. This represents a real threat to the future of a small Indigenous language.

5.5.6 Work experience (student free choice) and 'evaluation'

Towards the end of the CASLE year we had the option of gaining work experience in our own working sectors. Except for a few students who went back to *Kielâpiervâl* and the primary school, the work experience week in May was open for each of us to plan ourselves. Although we had been instructed in good time to figure out a task or a job for ourselves, according to Annika, there were some students who had not done anything in order to arrange a job even up to one week beforehand. In the end, everyone found something to do, but perhaps, as the whole CASLE year would be coming to end, we were no longer as active as we had been.

Quite a few of us were translating or writing at home and some felt that it was really hard to keep up their motivation and work independently. All and all, the things that we did during that week varied a lot. One student, a language teacher, organised and taught an AS Beginning Language course for the parents of *Kielâpiervâl* children; another, a priest, planned a mass that would be held in AS in August; yet another, a teacher of maths and chemistry, compiled vocabulary in these fields. One student translated the *Children's Traffic Book*; another planned a tour for the *Koškepuško* band; a third planned a student field trip to Njellim. One student trained at the Education office of the Saami Parliament and, among other things, proofread the new ABC book that was about to be published.

On the basis of our feedback, we would have preferred more instruction at the workplaces. The content of the work experience should have been planned more carefully, and the permanent workers/instructors should have been encouraged to commit more time and effort into instructing the students.

In general, the work experience created environments where it was positively a 'must' to speak AS intensively. We students realised that we could get along in AS even outside the classroom. Our vocabulary widened into new topics, idiolects and dialects. This work experience definitely encouraged us to use the language. Furthermore, it gave us a realistic picture of the work opportunities we would have after the CASLE year.

The AS work experience was extremely valuable because the community expected us to be highly qualified AS-speaking professionals. Most of us were already professionals, and when it comes to our AS skills, I think we managed remarkably well, after all. But, of course, our real 'language training' at work was about to start immediately after CASLE and continue for at least 10–20 years. Most of us already had jobs waiting for us where our language skills were needed. This motivated us even more to do our best. (The first reflections from our working lives as language transmitters can be seen in Chapter 7.)

In this chapter, the practical approach for the CASLE year has been described. Now it is time to illuminate the same issue from the viewpoint of project management, especially what it meant for people setting up CASLE as 'a new language training'.

Notes

(1)   The students have been promised full anonymity. Even giving age and gender would reveal within the local community who it is, likewise their occupation.

(2)   For many jobs, for instance in the municipal sector, knowledge of any Saami language is counted as an advantage. Sometimes, depending on the organisation and the nature of the job, it is even a requirement for candidates to have intermediate language skills. As yet, however, there is no official language test in AS. Some institutions have prioritised North Saami over AS although according to the Saami Language Act (Finlex, 2003) the different varieties should be considered equal.

(3)   Where some knowledge of a Saami language is required, the city council can pay a 'language bonus' on top of the basic salary. All the municipalities in the Saami region get government subsidies covering the 'extra costs caused by bilingualism'. Finland's Ombudsman for minorities, Eva Biaudet, has stated that municipalities

should encourage their employees to study Saami languages, and that knowledge of a Saami language should be required or at least stated as a preference when one applies for a municipal job in the Saami area.

(4) According to a study done in Norway, those Saami who suffer from psychological illnesses recover faster if the person who takes care of them is also a Saami (Kuokkanen, 2008).

(5) Petra Kuuva had been working in language nests and as a teacher of AS classes at primary school level. After Petra moved away from Aanaar she continued to contribute to the ASL community in many ways. She has, for example, taught AS through remote access on the internet. She has also given short language courses for adults and led summer camps for children with leisure time activities. She is now studying to become a teacher at the University of Oulu. She also speaks AS to her two children.

(6) Matti Morottaja was the first Chair of the *Anarâškielâ servi*, established in 1998 (see Info Box 17 *Anarâškielâ servi* [Aanaar Saami Association]). He was awarded an honorary doctoral degree by the University of Helsinki for his life's work in AS revitalisation.

(7) All study materials for CASLE needed to be created by the instructors.

(8) http://www.youtube.com/watch?v=e0YcIkUoEhc&feature=youtu.be

(9) Dried pike is said to be a symbol of the Aanaar Saami. In the past, it was used as a currency to pay taxes. Dried pike is a traditional AS delicacy and preparing it has been revived in informal gatherings called *Anarâš eehid* [AS evenings] (see p. 157).

(10) *Kielâkyeimi [Language Mate]* was published in 2011 (see Section 7.3.2 Funding the study materials).

(11) Burbot is a cod-like freshwater fish.

(12) My reflections here are based on Annika Pasanen's (2010a) report of CASLE's practical parts, student feedback forms and my own experience.

(13) See http://www.terralingua.org and the literature links given there for some of the research arguments; see also ICSU, 2002; Skutnabb-Kangas, 2000: Chapter 2; Skutnabb-Kangas & Dunbar, 2010: 75–78.

(14) Today, we sing and play all different kinds of music in AS, varying from pop to rock, and still sing cover songs as well as writing our own music. We have performed several gigs at local festivals and events. Some of the songs have been recorded and Saami Radio plays them regularly on their radio broadcasts.

(15) In AS the verb used for catching fish is also to 'kill a fish'.

(16) Aili Maarit Valle is also depicted on the book cover. In the photo she is fishing there with one of her apprentices, along with AS teacher Anna Morottaja and my son, Jussa.

(17) For example, if your ear is itching it will snow soon, just like if there is a halo over the moon or if snow grouses are sitting on the branches of a tree.

(18) For example, words for biology, geography, mathematics and music.

(19) Only a few Masters could write in AS because they all went to school in Finnish. So from this viewpoint, this was a very natural request.

(20) One AS teacher, Anna Morottaja, also a CASLE student, is now teaching AS to adults at the Saami Education Institute in Aanaar. While she was practising at the language nest and the primary school, she paid attention to children's eagerness to correct CASLE students' language. Anna thought she could perhaps try out a method in which the AS-speaking school children 'work' as Language Masters for her students. The meetings between students and children would be informal play dates, preferably at the children's homes, and would happen on the children's terms. This kind of revitalisation method was launched in spring 2012. As a sign of the tolerance of the AS community and its enthusiasm, all of the AS school children and their parents have given their permission to start this activity. According to Anna, the experiences during the first meetings between children and students have been very encouraging.

6 Complementary Aanaar Saami Language Education as a Project: CASLE 2009–2010

6.1 Introduction

This section (mainly written by Marja-Liisa Olthuis) introduces CASLE from the viewpoint of how to manage a language revitalisation project. According to Turley (2010: 1), in general a project is:

(A) A unique series of actions designed to accomplish a unique goal within specific time and cost limitations; (B) a temporary endeavour undertaken to create a unique product or service; (C) a temporary organisation that is created for the purpose of delivering one or more business products according to an agreed business case. In all definitions, a project creates a new product within a certain time frame, according to an approved plan.

I have used Turley's project frame *The PRINCE2 Principle* (2010) to describe CASLE's project stages, that is the manageable parts of the project, including the preliminary period, the realisation period and the closing. I highly recommend this internationally accepted project frame for the management of other revitalisation projects. Turley's project principles and project themes (see Section 6.4 Tracing the Critical Components of the Project) are key in setting up and carrying out the projects successfully. This may initially seem somewhat 'technical', but I experienced it as a great help in keeping track of the whole process.

This chapter is especially aimed at those people who plan and manage a revitalisation project, regardless of their official position in doing this. I start with a description of what happened before the project proper started.

6.2 Starting CASLE: The Preliminary Period

Before starting the project, there was a preliminary period consisting of the following stages: (a) *The first observations* (Turley, 2010: 150), which in this case came when a lack of AS-speaking teachers was observed by Lassi Valkeapää (see p. 15); (b) *The pre-project*, an investigation into what could be done to solve the observed problem (Turley, 2010: 150–151). CASLE's pre-project was field research into the needs of the community and numerous discussions with local employers; and (c) *The initiative*, that is the concrete suggestion to carry out a project (Turley, 2010: 151). As described earlier (see p. 20), the CASLE initiative came from the students in the revitalisation course.

During the CASLE pre-project, I started to create a new language revitalisation programme, using criteria introduced by Grenoble and Whaley (2006: 160–204). As a thorough assessment would have taken years, I chose to work with quicker preliminary surveys.

Firstly, language vitality had to be assessed. The results were alarming – the language could not be transmitted at home because the parent generation had lost the language. This is a common situation for many Indigenous peoples in the Western world, and is becoming more common elsewhere (see Info Box 2 Language Endangerment; Info Box 3 The Situation of the World's Languages). Thus the language transmission process had to happen outside the home. I had not assessed the exact ages of the AS speakers (see also Section 3.4 Aanaar Saami Use and Competence by Age Group) at that time, but I had a strong indication that most fluent speakers were already retired, and the youngest speaker generation consisted only of the approximately 40 language nest children. The working-age generation was even more constricted: I counted about 20 people in all professions. There were definitely too few of them for language transmission purposes, never mind the entire language-saving process. New language transmitters were urgently needed, and likewise a rapid enlargement of the young generation of speakers. As the total community was very small, one language nest was clearly not enough for these purposes. Expanding the language nests demanded more professionals who spoke AS.

Secondly, community goals had not been clearly determined. AS activists saw the language as essential to the community and promoted it. This meant in practice that the few well-educated members of the AS-speaking community were drowning in work. The elderly people had experienced very contradictory attitudes in their lifetimes: they had used the language in their childhood, but because of the *kansaškovlâ* (primary school) tragedy (see Section 3.5 Reasons for the Decline of AS) the language was suddenly banned at school. Later in their lives they had slowly grown used to the idea of speaking the language to each other, but they were not directly promoting it. For the L2 speakers, the language skills of 'ordinary' community members remained practically untapped. Adopting AICLS's (Hinton, 2002) Master–Apprentice (M-A) programme seemed to address this imbalance because it used 'ordinary' people as Language Masters. There were also other formally educated people who were committed to the community but who were unable to speak AS. Their valuable knowledge had to be put to use in the language transmitting process. I had to investigate, along with other community members, what kind of professionals the Saami employers needed and how many there should be. It was clear from the beginning that at least two professional groups would be needed: primary school teachers and preschool teachers.

Thirdly, when a language is seriously endangered, the human resources for revitalisation work have to be identified. There was an intention to have more AS-speaking professionals, but I was informed by local civil servants that the meetings organised for recruiting AS-speaking teachers had not delivered the desired results. Many teaching positions were permanently vacant or staffed by unqualified people because of the mismatch between (high) qualification requirements and the missing language skills. The normal teacher training programme could not solve the problem because the youth generation had lost the language. A new method had to be developed.

Fourthly, one has to consider potential obstacles and find strategies for overcoming them. The most challenging 'obstacle' which was considered in the development of CASLE's major project plan and its mission was actually a daunting task: How could the project replace the whole missing working-age generation with AS speakers? This implied far more than simply organising teacher training, which is the strategy mentioned in many manuals on revitalisation programmes. In this case, it was uncertain whether this aim was even achievable. Another obstacle had to do with the practicalities associated with replacing the missing generation: how could potential students be found, how could their studies be funded and how could a good study programme be set up for them? The study programme aspect seemed the easiest to solve because there was actually only one good possibility in higher education: the AS study programme at the University of Oulu. However, it was also clear that this programme would need to be modified, as for these purposes the language had to be learned mainly as a spoken language.

Fifthly, the formal education aspect of the programme must be developed. A curriculum needed to be developed, instructors to be found, and study materials for adult education to be created.

All of these aspects had to be addressed in order to create a new language programme. This challenge definitely needed more brainstorming. Therefore I asked Principal Valkeapää whether the Saami Education Institute would be able to organise a revitalisation course, and he agreed to do this. During the course the initiative for CASLE was formulated and concretised into a project plan, then sent to the Finnish Cultural Foundation and later to the University of Oulu. These were the first steps (i.e. the preliminary period, in Turley's terms) taken towards the realisation of CASLE. In the next section, the realisation period of the project is presented using the framework of the *PRINCE2 principle*.

6.3 The Realisation Period

According to Turley, the realisation period consists of two stages: initiation and delivery. These stages will be described from the viewpoint of project management.

6.3.1 The initiation stage

The initiation stage uses the pre-project investigation results as a basis, and a detailed project plan is worked out (Turley, 2010: 151–152). In CASLE, I as the Project Manager needed to be responsible for the following tasks:

(1) developing CASLE's educational contents;
(2) creating a management organisation for CASLE;
(3) dispensing the project tasks:
    (a) creating a project plan team
    (b) creating a study materials team
    (c) searching for the instructors and planning the courses to be taught
(4) selecting the students; and
(5) finding funding and elaborating the final budget.

6.3.1.1 Developing CASLE's educational contents

The creation of a good study programme was one of the most crucial issues in order to guarantee the quality of the final 'product', that is the new AS-speaking professionals who had to learn the language as well as possible in a very limited time period. Some background information was needed in order to specify the precise contents of CASLE; for example, the duration and the scope had to be clearly defined. There were, of course, linguistic requirements for the programme, including an estimation of how much teaching would be needed in order to achieve good or even excellent (proficient) communicative skills in AS. To determine this, I relied on my work experience as a lecturer of Finnish abroad. The basic study programme of 25 points (where each point corresponds to 27 hours of full-time work) gave a good basis for decision making, but if students were to reach a higher communicative level they needed more – at least 35 additional advanced study points, giving a total of at least 60 study points.

Several practical matters had to be taken into account in building up the study programme. During preliminary investigations, I interacted with a number of public servants in the Saami area to get a wider perspective of the needs of AS-speaking professionals. These discussions always turned to financial issues. The questionnaires given to potential students also clearly showed the need for secure funding, since they would need support comparable to their normal salaries for the entire study period. Secure funding would also obligate the students to do their best during the language studies; the employers as well as the funders would expect results.

There were, finally, three financial considerations that strongly restricted CASLE plans as well as the educational content of the programme. The first consideration was that the employers could spare their employees (the forthcoming potential CASLE students) from their jobs for a maximum period of one year. Although the project planning team considered lengthening the period to more than one year using unpaid time off, the few precedents indicated that this would not be accepted; it was expected by employers that their staff members would also study in their spare time. However, we knew that in the case of the CASLE programme, studying in their spare time would have weakened students' study results and their motivation for studying. Furthermore, it would have taken longer than a year for students to finish the programme successfully. As the expectations were extremely high, and getting new language transmitters was seen as an urgent matter, the programme had to be as short and efficient as possible. Clearly it could not be longer than one year.

The second financial consideration was that there was a strong restriction from one main potential student funder, the Ministry of Employment and the Economy. It accepted study only during normal office hours. This funder regularly bought individual student places from education organisers to increase the employment opportunities of unemployed people and those under imminent threat of becoming unemployed. The number of study hours per week had to be equal to the hours of a full-time job. A great number of potential CASLE students had the opportunity to use this funding because of their temporary contracts. The pre-investigations were worthwhile because in the end the Ministry of Education funded seven of our CASLE students. The final scope of the programme was thus determined by the norms of the Ministry. The number of work hours demanded of students was thus 1700 hours per year. This differed slightly from the normal academic requirement of 60 study points, which equal 1600 hours per year. Our complete study programme of 64 study points equalled 1706 work hours, which was thus equal to one year.

The third financial consideration was that, from the viewpoint of other potential student funders (and we had many!), the funding (e.g. student grants) could be guaranteed for a period of one year. This was another motivation for limiting the programme to a period of 12 months.

According to CASLE experience, solving student funding issues is a major key to a successful revitalisation programme. As we know from many colleagues and friends, this has been and is a major hurdle for most revitalisation programmes worldwide.

The next section describes how the programme was placed into existing organisations and how the CASLE organisation was set up.

6.3.1.2 Creating an organisation for CASLE

Because CASLE was envisioned by researchers, one of the challenges was how to create an organisation for CASLE from scratch, without any initial support from any organisations. Turley (2010: 22) sees a project as being based on a customer–supplier environment. For him, one party is the customer, who will specify the result and most likely pay for the project. The other party is the supplier, who will provide the resources, do the work and deliver the results. In CASLE's experience, a clear customer does not necessarily exist in a revitalisation project of this type: the programme, including the initial expected and final goals, had to be developed by researchers, who in this case can be seen as counterparts of the suppliers. One of my main tasks was to 'market' the principles of the programme and find suppliers. Once the suppliers were found, they also accepted the financial responsibility by sharing the costs of the educational part of the project. In this case, my personal networks and clear view of what a good study programme looked like helped support the project.

The only usable AS study programme, as already mentioned, was the programme at the University of Oulu. It had been created in 2000 and slightly modified a couple of times. However, it was theory based, and classroom teaching was the main teaching method. CASLE needed to implement strongly communicative teaching methods alongside classic classroom teaching. As there was no possibility of developing a completely new programme, it seemed natural to use the existing one as a basis and to modify it, adding several communicative parts. Initially, CASLE was 'marketed' to the University of Oulu in a manner which made Oulu CASLE's main supplier. However, the university did not have the human resources to implement the modifications. These had to be done by CASLE's planning team in *Anarâškielâ servi*, the Aanaar Saami Association, funded by the Finnish Cultural Foundation. Of course, the main supplier's wishes were taken into account.

The field teaching methods brought CASLE out of the classroom – but these parts could not be funded by the university. Therefore CASLE needed a co-supplier and funder, which were found in the Saami Education Institute. The team at *Anarâškielâ servi* planned several field teaching courses on behalf of the Saami Education Institute: three fishing courses, a cooking course and a comic art course.

The M-A programme was the most difficult part of the programme to organise. According to both suppliers, the M-A sessions were seen as 'private lessons', which could not be financed as such. Fortunately, the University of Oulu accepted this way of educating, provided that the funding questions could be solved. The CASLE planning team applied for a separate grant for the M-A part from the Jenny and Antti Wihuri Foundation. The necessary sum was granted, and thus this programme could also be implemented, managed by *Anarâškielâ servi*.

The University of Oulu, the main supplier, was responsible for 65% of the education budget, the Saami Education Institute for 15% and *Anarâškielâ servi* for the remaining 20%.

Once the organisation had been created, the project tasks had to be dispensed, as described in the next section.

6.3.1.3 Dispensing the project tasks

One of the tasks of the Project Manager was to create teams (see Turley, 2010: 22, 42–56) and guide their simultaneous work.

(a) Project planning team

The heart of CASLE was the project planning team. Once the main frame of the CASLE organisation was set up, this team had to work out the details. It created a detailed study programme and wrote a curriculum. The team marketed the programme to the field to find potential students and inform them about the curriculum. Once student selection was completed, the team contacted their local employers and helped to organise the students' absence from work for the period of 12 months from September 2009 to August 2010.

The team mapped out and arranged the funding opportunities for the students, contacting the Ministry of Employment and the Economy to 'sell' student places to them. It also took care of the students' grant applications for the Finnish Cultural Foundation and budgeted for the exact sums the students needed as a (supplementary) grant. They also applied for grants for certain additional parts of the programme, planned and organised the field courses on behalf of the Saami Education Institute, and finally carried out the programme in Aanaar as a subcontractor of the University of Oulu. The planning team also assisted the study materials team and the instructors' team.

Project administration also had to be worked out. There were several budgets and administrations of different organisations working side by side, so all costs and monetary transactions needed to be specified.

One team member, Irmeli Moilanen, was a specialist in administration and educational planning. She arranged the timetables, specified the main budget and several sub-budgets, arranged student funding, planned the cultural courses and took care of the practical arrangements like logistics during the project.

Another team member, Annika Pasanen, worked part-time (50%), taking care of planning and coordinating the practical training at people's workplaces as well as the practical parts of the M-A programme. The latter programme was extremely prone to changes because a great number of people, including the students and their Masters, had to be accommodated at the same time. Furthermore, the Masters, even though they were committed to the programme, had their own time-management systems that did not correspond to 'Western-type' bureaucratic agendas, so activities further ahead than a few days were almost impossible to plan. This definitely meant a new way of thinking for the coordinator as well; things just could not be planned in what we saw as 'good time'.

All of these stages needed very detailed plans that concerned the specific tasks, people and exact timetables. They are too specific to introduce in this book.

Parallel to the project planning team, there was a study materials team, whose activities are described next.

(b) Study materials team

Preparing study materials was a crucial part of the programme. This part definitely needed human resources and a separate budget, but CASLE lacked both. According to university regulations, there was no need for a separate budget because the instructors were responsible for the study materials during the courses and the preparation of them was included in their ordinary salary. However, an Indigenous or minority language that has hardly ever been taught before often lacks any study materials. Most often the instructor prepares them during his/her spare time, mainly during late evening hours. In this case, especially due to the expected rapid progress from the beginning level to the very advanced level, lots of materials were needed. During discussions with CASLE's forthcoming head teacher Petter Morottaja, it became clear that the shortage of materials would seriously affect the quality of the lessons. CASLE was an exception to normal study programmes and needed an exception (contingency) plan (see Section 6.4 Tracing the Critical Components of the Project; Turley, 2010: 80). The study materials were a 'must-have' issue because they were essential for the viability of the project, and their absence would have affected the project objectives.

In spite of the lack of a study materials budget, CASLE was fortunate, because the Saami Parliament was starting a study materials project for grammar school and adult education. The main authors of this study materials series were Petter himself and Petra Kuuva, one of the CASLE teachers. However, the time frame of this project was much slower than CASLE's, and financial resources were limited. I was asked to join the team, just to give a helping hand from the viewpoint of the CASLE programme. What I did not expect was that this part of the project would almost engulf me, mainly because of the strict schedule and lack of human resources. Adding this work to my daily routine very soon forced me to work 14–16-hour days from January 2009 until August 2010, a point certainly worth noting for future Project Managers.

New listening comprehension exercises were very time consuming to produce; the study materials team managed to do them for the first 12 chapters (out of 36). As the students' language skills progressed, CASLE used old Saami Radio recordings. An AS broadcaster, Anja Kaarret, was hired to search out and edit old broadcasts that would be suitable for the specific themes of our written material (see also Info Box 13 Saami Media in Finland). These broadcasts provided more authentic language than the team's listening comprehension exercises, which were more or less simplified and artificial.

When the CASLE programme started in August 2009, the last parts of the planned study materials were still in production. While Petter instructed the students in the classroom, I continued to produce materials. These were often given to students in photocopied rather than in printed form.

The creative process in preparing the materials took more time than we had estimated. We would now advise others to begin the materials planning even two years before the actual education programme commences. We see the lack of materials as a serious potential risk for the quality of the whole training (see also Turley, 2010: 104–107), to the extent that it might even be advisable to delay the start of the training if the materials are not ready. Even though the main CASLE materials were prepared beforehand and the materials work continued throughout the whole project (with the help of another instructor as well as ourselves), Petter as the head teacher still needed three or four hours daily to prepare for the following day's teaching. We would judge that the standard university norms for materials preparation covered only some 10% of the real study materials needed. In the case of materials development, we learned a great deal from our experience (see also Turley, 2010: 16).

(c) Team of instructors

One task of the Project Manager was to search for suitable instructors, taking into account their professional interests and specialities. This was paradoxical: on the one hand there was a lack of AS-speaking professionals, yet somehow the key people needed for CASLE's team of instructors were easy to find. Because of the programme's time-intensive nature, it was necessary to use several instructors.

The courses were mainly planned by the head instructor, but I was always kept updated with the contents and the students' progress. As a safety measure (see also Turley, 2010: 98–116), the main lesson plans were planned by two instructors. There was always a risk of absence (or other missed sessions), but postponing the courses was impossible. A few days without contact lessons might have been managed, but even that would have meant fewer language skills for the students. Risks were reduced through advance planning (see Turley, 2010: 104–106), and planning in pairs meant that there was always another instructor aware of the course contents and, if necessary, ready to take over. One positive result of planning in pairs was that the teaching methods, study materials and course contents were thoroughly considered, and could be planned as a logical continuum. The most critical feedback from students was received on parts that were planned and/ or carried out individually.

6.3.1.4 Student selection

I as the Project Manager was responsible for student selection, along with the local employers in the Aanaar area. Final selection was done by the *Giellagas* Institute and the Faculty of Arts at the University of Oulu.

In the beginning, local employers were asked to estimate their own employment needs in order to decide on the correct number of students to be selected from certain professional target groups. The aim was to educate, as much as possible, the exact number of professionals needed so that everyone could be employed after CASLE.

Appropriate student selection was vital for several other reasons too; it could either guarantee or diminish the quality (see also Turley, 2010: 57–75) of the 'end product', that is highly qualified professionals transmitting the language to the target groups. The 'wrong' student choice could have had a negative influence on the future development of the language. No 'normal' courses operate like this; it is a special feature of programmes like CASLE which are working with a very small, critically endangered language. Therefore the selected students simply had to be 'the right people' to be educated. They could be defined as follows.

(a) They had to represent certain professional groups defined by CASLE.
(b) They had to be (at least nearly) qualified and able/willing to continue their work through the medium of AS after CASLE.
(c) They had to represent particular age groups. For example, no young students were accepted because they would not necessarily have a clear vision of their forthcoming working life. On the other hand, CASLE students had to be young enough to stay in the labour market for at least 8–10 years after CASLE. This was due to the high investment put into each CASLE student position.
(d) They had to have a proven ability to learn other languages, that is they had to be as at least bilingual already.
(e) They had to be motivated to work with AS as well as to stay in the Aanaar area.

Student selection included one major risk (see also Turley, 2010: 98–116 and Section 6.4): as the Ministry of Employment and the Economy paid for several individual student positions, and as the payments were received for each student position separately, CASLE's final budget depended on the total number of students present. If even one student had withdrawn from the programme, the total budget would have been influenced negatively. Because this risk could not be avoided, its probability had to be reduced (see Turley, 2010: 208). This is why CASLE used a psychologist to help with the selection procedure. Criteria (a)–(c) above were general selection criteria. Criterion (d) was checked to gauge to what extend the applicants were capable of studying for the whole intensive year without experiencing learning difficulties. Criterion (e) assessed the applicant's motivation and whether or not it was strong enough to commit to the study programme as well as to the AS-speaking language community in general.

Still, although the backgrounds of the students were carefully investigated, the possibility of somebody withdrawing from the programme existed, possibly because of changing personal circumstances. This never happened, but the project had to accept this and be prepared for the financial risk. These circumstances could be managed by planning a risk budget (see Turley, 2010: 11; Section 6.4 Tracing the Critical Components of the Project), that is planning for more leeway in the budget at the beginning of the CASLE year and releasing the sum later. Applying for more funds would have been difficult in the middle of the project.

The strict student selection procedure had a positive effect on the quality of the results, because all of the students who started the programme finished the CASLE year. In addition, they completed the programme with even higher grades than normal for the university.

In this section we have only introduced one potential funding risk, but there were many financial aspects to be considered. These are discussed in the next section.

6.3.1.5 The funding and the final budget

Putting together the CASLE budget of €600,000 from several financial sources was the most challenging mission during the project. It took almost two full years.

The classroom teaching and the practical field courses organised for the whole group were the easiest part of the programme to fund, because the University of Oulu and the Saami Education Institute were able to pay the salaries of the instructors. However, there were a few parts of the classroom teaching that needed to be taught by two instructors simultaneously. It was very unusual for either organiser to hire two instructors with temporary contracts for the same course (although instructors with permanent contracts often cooperate), so the second instructor had to be funded by *Anarâškielâ servi*. This teaching method was used at the beginning for intensive conversation in the classroom and during the writing course where the teachers gave individual comments concerning the students' essays.

The M-A programme was financially the most challenging part of CASLE. As described earlier, these sessions were seen as 'private lessons' and could not be funded by the main suppliers of financing. The planning team thus applied for and was offered a separate grant from a private foundation for these sessions. However, during the time when the funding was still uncertain, this posed a potential risk for the whole programme (see Turley, 2010: 108–109); the CASLE programme had to be carried out even if the funding for the M-A programme had been denied. This risk could be totally avoided by strengthening the programme with three extra cultural courses carried out by the Saami Education Institute (see Turley, 2010: 108). Finally, when the funding for the M-A programme was secured, these extra courses were not necessarily needed, so they were included as optional parts of CASLE. Leanne Hinton (2002: 4) points out that the M-A programme could be implemented without funding. Our intention was to pay at least something to the Masters for their intensive commitment to CASLE; it would have been difficult to ask for such great favours and time commitments without any intention of reimbursing them.

The uncertainty of funding for student positions was resolved little by little. For CASLE it was important to know for sure that at least 10 students could be funded for a whole year, because this was the minimum needed to start the process. This represented a remarkable risk for CASLE, because the programme could not be carried out with too few students. We managed to avoid this risk (see also Turley, 2010: 107), because the funding for 10 students was guaranteed by the Finnish Cultural Foundation. The total sum granted by the Finnish Cultural Foundation was very flexible: it could be for 10 or even for more than 10 students, depending on many factors, that is the number of individual student positions from the Ministry of Employment and Economy, studying with normal salaries, and the funding of the Education Fund. As the result of a year of intensive work by Irmeli, all 17 students could be fully funded. Three students received a full grant from the Finnish Cultural Foundation to study for 12 months. Three students were able to study while receiving their normal salaries. The rest of the students received funding either from the Ministry of Employment and Economy or from the Education Fund, supplemented when necessary by a minor grant from the Finnish Cultural Foundation. In this way everyone could receive at least 80% of their annual net earnings. The CASLE planning team compiled a priority list for the funders instructing them in which order the students should be funded, in case the decisions by other funding sources were negative. This list was, fortunately, never used.

Once all aspects of the initiation stage were resolved, the delivery stage (see Turley, 2010: 12–15) of the project could be started.

6.3.2 The delivery stage

The delivery stage is the most crucial stage of the project, when the final product is created. Everything has to flow smoothly in accordance with earlier plans, and the finest details can be executed. All plans have to be kept up to date (Turley, 2010: 151–152). Many of the tasks at this stage have already been introduced above in part (a) Project planning team of Section 6.3.1.3 Dispensing the project tasks; see p. 7.

The whole CASLE programme year 2009–2010 has to be seen as the delivery stage. The study programme and the learning process are described in detail in Chapter 5.

6.3.3 Closing

The *Closing* is the final stage of the fulfilled project when the final work has to be done and the final product can be utilised (Turley, 2010: 208–215). In CASLE, the closing stage has taken more than two years. The administrative as well as the final reports had to be prepared first. In addition, the whole project had to be documented thoroughly; this book represents a large part of that documentation process.

We had already started the preparations for closing the project in the early stages of the CASLE year. Some students were recruited into the programme with the vision of the language nest activity of *Anarâškielâ servi* being extended in the near future. This seemed to be the right moment to extend the language nests, as the language community was getting new AS-speaking professionals. I as the Project Manager, together with the Finnish Cultural Foundation, discussed language nest funding issues with the Ministry of Education and Culture. The result was that the funding for two new language nests was made available in May 2010, three months before the end of the CASLE year. Furthermore, the local primary schools also needed AS-speaking teachers. When CASLE finished, there were eight new posts for former students in the language nests and primary schools. Other students wished to return to their own jobs, adding the new language into their daily work.

Some students found other positions. One of them, Anne-Marie Kalla, interviewed the former Masters and wrote a report about how they saw their own roles as Masters in CASLE (Kalla, 2010). The results of her report have been used in this book.

The wish of the Finnish Cultural Foundation as well as of many fellow researchers was to document CASLE as thoroughly as possible. This task has been Marja-Liisa's and Suvi Kivelä's pleasure as insiders, and Tove Skutnabb-Kangas has played a significant role as an outsider.

6.4 Tracing the Critical Components of the Project

The revitalisation of any Indigenous language should, of course, represent a success.

Using Turley's project themes and principles (2010: 16–24), I recapitulate the most critical components of CASLE. Turley's themes and principles are used worldwide for all kinds of projects; therefore we expect that these might be key issues for other revitalisation projects as well.

(1) Plans

Every revitalisation project has to be planned thoroughly. Turley distinguishes between four types of plans: project plan, stage plan, team plan and exception (contingency) plan (Turley 2010: 78).

The *project plan* has to be created at the start of the project (Turley, 2010: 78). CASLE's project plan described the following issues: (a) the results of the pre-project (see Section 6.2 Starting CASLE: The Preliminary Period), that is the results of the field investigations regarding why, where/by whom/how many AS-speaking professionals were needed; and (b) the initiative, that is the fact that CASLE was the right 'product' to be developed to cultivate AS-speaking professionals. The project plan cannot be stressed too strongly because it convinces (or disappoints) the funders and suppliers. CASLE's project plan described the initiation stage (see Section 6.3.1 The initiation stage) and the idea of how to carry out the CASLE year (described in Chapter 5 The CASLE Year). Finally, it estimated the time frame and costs of the project.

CASLE needed several *stage plans* (see Turley, 2010: 78). It was important not to start the CASLE year before all preparations had been made, so the following stage plans were made for the initiation stage: (a) student funding (see Section 6.3.1.1 Developing CASLE's educational contents; Section 6.3.1.5 The funding and the final budget); (b) study programme and curriculum (see Tables 5.1, 5.2 and 5.3; pp. 57–59, 69 and 79); (c) setting up the organisation (Section 6.3.1.2 Creating an organisation for CASLE); and (d) setting up the teams (Section 6.3.1.3 Dispensing the project tasks). The teams operated with their own detailed stage plans, that is weekly/monthly work plans (which have not been described in this book). During the CASLE year many stage plans were made, that is for each course and teaching period.

According to Turley, *exception* (contingency) *plans* are needed when something falls outside the tolerance. The Project Manager must have leeway when it comes to factors like time, cost and scope; other organisers/partners must be informed that there is or might be a problem (Turley, 2010: 78). In CASLE, there were several exception (contingency) plans that corresponded to the project's risk management. These issues concerned funding, human resources and the quality of the programme. They are described in detail below in clause (5) Risks, p. 122.

(2) Cost–benefit justification[1]

In addition to the project plan, the suppliers and funders are interested in costs. Because revitalisation programmes like CASLE are expensive, a cost–benefit justification should prove that the project is worth investing in. A revitalisation project is worth the investment when it has long-term influence, from at least five to 20 years, on the language revitalisation process. This plan should show by whom and why the project should be implemented, as well as its costs, the expected benefits and time frames (see Turley, 2010: 21–22). It can be said that the cost–benefit justification is as important as the project plan.

(3) Organisation

Like all projects, a revitalisation project needs an organisation (see details in Turley, 2010: 43–52). There are a few criteria for setting up the organisation and choosing the main suppliers of language education. Firstly, organisers should be able to give students an official certificate on completion of their study programme. Another criterion is a good study programme – if this does not already exist, it should be created based on the same criteria. In our experience, the main supplier can be a university or a language institute or a combination (see Section 6.3.1.2 Creating an organisation for CASLE). We chose a combination, where the University of Oulu offered the academic standards and the Saami Education Institute provided the local knowledge as well as excellent logistics and facilities in a sparsely populated area. The management and administration they provided were of great help to us in carrying out the project.

It may happen that the teaching location is not near the suppliers. An important consideration is whether or not the project needs a physical and geographical base. If a base is desirable, any related funding issues have to be resolved. In CASLE's case the main supplier, the University of Oulu, was 600 km south of Aanaar, and the CASLE students were officially students of Oulu. Unfortunately, a local base in Aanaar could not be funded by the university but, on the other hand, a possible lack of a physical base was a moderate risk for the programme, which needed students to be satisfied and courses to run smoothly. This problem was solved with the grant from the Finnish Cultural Foundation, allowing the project planning team at *Anarâškielâ servi* to continue during the CASLE year, acting as a partner of the University of Oulu in order to carry out the programme locally. All in all, *Anarâškielâ servi*'s presence as a partner with an independent and flexible budget was very beneficial for the project, making it possible to carry out even the finest details according to the stage plans.

(4) Quality

Indigenous languages deserve the best possible care, so revitalisation projects should pay close attention to quality requirements. Turley defines quality as 'a useable and desired product that should be considered already at the start of the project'. He states: 'If quality is defined insufficiently, the project might possibly result in developing a wrong product'[2] (Turley, 2010: 59). The quality can be determined by asking the following questions. Firstly, what is the intended end product of the project, and what does it look like? And secondly, are there any other products, for example tools, that need to be developed in order for the final product to be reached? CASLE produced two 'products': a study programme as a tool to produce the 'end product', that is new AS-speaking professionals.

There were several keys in producing quality in these products.

(a) How could the quality of CASLE's 'end product' – AS-speaking professionals – be ensured?

The quality of the end product has to be specified first. It is essential to determine from which professional groups the candidates come. It is also necessary to get the 'right' students. The opinion of the local employers is also needed. Do they wish to educate their own staff, or should professionals be recruited in another way? The 'ideal' candidates have to be determined as well as their age, working experience and commitment to the area and/or the community. Their motivation and capability to learn languages should be examined, that is to determine the following issues: (i) What languages do they already know and how well? (ii) Where and how did they learn them? (iii) How long did they study? (iv) What was their motivation to learn these languages? (v) How did/do they use these languages since learning them?

(b)   How can the quality of the study programme be ensured?

There were several criteria established for creating a high-quality study programme for CASLE. The programme had to stress practical language skills, oral proficiency and written proficiency (see Tables 5.1, 5.2 and 5.3, pp. 57–59, 69 and 79), instead of heavy linguistic theory. The students had to learn everyday language and the vocabulary of his/her own profession. According to our experience, between 1600 and 1700 learning hours are absolutely necessary to reach this aim. According to the new quality requirements of the municipality of Aanaar, for a L2 speaker to qualify as a teacher she/he needs to have studied Aanaar/North Saami for at least 60 points (equal to 1600 hours).

In our experience, the programme becomes more interesting and adaptable to students when it offers both classroom and field teaching. The basic language skills are taught in the classroom, and when students' skills improve, the learning process can begin in the field, interacting with 'ordinary' language speakers. We have discussed whether the field learning period could have started earlier (see Section 5.3.2 Diving into the culture: student view). I am not convinced by this. According to the students' feedback, the timing of the field study period was good because it came after learning the basics in the classroom. Also during my personal discussions with the Masters I had the strong impression that the Masters were not willing to act exactly as the Masters in the AICLS's M-A programme had done (see also Hinton, 2002), that is by starting at the beginning level. All in all, both Apprentices and Masters enjoyed their deep discussions in AS. If an early start is considered, there should at least be a different kind of training for the Masters and Apprentices (see also Hinton, 2002: 91–99). In other words, more elaborate training would be needed, compared to CASLE's small-scale training sessions (see Section 5.4.2 Master–Apprentice training). When this issue was discussed with a few Masters, one of them immediately recalled how it was in the submersion schools, where Saami children did not speak the majority language but were forced to use it anyway (Kalla, 2010). It has to be asked whether the Masters would experience an early start in the field as language immersion, or if they would be painfully reminded of their own language shift when they were forced to use the majority language in schools without knowing it. If an early start of the field learning period is considered, such feelings on the part of Masters or Apprentices should be taken into account. Of course, there are examples of past researchers who have learnt the language almost completely in the field, as Lea Laitinen did (see Section 4.4.2 Documenting earlier individual AS Master–Apprentice 'training' experiences). However, at that time the role of the Masters was different; they had acted as language teachers, mostly with a small salary. In addition, the language loss in that context had not progressed so far. At present there are not many AS speakers, so the Masters clearly experienced their AS-speaking CASLE Apprentices as 'familiar chat mates'. If I could do it again, I would do it in the same way, teaching the basics first in the classroom and having students take that knowledge later to use in the field with 'ordinary' elder speakers.

As already stated, the classroom part of the programme needs plenty of study materials. To guarantee their quality, it is advisable to form a team to prepare the materials beforehand. Because the classroom leaning period was going to be long, Petter chose to write texts with hilarious protagonists. One of them in particular, Rávnár, helped the students to remember the stories and to learn the new words (see Figure 6.1).

The CASLE study materials team did not manage to produce actual study books, but the structure of the lessons was thoroughly planned for the first four and a half months. The team produced 36 chapters, each one beginning with a text, followed by a vocabulary list, a compact grammar section and a set of exercises. The exercises consisted of questions about the contents, idioms, reading and listening comprehension, grammar, vocabulary and writing. Each chapter ended with an additional 'B' text, which was more difficult than the main text. After the first four months, the students could also use other academic study materials which had been developed a couple of years earlier for AS studies, but even these were adapted by the instructors for CASLE purposes.

A language education programme like CASLE certainly needs at least a few instructors, which allows for team work and planning in pairs, the covering of absences and a variety of teaching styles for the students.

Vagabond

Hendâ is frying fish when he hears a knock at his door. He opens the door. There is a strange man outside.

Stranger: Good evening!
Hendâ: Who are you? Good evening …
Stranger: I am only a vagabond.
Hendâ: What do you want?
Stranger: Thanks for asking. Fish, that's what I would like to have!
    Hendâ serves fish to his guest. Oh gosh, the guest eats a lot.
Stranger: This is delicious!
(**Hendâ**, thinking: Who is eating it up?)
Stranger: My name is Äijihjäävri Rávnár [R. from Äijihjävri]. I go from one village to another.
Hendâ: Where do you live?
Stranger: I don't have a home. But I will move to your house!

Translated by Marja-Liisa Olthuis

Figure 6.1 KOLGOLÂŠ_VAGABOND

In our experience, this positively influences the quality of the education, and the risk of cancelling lessons due to absences can be markedly reduced.

CASLE would not have offered the level of quality it did without the thorough planning of the practical parts of the study programme. Therefore the project planning team in Aanaar was irreplaceable as a partner of the university.

(5) Risks

Each project should be prepared for risks because, should they occur, they will have a negative effect on achieving the project objectives (Turley, 2010: 99). The risk tolerance as well as *each* potential risk should already be evaluated at the beginning of the project. Firstly, the risk should be categorised: is it high, moderate or low? Secondly, ways to handle each risk should be evaluated. Can it be managed? Can it be totally avoided with a fall-back measure? If the risk cannot be avoided, there must be an analysis of whether the risk or its impact can be reduced. If the risk cannot be managed, avoided or reduced, it just has to be accepted (Turley, 2010: 101).

It should be noted that the risks of a revitalisation project should not be bundled according to certain themes but analysed separately, risk by risk, because their impacts are different on different parts of the project, meaning that they have to be solved in different ways. Revitalisation projects like CASLE are mostly low risk-tolerance projects because of the very limited financial and human resources, the fast pace of the language loss and the sensitivity of language revitalisation matters, so it is essential to map out the risks as far as possible before they happen.

All of the following risks have already been introduced above. These risks have to be seen as fundamental for CASLE, but they were not observed by all counterparts. Now it is time to analyse them from the viewpoint of risk management. This view is very mechanical.

Risk 1 No suppliers/potential students

Risk level: low (for finances); high (for the revitalisation process).

Reasons for the risk: AS language education is a new phenomenon. Neither the revitalisation process nor the loss of language were taken into account in academic language education before CASLE.

Impact of the risk: If there is a lack of suppliers/students, the programme is not (yet) worth the investment; for the community this means continuing language loss.

Timing of the risk: For the project this risk exists in the preliminary stage and possibly at the beginning of the initiation stage.

Managing the risk: The project should be put on hold. Attempts to address language revitalisation should be continued and the viewpoint should be reconsidered.

Remaining risks: There are no remaining financial risks for the project, but language loss in the community will progress if nothing is done.

Managing the remaining risk(s): There should also be an analysis of what else can be done to revitalise the language. If the same end product is still the aim of the community, then other methods should be found for recruitment and marketing.

The result: CASLE Project Management had to accept uncertainty for a while; there were no answers in the beginning regarding whether suppliers/students could be found, especially as the project had to be set up from scratch. In our experience, the best approach would be to find suppliers first and after that continue with student recruitment. If uncertainty remains, then the project will remain in the preliminary stage until this problem is solved.

Learning from experience: CASLE could not be started immediately. The viewpoint had to be changed many times, until the right viewpoint bore fruit. Language revitalisation is hard work, all in all.

Risk 2 Funding of the selected students

Risk level: High.

Reasons for the risk: Normally university students take care of their own funding when they apply for a place. CASLE worked differently: it recruited students who were already qualified and working in branches that were crucial for the language revitalisation process. Normal funding options were not applicable to this case.

Impact of the risk: If individual funding questions had not been resolved, the programme would most probably have missed out on the most capable students or produced fewer, less capable language transmitters.

Timing of the risk: This risk showed up in the preliminary period as well as at the initiation stage. It should be solved before the delivery stage.

Managing the risk: In the case of CASLE, the probability of the risk could be reduced by negotiating secure funding for at least 10 students. This number of students was the minimum to ensure that language training could be initiated.

Remaining risks: The university had selected 17 students, but the possibility remained that the Ministry of Employment and the Economy would have supported less than the maximum of seven study places. This would most probably have meant that fewer students could receive the language training.

Managing the remaining risk(s): CASLE compiled a priority list of students to be given grants by the Finnish Cultural Foundation. It also accepted the remaining risk that not all 17 students would be funded. Concerning the whole project, the remaining risk was low because the language training could be carried out with the minimum number of students.

The result: The funding issues were resolved as initially planned. Compiling the priority list was the quickest and safest way to exclude Risk 1 (no/not enough students) and to continue project planning.

Learning from experience: The Project Management has to be willing to spend a lot of time organising the language training, being uncertain about the total number of students in the programme and trying to arrange funding for as many students as possible. When there are 17 selected students, there are also 17 different kinds of funding needs. Securing funding for the minimum (10 students in this case) was essential so that at least some students could be promised positions and could start arranging their leaves of absence for a year. The rest had to wait for the decision of the Ministry of Employment and the Economy. These financial arrangements for the students were an exception, because normally suppliers will not arrange student funding for already-qualified people.

Risk 3 Students withdrawing from the language training

Risk level: High/moderate.

Reasons for the risk: Even using strict student selection procedures, the risk of losing individual students remained. The main supplier was paid for each individual study position, while the project was paid only for existing students.

Impact of the risk: Student withdrawal from the programme would have reduced the total budget by a significant sum, that is the project would have lost between €6000 and €12,000 per individual (from the Ministry of Employment and the Economy), depending on the timing of the withdrawal.

Timing of the risk: Both the delivery stage and throughout the year; the impact of the risk would have been highest in the first half of the training, reducing gradually throughout the year.

Managing the risk: The probability of the risk could be reduced by using a strict selection procedure that involved a psychologist.

Remaining risks: The main supplier did not wish to accept the costs of hiring a psychologist; the risk of withdrawal always remained.

Managing the remaining risk(s): CASLE's Project Manager negotiated with the main supplier to accept the expense of conducting student selections using a psychologist even though it was slightly higher than normal. The best argument was that the salary of the psychologist was a minor sum compared to the loss of major financing due to a withdrawal. The remaining risk of withdrawal had to be managed with a risk (contingency) budget. CASLE calculated the withdrawal of three students and kept the funders aware of the risk (contingency) budget as a final fall-back measure.

The result: All students completed the CASLE year.

Learning from experience: The strict selection procedure and the risk (contingency) budget as fall-back are advisable for reducing the financial risks.

Risk 4 Lack of funding for M-A training

Risk level: Moderate.

Reasons for the risk: This part could not be funded by the suppliers.

Impact of the risk: The aim of M-A training was to expose the students to 'ordinary' AS speakers and to give the students an opportunity to establish their own places within the community. The worst that could have happened would be that the M-A programme would not have been funded at all. Because the CASLE programme was designed to consist of 64 study points, with or without M-A training, the project had to plan for alternatives to M-A training.

Timing of the risk: Initial stage; after this stage, the risk had to be totally avoided.

Managing the risk: The CASLE project planning team had to solve the problem with two fall-back measures. Firstly, we applied for a separate grant from a private foundation for the M-A training. Secondly, as a final fall-back measure to avoid the risk, CASLE was prepared to organise another kind of field teaching in groups instead of M-A training. Classroom teaching was also one possibility that could have been funded by both suppliers, but it did not offer the necessary variety of activities for the students. Field teaching in groups focusing on practical cultural activities could have been paid for by the Saami Education Institute. Because the M-A training was very practical and had been planned to take place in the community, we chose to conduct three extra cultural courses organised by the Saami Education Institute. Of course, the organiser was informed about the fall-back measures.

Remaining risks: –

Managing the remaining risk(s): –

Learning from experience: This time the M-A training could be included in the university programme with special funding. M-A training brings students to the heart of the culture, in situations where the language still can be used in daily life, and we feel it is essential. From the perspective of language revitalisation, academic education programmes urgently need to develop ways to benefit from these nearly untouched language resources.

Risk 5 Limited possibilities for teamwork in planning and teaching due to university bureaucracy

Risk level: Moderate.

Reasons for the risk: The specific needs of a small minority language are not considered in the bureaucracy of the university.

Impact of the risk: The CASLE instructors who worked as freelancers would have been forced by the university to work individually in situations where teamwork was desperately needed. One issue was that two freelancers were not permitted to teach the same group concurrently. This problem arose during two courses: the Beginning course and the Writing course. Because students were expected to speak the language fluently very early on, they needed extra guidance in conversation, and because the programme stressed oral use of the language, there was automatically less time for writing. This is why the students needed personal guidance instead of simply analysing their texts in groups. One instructor would be unable to respond to these needs alone.

The second issue was that CASLE instructors needed to prepare their lessons in pairs. This was a safety measure, as stated earlier, to avoid missing lessons due to absences and to offer better educational quality. The absence of instructors would have been harmful to the quality of the programme, leaving students on their own. Planning in pairs would reduce the impact of the risk because, if one of the instructors was absent, the other could easily take over his/her tasks. Planning in pairs was not the normal procedure of the suppliers, but it had a positive impact on the quality of the education. In both cases, proceeding with one instructor would have had a negative impact on the quality of the lessons.

Timing of the risk: During the whole delivery stage.

Managing the risk: The risks could be managed and avoided by paying the salary of the second teacher from the budget of *Anarâškielâ servi*. The extra planning time of the head teacher was paid for by the main supplier, but from a separate budget. This reduced the impact of the risk.

Remaining risks: –

Managing the remaining risk(s): –

Learning from experience: When the project comes from the outside to the suppliers' desks, it does not have the same starting position as a project developed by the suppliers themselves. Planning and teaching should ideally be teamwork, performed under secure circumstances. The CASLE instructors formed an outstanding team, all taking responsibility for carrying out their tasks to the best of their ability. However, it would have been easier for the project if the instructors had been given longer contracts, at least for the whole study year 2009–2010. It would have been better if there had been more time for the Project Manager to explain all of the specific needs of the programme to the suppliers before the programme began. Unless they have better knowledge and understanding, university bureaucracies use standard regulations everywhere, and all exceptions face 'too much' resistance.

Risk 6 Lack of study materials

Risk level: High.

Reasons for the risk: The intensive language education programme needed a lot of study materials. There were not many materials produced before this point. According to the standard regulations of the university, there was no consideration of the need to produce materials beforehand.

Impact of the risk: The lack of study materials was seen as a factor that would reduce the quality of the CASLE programme; it would have negatively affected teaching and learning.

Timing of the risk: During the whole study year 2009–2010; the most critical period was expected to be the first four and a half months, because students' language skills were expected to improve rapidly to a fair level of proficiency.

Managing the risk: Study materials were partially produced in cooperation with the Saami Parliament study materials project; I also had to add materials work to my daily tasks, and together with Petter I prepared extra materials even after the CASLE year had started.

Remaining risks: The study materials never seemed to be completely ready during the CASLE year. The team had to endure extremely long work days, along with the feeling that still more should be done. These issues caused extra stress for the instructors.

Managing the remaining risk(s): The only way to manage the risk was to cooperate as much as possible with each other, to prioritise needs for certain materials, to respect students' and instructors' wishes as much as possible, and to continue trying to produce as many materials as possible.

Learning from experience: The study materials have to be prepared in good time, by a team. This task should not be left to the instructors on top of their daily teaching tasks. Even though our team worked fast and produced a lot, we were not able to do everything – and we were not even trying to produce study books for CASLE. The idea was to produce texts and exercises and to finish the book after the CASLE year was over. Our team has asked ourselves afterwards what the result would have been had we not produced this amount of materials for CASLE. We do not even dare to imagine. At least we could say that the language skills of the students would have been less developed. Petter and Petra finished the first part of the study book just before Christmas 2011 (Morottaja *et al.*, 2012), which was almost one and a half years after the CASLE year. One-third of the book is composed of CASLE materials, and the rest was supplemented after the programme. And after all these years of effort, there is still plenty of work to do on study materials. This part of the CASLE project should have been monitored and prepared a lot better, but the funding issues of this part remained unresolved: no extra human resources could be hired. Regarding this part of the project, the only option was for us to do our best and believe that it would be much better than nothing.

Finally, when all the details have been planned, then everything has to be evaluated.

(6) Control the progress

The last theme of Turley (2010: 24, 137) is the monitoring and evaluation of the progress. This means checking the development of the project in relation to the plan, checking the project viability and controlling for any deviations. Checks *must be done* periodically to ensure that the implementation process is working correctly. It is necessary to evaluate the project throughout its life cycle, whether or not the project will be continued.

Once students have been selected, the education programme cannot be stopped, because there are too many people involved in it. The preliminary period has to be executed in a way that even the smallest details are thoroughly considered. The CASLE programme had to be developed and executed by separate teams, and the pieces had to fit together from the beginning. The Project Manager needs to follow the project strictly. In a project like CASLE, there is actually not much space for individual work. The people selected for the teams need to be good team players. It might be advisable for team members to spend a few days together to get acquainted before starting the whole project. The team members should easily find their places in the project and be able to cooperate with each other and with the suppliers/employers/students. This part of CASLE could have been conducted more effectively. We are aware of the fact that real professionals prefer their work to 'playing games' but, for the sake of team spirit, even a couple of days together might have saved the teams from a few difficult discussions. I as Project Manager initially felt that real professionals did not wish to be 'controlled' so often. I feel that I should have explained to team members even more clearly that regular reports or meetings or chats over a cup of coffee belong in normal project control processes – they do not imply any kind of mistrust of the staff. Such reports and chats give valuable information to all the team members so that the separate pieces can be fitted together or so that fall-back plans can be created. In a project like CASLE, no-one should be irreplaceable. Luckily nothing serious happened to the team members or students, and the project could be carried out successfully through to the end.

Now that the risk analysis has been done, we can have a look at CASLE's results in the final chapter.

Notes

(1) Turley calls this theme a 'business case' (2010: 21). The content is the same.
(2) Developing a 'wrong product' is a technical concept. In CASLE's case it would have meant, for example, educating people who were incompetent in transferring the language.

7 What Has CASLE Achieved?
What Does the Future Hold?

7.1 Introduction

The AS community has grown since the CASLE year of 2009–2010, just as we had planned and hoped. Due to CASLE, the growth process has been extremely rapid, and a great deal of work has been done in the local community to fit the new services into AS society: two new language nests were opened in 2010 and 2011; the teaching of AS has tripled lately in primary and secondary schools; slightly more study materials are now produced, as compared to the last five years before CASLE; AS has received status as a major subject at the University of Oulu; AS community activities have been extended; AS can be heard in church again, after a break of more than 20 years; and, last but not least, CASLE graduates have helped the elder AS speakers to revitalise their mother tongue. In this final chapter, the influence that CASLE has had on various sectors of Saami society is described in detail mainly by Marja-Liisa Olthuis and Suvi Kivelä in terms of concrete results. This chapter also gives our views on the new situation, with (mainly) Tove Skutnabb-Kangas then placing it in an international context.

7.2 Language Nests

Marja-Liisa: The extension of the language nest activities has succeeded. Two separate steps were needed: (1) educating the AS-speaking professionals in CASLE; and (2) seeking funding for the new language nests from the Ministry of Education and Culture. As a direct result of CASLE, two new language nests have been opened, one in Aanaar and the other in Avveel. As stated in Section 4.5.2, the pedagogical views of the language nests were revised in Aanaar: children up to two and a half years old were placed in the old language nest, *Piervâl*, and the older children from two and a half years up to school age in *Piäju*. It is still too early to comment on the learning results, but according to teachers the first experiences have been positive: *Piervâl* uses basic terms with the small children so that *Piäju* can concentrate on more difficult language structures as well as teaching more vocabulary.

There are three CASLE graduates working in the new language nests, two as teachers in language nests (Riitta Vesala and Tanja Kyrö) and one as an administrative secretary (Varpu Falck). All language nest staff use only AS at work. The secretary uses mainly Finnish for administrative tasks and AS with her AS-speaking colleagues. Some AS language nest staff are native speakers and others are second-language (L2) speakers.

There are enough staff in the language nests at the moment, but the situation is still vulnerable because in practice no-one can be spared. The number of staff needs to be increased in the near future; some will retire soon, and there is competition for some employees. The recruitment process has begun in the municipality of Aanaar for qualified professionals to attend the forthcoming AS language courses at the Saami Education Institute. The ideal number of AS language nests would be more than 10 if we want all the children in Aanaar to be served and if we wish to extend language revitalisation to towns in other parts of Finland with parents who want their children to learn AS. Most of these would probably have Saami ancestry. Extending AS language nest activities would thus mean doing more revitalisation work outside the Aanaar municipality and even outside the Saami area. This will be the next great challenge for AS revitalisation work.

Among the North Saami, people have become more aware of the current situation of their own language and have started to worry that even their language is not necessarily being transmitted to children at home or by the reindeer corral. As a result, the North Saami have followed the example of AS and there is a need for language nests – just as we followed the example of the Māori (see Info Box 8 Immersion Programmes) and the Hawaiians (see Info Box 12 Advice From Revitalisation in Hawai'i).

The language nest method appears to be the strongest possible revitalisation method for children. We think its name should be 'protected' worldwide; other activities that have been organised for children in minority languages, such as club activities, camps and other events, are necessary but they should not use the 'language nest' label. If this happens too often the concept will be diluted, which could harm the effectiveness of the language nest method, and might endanger the language revitalisation process in its efforts to produce new young language speakers.

Suvi Kivelä, as a mother: I can really observe the effects of CASLE on the language nests every morning when I take my son to *Piäju* and each afternoon when I collect him. Before CASLE it was of course not possible for me to chat in AS with fellow parents or language nest staff. Today the situation has changed completely, and the main language of communication between parents and language nest staff is AS. There were three mothers with young children in CASLE, and we now have a total of four children in language nests. Furthermore, when one of the CASLE graduates, Anna Morottaja, started to teach AS at the Saami Education Institute in 2011, four new mothers of language nest children (who have six children altogether) participated in the AS study programme. A couple of language nest parents already knew AS, which facilitates communication in AS at the language nests. Suddenly, families that do not use AS are in the minority. It is also noteworthy that all of the parents who have learnt AS are women/mothers, and apart from two, they all come from outside the community. As far as I have noticed, the children have started to use AS more actively between them. In 2010, when my elder son was in the language nest after school in the afternoons, it was typical for children to speak AS to the staff but Finnish to each other when playing together. Today, Finnish is still there, but I would claim that children use AS more frequently between themselves. The number of AS-speaking adults involved in the lives of language nest children has also increased significantly. Before CASLE, many language nest children had only the language nest staff and a couple of regular visitors with whom they could speak AS. Through the practical training periods (see Section 5.5) children got to know a whole new group of adults with whom they grew accustomed to speaking AS. Nowadays, when I meet any of these language nest children on any occasion, they automatically greet me and start to speak to me in AS.

7.3 Schools

7.3.1 How did CASLE influence the schools?

Marja-Liisa: Table 7.1 shows the number of pupils learning AS in schools just before the end of CASLE (2009–2010) and for the first two years after CASLE. As the table shows, teaching through the medium of AS has remained stable in primary and secondary schools, but the teaching of AS as a L2 subject tripled immediately after CASLE. This was expected, because the CASLE students could act as new teachers, and the L2 teaching of AS could not be expanded before the number of new AS-speaking teachers was increased through CASLE. The number of former language nest children who were already learning through the medium of AS has remained unchanged.

Table 7.1 Participation in the teaching of AS

Teaching of AS	Pupils in 2009–2010	Pupils in 2010–2011	Pupils in 2011–2012
Through the medium of AS	12	13	14
AS as a L2 subject	12	32	33

Source: The Saami revitalisation report (Ministry of Education and Culture, 2012) and statistics from the municipality of Aanaar (2009–2012)

In Aanaar, three of the four primary teachers teaching through the medium of AS in 2010–2012 were CASLE graduates: Maijukka Pyykkö, Yrjö Musta and Éva Kelemen; the fourth teacher was Miina Seurujärvi, who had worked as a Master for some CASLE students. (Miina learned AS as an adult and speaks it to her three children.) Avveel's only teacher, also a CASLE graduate, Teija Linnanmäki, teaches AS as a L2 to full classrooms of students. She also teaches AS in upper secondary school. For the first time in AS history, AS as a L2 teaching could be started in primary schools in the city of Rovaniemi in 2011, and here too the teacher is one of the CASLE graduates, Mervi Skopets. She cooperates with her colleagues in Aanaar, in particular by exchanging study materials.

The teacher supply situation has improved slightly since CASLE, but the AS teaching situation is still not stable because only two of the teachers (the CASLE graduates) are fully qualified. However, all of those (six persons) who (intend to) teach (through the medium of AS) at the primary level are presently (in 2012) studying for their teaching qualifications and will finish their studies in the near future. Because the community is still growing, a few more primary teachers are needed to teach (in) AS. Therefore, the recruiting process to find suitable qualified teachers for AS education programmes needs to be continued.

Suvi, as a mother: When I heard that a fellow CASLE student was going to be my son's teacher I wondered how she would manage language-wise. After all, I could have been in exactly the same position. After a little hesitation I thought I would have to give her a chance and trust that everything would be fine. I knew what CASLE was designed for, and this was what I wanted for my children. There would not have been any point in participating if the language immersion programme had stopped right after the language nest.

The next natural step from there was the primary school. I decided I would pay extra attention to my son's school attendance and help him in every way I could. Luckily, everything went much better than I had expected. During that year he learned to read and write properly in both AS and Finnish. I felt like all the struggles had been worth it when the teacher said to me: 'One can tell that your son also hears and speaks the language outside school.' I was more than happy to be able to help my son with his homework, to comfort and explain things to him when he did not understand something and felt stupid. Some books that were translated from Finnish into AS were extremely difficult to understand, and we really needed a dictionary for those. In the autumn of 2012 there were more changes: his teacher moved away from Aanaar, and there was a period when we didn't know who his new teacher was going to be. Although it is not ideal to have a new teacher every year [and this is uncommon in our culture], I will be happy as long as he can study in AS. I am quite confident that whoever the teacher is, the main thing is not just how well the teacher knows the language. Learning is a process and children learn from so many sources; it is no longer only the teacher or the textbooks that provide the information. Luckily the immediate future looks even better: there will be more qualified AS-speaking teachers in a few more years (p. 138).

7.3.2 Funding the study materials

Suvi: The poor situation regarding study materials improved during and after CASLE. The very first positive step was the extra funding given for AS study material as a result of the schoolbook delegation *Karvakenkälähetystö*, which consisted of about 40 AS school and language nest children, parents and teachers. This delegation lodged a complaint concerning the lack of AS schoolbooks to Finland's then-Minority Ombudsman, Johanna Suurpää, on 20 November 2009 in Helsinki. According to the complainants, the lack of schoolbooks in AS constituted ethnic discrimination, and put AS children in an unequal position compared to other children in Finland. The complaint was addressed to the Finnish government.

The delegation met the president of Finland, Ms Tarja Halonen, at an event that had been organised to celebrate the 20th anniversary of International Children's Day. The President promised to do everything she could to promote the cause. The delegation drew a lot of media attention and publicity. President Halonen called for a new language policy that would consider all of the languages spoken in Finland. She said: 'There are people in Finland who feel that their language rights are not being realised' (*YLE News*, 21 November 2011).

After about a year, the delegation was informed of the reply given by the Ministry of Justice to the Ombudsman. The delegation then formulated a further appeal to the Ministry of Justice, which was sent to the present (as of May 2012) Ombudsman, Eva Biaudet. After researching the case, Biaudet recommended that the Ministry of Justice take immediate action to increase the school book funding. She also urged the Ministry to deal with this need when preparing the next governmental programme and budget (YLE, 5 November 2010). Besides the accomplishments of all the public statements made by MPs, the Ombudsman and the President, perhaps the most significant result was to get the revitalisation programme documented in the governmental programme released in June 2011. This was also one of the main targets of the Saami Parliament. Furthermore, the language strategy that President Halonen had called for was likewise written into the governmental programme.

The delegation also achieved financial results. On 1 July 2010 the government released its third supplementary and amended budget (http://www.finlex.fi/data/sdliite/liite/5826.pdf), in which the subsidy for producing schoolbooks was raised by €20,000. Hannu Kangasniemi, the Secretary for study materials at the Saami Parliament, saw this as a direct result of the *Karvakenkä* delegation. For the year 2011, the annual amount was raised from

€258,000 to €290,000 in the governmental budget (see the Saami revitalisation report of the Ministry of Education and Culture: OKM, 2012a: 32).

7.3.3 New study materials produced by CASLE professionals

Marja-Liisa: The professional skills expended by CASLE have clearly increased the production of AS study materials. The study materials package used by the CASLE students during their learning period has now been published as a study book: *Kielâkyeimi 1* [*Language Fellow 1*] (Morottaja *et al.*, 2012).

While *Kielâkyeimi 1* was produced by CASLE teachers, CASLE students also participated in AS study materials production. Firstly, Pia Nikula and Anne-Marie Kalla translated Heather Amery's book *The First Thousand Words in English* into AS during their study period. This book, *Vuosmuš tuhháát säännid anarâškiellân* [*The First Thousand Words in AS*], was published by the Saami Parliament (Nikula & Kalla, 2011), and is in active use in the language nests as well as in people's homes. Secondly, Tanja Kyrö translated the mathematics study book *Lohosierâ 1* [*Counting Game 1*] into AS (Kyrö, 2012). Thirdly, as teaching in AS is being extended in primary schools, there is always the need for specific vocabulary. Teacher Maijukka Pyykkö has created a special set of vocabulary for history.

The CASLE graduates are aware of the increasing need for study materials in AS and are willing to expedite the production of new materials. Currently they, as well as Anna Morottaja's second/third generation AS graduates and students, are participating in several study materials projects.

7.4 Aanaar Saami Revitalisation and Teaching at the University

Marja-Liisa: Between 2011 and 2012, a lot has happened in the community and in my personal working life, mainly due to the positive impact of the growing language community and the active CASLE graduates, but also due to massive reorganisation of higher education by the Finnish state. The centre of research on the Saami languages has been moved to the University of Oulu (http://www.oulu.fi/giellagas) from Kotus, the Research Centre for Languages of Finland (http://www.kotus.fi/). At the same time, AS has received a new status at the University of Oulu as a major subject. Now it is possible to graduate with a Master of Arts in AS. The first six students began their studies in Oulu in 2011; five of them are CASLE graduates.

The traditional fieldwork done by *Kotus* did not fit very well into the work description of the University, but it was partly included in my new job anyway. I see a major conflict between the main task of the University, i.e. educating students, and coordinating revitalisation work in the field. The traditional academic way of thinking prioritises education, and the expectation is that language revitalisation will be offered as part of the study programme in a way that allows students to earn as many study points as possible. The needs of the field differ considerably from the idea of just earning study points (which some 'ordinary students' might be mainly motivated by): the language nest activities should be managed and increased, and a new complementary form of education should be set up. New professionals are needed to fill positions at primary schools, language nests, the media and churches. There is a need to create more natural and authentic language domains for AS. In other words, there should be an organisation stronger than the university to coordinate revitalisation work in the field. This was the actual work distribution of Kotus and the university until the end of 2011, but the benefits were unfortunately lost as a result of integrating the work of Kotus into that of the university. In practice, the current state of affairs means that revitalisation work in the field has to be kept up more and more by voluntary workers. If this fails for some reason – which is very possible because of lack of both human resources and positions, the revitalisation work could easily slow down or even be prevented. Also, wrong decisions can be made. This is partially due to the fact that no-one has the ultimate responsibility for language revitalisation work in the field. The AS Association keeps up the language nest activities. It could do even more for language revitalisation, but more salaried positions would be needed. At present the association does a great deal of language revitalisation as voluntary work, for instance in the management of the language nest activities. The problem is that, as workloads and responsibilities increase, they may become unendurable for voluntary human resources. This is a very common problem for most Indigenous peoples in the world – there is a grave risk of burn-out.

The most remarkable change in my personal situation has been the removal of a great deal of language nest responsibilities to *Anarâškielâ servi*'s new language nest issues secretary. Besides her daily administrative tasks, she also takes care of the practical arrangements on funding issues, as well as assisting in personnel management. However, the final responsibility for the three working language nests still remains with me, meaning that in practice my work as general manager of the language nests has to be done during my spare time. This is very time-intensive work; the total budget of the language nests is over €400,000. The start-up period as well as the first few months of the language nests were especially hectic; a new management system had to be set up and responsibilities delegated. We have, however, started negotiations to transmit the general management of the language nests from the AS Association to the municipality of Aanaar.

AS has reached its new position rapidly, with the result that there is still a lack of university personnel. There are still no permanent university teachers besides me, and AS shares the professorship with North Saami. This means in practice that the teaching of AS has to be organised on a small scale and in cooperation with the Saami Education Institute in Aanaar. There is not much time or space for potential new revitalisation projects at the university.

It has been challenging to determine the order of priorities for promoting AS at the university, especially because the needs of a small Indigenous language differ from traditional academic education. AS revitalisation still needs the combination of complementary language education and traditional academic education. The situation of total language loss in the generation of young students is a new phenomenon for the university; in the AS case, practically speaking, no young students can be expected to learn AS in the next five to seven years in a 'normal' way. This situation calls for a different approach to recruitment, and it has to be done in collaboration with local employers in the Saami area. Because of the language loss, it is to be expected that students will be of working age, as they will not come straight from secondary school. However, from the point of view of the university, it is time-consuming to recruit from the field – especially as the contents of language education should be focused and prioritised, rather than taking so much time to find students. It seems that, from an academic point of view, educating professionals who need complementary language education has to be seen as an exception, not as a normal routine. This approach to education requires extra human resources, which can be viewed as an overly high expense at first. However, in the case of CASLE, this complementary form of education was in fact extremely profitable for the university, because the state support received for each student position generated pure income. As CASLE-style complementary education is used as a way of educating new professionals, it may be necessary to inform the management of the university and other organisers as well about the management and administration of the project. Our experience is that it certainly differs a lot from traditional ways of university doing and thinking.

One major inconvenience is the fact that neither the academic study programme nor the university as an employer offer any project management resources for carrying out (revitalisation) projects. It was even more complex to carry out CASLE than to conduct 'normal' linguistic projects because CASLE had to be simultaneously executed by several teams and suppliers in several locations. Unfortunately, there are still no standard solutions for defining 'correct' working methods for these kinds of projects, except for Turley's (2010) wise advice: learn from experience. In the case of CASLE, discussions with two experienced Project Managers working in the chemical industry helped me. The idea of using Turley's *PRINCE2* principle for CASLE came from these projects. I see the *PRINCE2* principle as extremely useful for revitalisation projects, because its themes and principles create a strong frame for the whole project. The basics of how to guarantee project quality would be extremely valuable for academic researchers as well.

Judging from my experiences, the university is too traditional and constrained to accommodate the needs of a modern revitalisation programme. In summary, I suggest that a separate research unit should be established for revitalisation issues.

7.5 Aanaar Saami at the Saami Education Institute

Marja-Liisa: One year after CASLE, in the autumn of 2011, the Saami Education Institute started a full-time year-long AS language and culture course, following the AS curriculum of the University of Oulu. This was the original initiative for CASLE, which responded to the late Principal Lassi Valkeapää's worries about the lack of AS teachers.

After CASLE, the Saami Education Institute hired an AS-speaking teacher, CASLE graduate Anna Morottaja. Anna's starting point was easier, compared to CASLE, because she already had all the study materials from CASLE, and the first two parts of the CASLE materials were already available as a study book (Morottaja *et al.*, 2012). Of course, she also needed to produce new materials.

Anna's first student group (2011–2012) consisted of 13 women and the second group (2012–2013) of 10 students (female and male). These are then the second and the third AS-speaking L2-generations. Many of these graduates/students are parents of language nest children. The second group also consists of some 'outsiders'. Like our CASLE graduates, these graduates/students are extremely motivated. The main difference between the CASLE group and Anna's graduates/students is that Anna's graduates/students are younger. Many of Anna's students also have AS grandparents who act as Language Masters for the new group, which includes highly qualified returnees to the area. The language community expects a lot from them. The Saami Education Institute intends to continue with AS education in the future.

7.6 Aanaar Saami Community Activities

Marja-Liisa: Reviving a language in a small community creates a snowball effect. A colleague told me recently: 'One hears and uses AS more and more. I always meet AS-speaking acquaintances at the supermarket, at the swimming pool, everywhere in the village.' It is easy to agree with him: the CASLE graduates have organised activities for elder AS speakers as well as AS evenings and leisure activities for young people and children. Even people who did not use AS before use it now everywhere and whenever possible. Some people have said that today it feels like AS is heard and spoken in Aanaar even more than North Saami is. Because the language community, including children, elders and 'novices', was brought together, AS speakers were no longer ashamed of speaking AS with one another, no matter where they met.

To give an idea of how the community has expanded and the active roles that CASLE graduates have played in this process, we give a few examples here.

Firstly, Teija Linnanmäki, who is active in teaching AS as well as producing study materials, has organised conversation activities for elder AS speakers. Her *ákkukerho*, literally 'old ladies'/grandmother club', has become a success in two villages, Avveel and Njellim. As the name shows, the participants are mainly AS-speaking elderly women. However, even a few men have been participating recently. I talked to one of the village elders in Njellim just before Christmas 2011. The woman wiped tears from her eyes as she thought of Teija: 'Teija has found us here. We were totally forgotten and lost. She taught us who we are. She has given our lost language and our identity back to us. We are so happy now.' An 80-year-old AS man, also a member of the retirees' club, told his story in the local newspaper *Inarilainen* (2012). He explained how difficult it was to speak AS during the first conversations conducted in the club. After that, he finally rediscovered the language of his childhood and now speaks it fluently. This activity started by Teija has also been essential from the viewpoint of elderly people's social contacts.

Secondly, Suvi has organised 'AS evenings' in 2011–2012. The programme of these evenings brings AS speakers together, creating a natural domain for speaking AS. The programmes have a broad focus: playing games, singing, watching AS films and photos, fishing, fixing fishing nets, cooking, picking berries, organising bird watching and mushroom identification trips, drying pike, etc. The idea of these evenings has unified the AS-speaking generations. This is absolutely necessary because many elderly Masters do not know the young AS speakers at all, and elder speakers still have a lot to offer to younger speakers. The evenings have become a great success; they have had a total of 83 participants in 2011–2012, representing approximately 24% of all AS speakers. It has been marvellous to see new faces participating in the evenings each time. These people call themselves passive AS speakers, and they wish to reactivate their mother tongue gently. The regular participants have often been amazed because they did not even know these people as AS speakers previously.

Thirdly, there are many ideas about the future of AS revitalisation, but perhaps the most urgent activities target young people. The latest activities are AS evenings for young people. It has been a great challenge to get the first language nest children back into the language community. As we write this book, there is still too little experience and no permanent funding for youth activities, even though there would be professionals available to guide the young AS speakers. Even before CASLE there were a few workshops for young AS speakers on various themes, for example animation, theatre, filming and camps. The AS rap artist AMOC, alias Mikkâl Antti Morottaja, has shown a way through his music to revitalise the language among young people and tell the story of AS as a small Indigenous language. Planning the continuation of young speakers' language activities is one of the most urgent issues to be addressed in the near future.

7.7 Aanaar Saami in Church

Marja-Liisa: Before CASLE, there was a period of almost 25 years when no-one spoke AS in the entire Finnish Evangelical Lutheran church system. When the local AS-speaking priest retired at the end of the 1980s, there was no plan to replace him with another AS speaker. Thus AS came to an end, not only in the Aanaar congregation but also in the whole church system. Then Pastor Tuomo Huusko studied AS in the CASLE programme. He now uses AS at work, mainly in ecclesiastical ceremonies and with his personal contacts. Taking into account that his large working area includes the entire Saami region in Finland and the need for three languages – AS, North Saami and Finnish[1] – it is clear that the church should strengthen the Saami knowledge of its employees much more. Furthermore, there is much ecclesiastical work to be done. No spiritual literature apart from the Catechism exists in AS. The Bible and prayer books should be translated, and the AS hymnal should be enlarged. The translation of all four Gospels is about to begin in 2013, as well as the epistles of the whole church year. The main translator of these will be Mervi Skopets, a CASLE graduate who is an Orthodox theologian. The church also lacks Aanaar-/North Saami-speaking youth leaders and social workers. Two colleagues of Pastor Huusko speak North Saami in the Finnish Saami area, but both will be retiring soon. If nothing is done, the use of North Saami is expected to diminish. The Christianity Chapter of Oulu (located in the city of Oulu), to which Aanaar belongs, is aware of this and has discussed the matter thoroughly, for example during the April 2012 seminar *The Saami People in the Church*. This is the situation as of August 2012. All these challenges may have been solved – or not – by the time this book is published.

Both of the Saami languages used in the Finnish Evangelical Lutheran church should be promoted in the same way as the South Saami language in Norway and Sweden. South Saami number approximately 500 speakers, with four church employees dedicated to South Saami issues. As the South Saami Pastor Bierna Bientie stated (in a private email in March 2012), the financial situation of the Norwegian church is stable, which makes the strengthening of the local language easier. Also, the attitudes vis-à-vis Saami issues in the Norwegian church are positive. However, Pastor Bientie states as a negative fact that he is the only South Saami person in the church who is able to write the language.

In the Finnish church, some traditional viewpoints need to be urgently revised, such as the matter of having the number of employees calculated according to a certain number of parishioners. This stance keeps the issues of the Indigenous language immutable, since the Saami are always in a small minority. In addition, there is resistance or aloofness on the part of individual employees regarding the importance of mother tongue issues, and these attitudes can be harmful for Indigenous languages.

We have been asked why CASLE did not recruit harder in the church when the lack of AS-speaking employees was so visible. This was because AS lacked a whole generation of language transmitters. The daycare professionals and teachers were needed first, and there were only a certain number of student places available. However, from now on, church professionals will be actively recruited. As the local Aanaar congregation is not a large one, the recruitment will have to be enlarged to the whole Oulu chapter, and perhaps to the whole country. The church's committee for Saami issues is working on the same matter and preparing language-related plans for the forthcoming five to 10 years.

It is also worth noting that the Swedish church has recently actively criticised minority policies in all of Sweden (see Info Box 1 Criticism of Sweden's Current Minority Policies and Practices). Maybe some Nordic churches are learning from Latin American liberation theologians. . . .

7.8 CASLE Graduates at Work in the AS Community

Marja-Liisa: As Llurda pointed out (p. 42) it is an interesting issue as to how the AS L2 experts feel in their new language surroundings and their new roles as language transmitters. A year and a half after CASLE, I have some observations about them. During the CASLE year, as a Project Manager, I saw the CASLE students as 'ordinary' students. Since CASLE, my perspective has changed, and now I see fully capable and talented individuals working in the AS community. Some of them have become my colleagues and close personal friends. (I could not have imagined this happening during the CASLE year.) There are some other CASLE graduates who I know well but from a certain distance, mainly because we do not have such close professional connections. A few graduates are still quite reserved, and I know them only through infrequent contact. I have not interviewed them, so the observations I make below are very subjective. In my view, all CASLE graduates are aware of their specific roles as language transmitters, but the ways they function in AS vary a lot.

Some CASLE students are parents of language nest children and speak AS at home to their children. Convincing people to commit themselves to the language community has been my dream as the Project Manager, at the same time as it has given me great satisfaction to have (indirectly) helped create a young generation of AS speakers. This young generation even has the motivation to learn the language better. It is also a pleasure for me to see Anna Morottaja's graduates/students taking an active part in AS life.

CASLE graduates working daily with AS do so with clearly conflicting thoughts: they are happy with the idea of serving the language community, but unhappy with their 'insufficient' language skills. They seem to be perfectionists. We have very often heard about their feelings of frustration because they have not reached 'the level of a native speaker'. According to them, they are still missing lots of expressions in AS, but fortunately not so much of the vocabulary. One CASLE graduate once described this feeling, using what was in my opinion fluent AS: 'Just imagine the situation where your hands are cut off but you still have to function fully with the stumps. It's impossible!' This graduate even has a beautiful AS accent in her speech and she hardly ever makes a mistake in the language. Some graduates who we know well and who use the language regularly have this attitude: 'I will do my best and see how it works.'

Although all CASLE graduates are very talented, a few of them have developed nearly full daily fluency. When they sometimes make errors, native speakers will correct them immediately. I have tried to remind them of their excellent language skills, and I myself have suggested these minor corrections in the form of small compliments. On one occasion I spoke to one of the CASLE graduates who had been using North Saami for a few hours before the appointment. Initially, s/he retained a slight North Saami accent. However, as the AS conversation proceeded, this accent disappeared and was replaced by a flowing AS accent. Of course, in daily conversation it sometimes happens that AS words are every now and then replaced by Finnish words. However, this is also very common in the speech of AS native speakers.

Some CASLE graduates who do not use AS daily say that their AS is getting rusty because they have difficulty in finding the right words and expressions. However, these graduates sound fluent in daily conversation. Their language capacity means a lot to the AS community, so these graduates need to be encouraged to keep up their current level of AS by taking part in AS activities. It could also be an option to talk more to their employees in AS in order to put their language skills to more active use at work.

The consequences of stressing communicative language skills during CASLE have had some slightly negative effects, as expected. Some graduates of CASLE now have the impression that their writing skills are not at the same level as their oral skills. They feel that they should be able to write in AS quickly and impeccably. These skills have to be practiced now that CASLE is over. There are some practical methods for this. For example, the hand-written Bible translations have to be typed out, which would be good practice for achieving rapidity and routine. Some pieces of texts and study books could be re-translated and compared to existing translations. And, of course, there could be completely new texts produced.

Some of the CASLE graduates want to use AS as much as possible, in their private lives as well as at work. They are eager to learn more. Some of them have even thought of leaving their current jobs and finding new ones that would give them more contact with the target language.

There are also CASLE graduates who strongly question their roles in the AS community, mainly due to having few human contacts and friends in the area. Not to criticise the selection of these students, but some lessons can be learned from these cases for the future; that is, the selection committee should pay even more attention to whether or not applicants have close links to the local area where the language is spoken. Apparently, having too few or too loose human links to the area can be a problem later, if homesickness wins over job possibilities and revitalisation aims. We could say that there should be at least another kind of revitalisation aim in mind for those capable candidates living outside the main speaking area of the language. There is one motto for revitalisation efforts here: strong links to the language community carry the new L2 speakers to success.

Suvi: The reason why I was recruited to CASLE, namely to function in AS as a journalist, never materialised. At least it has not happened so far. I ended up resigning from YLE, Finland's national public service broadcasting company, because there was no work for me at Saami Radio. I wanted to continue working as a journalist but no longer in Finnish, as I had done before. Before CASLE, the CASLE team and I had some quite realistic ideas about how I could contribute to the radio, which at that time and even today has only one part-time employee. The resources for AS broadcasting, however, have not increased at all, even though there are now whole new audiences and needs for new programmes both in radio and on TV. What a shame for the radio and the AS media in general! But fortunately I found a completely new job and career where I can promote the AS language and culture. As the person responsible for the Saami Archives, which were established in 2012 as part of the National Archives services in Finland, I can contribute to the study of Saami culture and languages in Finland, and collect, gather and offer historical information to researchers. I use a lot of AS at work, and often when communicating with North Saami customers and colleagues at the new Saami Cultural Centre *Sajos*, which has many Saami organisations, including the Saami Parliament, under the same roof. I have been asked to start writing AS news and articles for the regional newspaper *Lapin Kansa,* but so far I have not found the time to do that. Besides organising AS evenings (see Section 7.6 Aanaar Saami Community Activities) and film workshops for school children, and speaking AS at home with my kids, I realise there are many possible ways in which I could advance the revitalisation process. Awareness of these possibilities and things that should and could be done makes me tired sometimes, and quite regularly I have to ask myself: what is the point of all this? Is there going to be any future? Thus far I have always been able to answer my own questions and have found the reasons and the will and desire to go on, speak out and act. Referring to Marja-Liisa's remarks above, I also feel that my language skills are still not nearly as good as native speakers. But I get by. Every day I learn new words and make fewer mistakes. And I understand the hard, self-critical feelings that those primary language transmitters, like teachers, are going through. To be honest, I am happy not to be in their shoes. I admire them more than words can say.

When it comes to my fellow CASLE graduates, I think we all have done a pretty good job. We are all different and our strengths lie in different areas. It is only now, a couple years after finishing the CASLE year, that we are starting to find our ways in the language community. Most of us are in the middle of our peak years, and really busy with our careers and families. It takes time to make radical changes like changing one's career; if serving the AS community in one's present job is not possible, there are several other jobs that would serve the community. Finding them and changing to them, however, demands courage and a great deal of idealism. But it is possible, and many of us are living examples of that.

What I am most scared of is that people get passive. Even knowing that everybody is busy dealing with their own business, I have often been sad about the fact that, for example, AS evenings did not attract former CASLE students. Only a few of us have taken part occasionally. I had partly planned the AS evenings to be a forum where we could meet and chat, exchange experiences and share solidarity after the intensive CASLE year. Understanding how difficult it was for people to arrange the time to maintain contact and prioritise leisure-time activities, I ended up creating a Facebook group where we could all meet, chat, inform each other about events, link news and stories concerning AS issues, share experiences, share photos, etc. That group, called *Anarâškielâ orroomviste* [AS living room], now has more than a hundred members, and I think it has really brought AS into today's world, making it a normal language for everyday communication. It is fun to see how teachers are typing, while teaching in the classroom, to ask the meaning of some words or looking for the right words, phrases or synonyms, and almost instantly somebody answers them. I think Facebook as a new social media domain has affected the AS community in a way that has lowered the threshold one must cross to be able to write the language. There are, of course, a lot of passive members who hardly ever join in the conversation themselves, but I think that even they are following, reading, seeing, observing. Facebook makes AS more visible than ever. I was happy to notice that even the largest Saami society in Helsinki, *City-Sámit*, had copied our name. They organise monthly gatherings in Helsinki under the same name (*Orrunlatnja* in North Saami), and they have a Facebook group with the same name too.

Marja-Liisa: Since the summer of 2012, a new challenge awaits CASLE graduates and the whole AS community: the need to enlarge the AS-speaking area in Salla, about 370 km southeast of Aanaar. This area suffered a total language loss in the 19th century when the local Saami language, Kemi Saami, became extinct (Salminen, 2009; Sarivaara, 2012: 32–41). However, the local Saami culture is still alive (Sarivaara, 2012), and the Saami in Salla wish to put AS into use in the area because it is seen as the closest related language to Kemi Saami. This means that AS should be exported from the municipality of Aanaar to the municipality of Salla. The language import to Salla has been a wish of Metsä-, kalastaja- ja tunturisaamelaisten yhdistys [The Forest, Fisher and Fell Saami Association], founded in 2012. This proposed revitalisation programme is mainly the initiative of my colleague, Dr Erika Sarivaara. As far as we know, this kind of language export has never happened before with any minority language. CASLE graduates are intended to act as potential language transmitters, together with AS native speakers. The language learning method for the language import is planned to be the CASLE programme, implemented again but in a new context.

7.9 The Elder AS Language Masters After CASLE

Marja-Liisa: The elder native speakers became vital language transmitters for the CASLE students. However, CASLE also affected the language use of this generation, because the elders who had not been language transmitters before now got a chance to activate their speaking skills. They made new contacts and also started to use AS with each other.

In the past year (2012), I have visited a great number of CASLE's former Language Masters with Pastor Tuomo Huusko. During our visits, we have witnessed some of the sadness, as described by Suvi in Section 5.4.2.3 Short profile of CASLE's Masters, where many of them claim that their language skills are only fair, or even poor, because they have not used the language actively for a long time. Some of them have said that they did not have the courage, or the opportunity, to use their mother tongue for many years before they participated in CASLE.

Even the strongest speakers feel that they have forgotten and lost a lot of what their parents and grandparents certainly knew. On the other hand, they are happy about the recent developments in AS and the new 'renaissance' of the language. At the same time they feel unhappy with the most recent vocabulary, and with being unable to follow the 'newest' AS. The Masters are mainly unable to write their language, and as they read modern AS, they are unable to understand some things. For example, they have difficulty with study books because of the use of modern terminology, and because most of them had little formal education – and what they did have was all in Finnish. For example, while pupils discuss space shuttles fluently in AS with their teachers and fellow pupils, elder speakers probably cannot share in these conversations at all.

Whenever we visit the elders, however, there has always been a warm welcome, with a hot meal and fresh coffee. We have heard plenty of joyful details concerning past daily programmes of the Masters with their Apprentices and a great number of stories from old times. Some of the Masters feel sorry that their teaching periods are now 'over', showing how much they loved their roles as Masters. They wish that someone would still come and see them, just for a conversation or for another M-A period or even a full day. Once these 'ordinary' people were given the opportunity to transmit their language and to work as respected Masters, they and other elders around them realised the true value of their language. The Masters seem to be proud of this. We are sure that elder AS speakers got a piece of their lost identities back through working with the CASLE students.

7.10 How Threatened is the AS Language Since CASLE?

Marja-Liisa and Suvi: Despite the revitalisation aspirations of the community during the last 15 years, AS is a still a small Indigenous language with a very low number of speakers. However, we argue that the AS revitalisation work has produced observable results. Today all of the age groups which had no or very few speakers in the past now have AS speakers. The level of their language skills varies considerably, but since CASLE the total number of speakers has increased and continues to increase. Therefore the degree of endangerment of AS should be re-estimated. UNESCO's (2003) Degrees of language endangerment in Table 7.2 (p. 146) can be used to evaluate the endangerment grade of AS. These degrees assess the intergenerational language transmission process.

We would argue that in the last 15 years AS has moved from being a 'severely endangered language' to being close to the definition of an 'unsafe language'. It has jumped over one category. Before the establishment of the first language nest, AS was, with very few exceptions, spoken only by grandparents and the older generations. AS belonged clearly to the category of severely endangered language.

It might be logical to think that, with the revitalisation activities, AS took one step forward and rose in the UNESCO categories to the level of a 'definitively endangered language'. However, that category never seemed valid in the case of AS, because the parental generation had lost the language altogether. As a home language, AS had been lost. The UNESCO definition does not take into account the notion that a revitalisation process can also start outside the home environment. Going forward with the second language idea, AS clearly comes close to the UNESCO stage of 'unsafe' (most but not all children speak the language as their first language) because the parents who have learnt AS as a L2 transmit it to their children at home. In this case, the language can be classified as one of the children's mother tongues. This is, however, a very recent phenomenon. These parents have learnt AS during or since CASLE.

In our opinion, it is possible that AS may reach the stage of 'stable yet threatened'. This will take time and it depends on many things, basically on how hard AS people themselves are prepared to work for their language and how 'others' at the local, regional, state and even international levels view

Table 7.2 UNESCO's (2003) Six degrees of endangerment with regard to intergenerational language transmission

Safe (5)	The language is spoken by all generations. There is no sign of linguistic threat from any other language, and intergenerational transmission of the language seems uninterrupted.
Stable yet threatened (5−)	The language is spoken in most contexts by all generations with unbroken intergenerational transmission, yet multilingualism in the native language and one or more dominant language(s) has usurped certain important communication contexts. Note that multilingualism alone is not necessarily a threat to languages, but that encroachment on certain domains by one language may limit use of another.
Unsafe (4)	Most but not all children or families of a particular community speak their language as their first language, or this language may be restricted to specific social domains (such as the home where children interact with their parents and grandparents).
Definitively endangered (3)	The language is no longer being learned as a mother tongue by children in the home. The youngest native speakers are thus the parent generation. At this stage, parents may still speak their language to their children, but their children do not typically respond in the language.
Severely endangered (2)	The language is spoken only by grandparents and older generations; while the parent generation may still understand the language, they typically do not speak it to their children.
Critically endangered (1)	The youngest speakers are in the great-grandparent generation, and the language is not used for everyday interactions. These older people often remember only part of the language but do not use it, since there may not be anyone to speak with.
Extinct (0)	There is no-one who can speak or remember the language.

Source: http://www.unesco.org/culture/languages-atlas/

and support the goals of the AS community. Perhaps, and hopefully, the awareness of AS will increase. Where AS is not noticed, or where it is left in the shadows of the dominant languages, it is often not about people being mean but rather about their being ignorant. Even in the area where these languages are spoken, not many people realise that AS and North Saami are different languages altogether. It is easy to bundle them into one. North Saami has been the 'norm' and 'Saami language' has been a synonym for North Saami for such a long time that it will take more time to raise awareness.

It does not seem possible that AS will ever rise up to the highest UNESCO category of being 'totally safe'. Perhaps AS will be spoken by members of all age groups in the future, but because of the small number of speakers the language will always be under the threat of more dominant languages in its surroundings.

One great challenge in the long run is to make AS a first language again. According to our estimation, about one-third of AS speakers speak AS as a L2, and L2 speakers are becoming more and more dominant in AS-speaking society. One big question for the near future is how to continue to revive the language even if we reach the point where there are fewer or even no more first-language speakers. This issue is common to all languages undergoing revitalisation. In Hawai'i in particular, people have given a lot of thought to this – see, for example, Wilson and Kamanā (2009) for a very reflective and optimistic account, including a vision and a plan about how to realise it (Info Box 12 Advice From Revitalisation in Hawai'i). Despite the fact that AS will lose its strongest speakers in the near future, at the very latest in about 25–30 years, it has to survive, develop and be passed on to other generations. This means that the quality of today's language documentation will become more and more important.

7.11 The Community's Degree of Openness Towards Second-Language Speakers

Tove: The AS community has been open to people with no AS background if these people have been willing to try to learn the language to an extent where they can communicate with native speakers and have shown an interest in cultural traditions. Annika Pasanen (see 2005, 2006, 2010b) sees this as one of the central factors in the revitalisation movement, along with the pattern of using (even slight pressure to use) AS at the AS Association meetings, regardless of how recently learned or halting one's proficiency is. The Masters in CASLE are a good example of this openness, and the support that is given to AS second-language speakers. Not even all of the other Saami communities have been equally accepting of L2 speakers, and there is tension among some North Saami communities in Finland around this issue. Similar tensions may exist among other Indigenous peoples too; for an example, see the discussion with two Hawaiian shamans in Aikio-Puoskari and Skutnabb-Kangas (2007). It seems to us that there is no alternative for very small endangered languages other than to accept L2 speakers – unless one wants the language to disappear. In any case, accepting (and welcoming) new speakers has historically happened millions of times, for example in connection with marriages. Obviously this is one – but only one – of the factors that develops and changes languages; it is a normal process.

7.12 Aanaar Saami Language on the Internet

Suvi: The *internet* can offer a host of new tools for saving endangered languages. In the late 1990s and 2000s there were some case studies of internet use in connection with specific endangered or minority languages. According to Danet and Herring (2007), few of these studies were truly evaluative and empirical in orientation. However one of the two exceptions were from Hawai'i.

In the early to mid-1990s, there was an internet-accessible telecommunication system called Leoki [Powerful Voice]. It included private email, chat space, discussion lists, a 'newsline', vocabulary lists, current and back issues of a newspaper, an area for cultural resources like stories and songs, and information about agencies supporting Hawaiian studies and language learning – all in Hawaiian only. Many of these functions, except for the chat space, are available in AS on *Nettisaje* [the internet place], an AS Wikispace where AS-speaking people can share information, materials and written discussions in AS (http://nettisaje.wikispaces.com/). *Nettisaje* was created by teachers and it seems to be best used for educational purposes. However, daily interactions between younger AS speakers happen via social media and in a special group, *Anarâškielâ orroomviste* [AS living room] on Facebook (see Info Box 13 Saami Media in Finland).

According to Mark Warschauer (1998), who carried out an ethnographic study on Leoki, the site represents an excellent model of a group of people working to positively amplify existing linguistic and cultural practices in an online environment (quoted in Danet & Herring, 2007). In Hawai'i the challenges were similar to those encountered by the AS community. Many Hawaiian natives could not access the system from their homes because they lacked computers and even telephones (Warschauer, 2003; quoted in Danet & Herring, 2007). Likewise in Northern Lapland, there are still places where the internet cannot be accessed. However, the world is changing rapidly even in Northern Lapland, and better and faster internet connections are being built all the time.

Another internet page where AS can be read, a static one, is the homepage of Anarâškielâ servi, the AS language association: http://www.anaraskielaservi.fi.

7.13 Back to Worldwide Debates and the Future

7.13.1 Colonialism continues: The example of Arizona

The starting point for the AS project was, in terms of the need for maintenance of the language, similar to many other Indigenous situations all over the world. These are described by Indigenous peoples year after year at the two-week sessions of the *United Nations Permanent Forum on Indigenous Issues* (see http://social.un.org/index/IndigenousPeoples.aspx). There are literally thousands of books (including popular fiction) and tens of thousands of articles and reports about the general situation of various Indigenous peoples. Much of this literature makes one both sad and furious – the injustice and exploitation are so enormous, and most state action violates Indigenous peoples' human rights in really brutal ways.

It is important to analyse the injustice done to Indigenous peoples in terms of their earlier historical and still continuing colonisation. If their situation is not placed in the context of colonialism and neo-colonialism, it is impossible to understand today's linguicist[2] and racist ideologies, structures and practices, also visible in educational language policies. The language ideologies that were formed during the historical colonisation have penetrated very deeply into the consciousness of both the colonisers and the colonised,[3] and this is of course true also in Finland in relation to the Saami. The rank order of dominant and dominated languages and their users, and people's images of these languages and users, have permeated the discourses about educational models and the languages to be used for teaching and learning. This means that the dominant languages and their speakers are glorified, the dominated ones stigmatised and the relationships between them rationalised. These discourses always show the former as 'doing/being good' for the latter, who should, in their own interest, assimilate into the dominant people, languages and cultures, and leave their own languages and cultures – and knowledges – behind. This is how subtractive learning situations are 'normalised'. Today's silent ethnocide – a low-intensity warfare waged through formal education – is part of 500-year-old Western nation-state logic and Western cosmology. Authors in Meyer and Maldonado Alvarado (2010; see also the review of this by Pérez Jacobsen *et al.*, 2010) state that, when the elites in 'Latin America' created states independent from their European colonial bases, they did not liberate themselves from the colonial cosmologies. Ideas about the superiority of the white man (and it was indeed males) over dark-skinned people, about wellbeing understood as only human wellbeing, about the necessity of a culturally and linguistically homogeneous nation-state, and about development, all became the founding principles of the new Republics. Schooling was, and is, the tool *par excellence* for perpetuating this cosmology: it was also 'the principal instrument of the state for exterminating Indian peoples' (Esteva, 2010: 116). Today, the 'political function of the school is ethnocidal domination, the eradication of languages and customs of indigenous peoples by means of an interventionist army – teachers and schools' (Maldonado Alvarado, 2010: 375).

The states that have managed to either kill or bring very close to extinction the largest number of Indigenous languages during the last 200 years are Australia, Canada and the USA. These countries, along with New Zealand, were the only four countries that voted against the United Nations *Declaration on the Rights of Indigenous Peoples* (UNDRIP) in September 2007, even if all have since repented and now accept it.

Here is just one example of this language situation. In Arizona, USA, among all except the largest Native American tribes, Indigenous language 'speakers tend to be middle age or older and beyond childbearing age. Thus, when elderly speakers die, their languages die with them. . . . Native American children increasingly enter school speaking English as their primary language' (Combs & Nicholas, 2012: 105; see http://ourmothertongues.org/LanguageMaps.aspx for a map of North American Indigenous languages). Proposition 203 in Arizona (which is similar to Proposition 227 in California, designed to ban bilingual education) states: 'All children in Arizona public schools shall be taught English by being taught in English and all children shall be placed in English language classrooms' (ARS Statutes, 15, §3.1-752; to be found at http://www.azleg.gov/ArizonaRevisedStatutes.asp?Title = 15). Indigenous immersion schools (e.g. Rock Point, Rough Rock, Fort Defiance, Puente de Hózhó, etc.) have consistently shown positive results, where Indigenous students taught in their own language outperform Indigenous children who are in English-medium education, in English, mathematics and, of course, in their own language. Teresa McCarty's assessment is, for instance, that 'the Fort Defiance data demonstrate the powerful negative effect of the *absence* of bilingual/immersion schooling and, conversely, its positive effect on the maintenance of the heritage language as well as on students' acquisition of English and mathematics' (McCarty, 2003: 156; see also other references to McCarty's work).

But the good results are not the point – in fact they have not counted at all in the power games, which are clearly still largely influenced by colonial mentalities. The USA Federal state, through the *No Child Left Behind Act* (something many of us call the *No Child Left Bilingual Act* – see, for example, Hornberger, 2006 for a critique of the Act):

> seriously limits tribal exercise over how Indigenous children should be educated and in what language (Winstead *et al.*, 2008). Arizona state policies that dictate how Indigenous children should be educated and in what language similarly challenge tribal sovereignty and efforts to revitalise Indigenous languages (Combs & Nicholas, 2012: 115).

Combs and Nicholas (2012: 115) tell the sad story about how the state has intervened to discourage tribal educational decision-making. That Navajo students were excelling in both Navajo and English was beside the point; because tribal leaders opposed state English Only mandates, state authorities felt compelled to discipline them (somewhat like an authoritarian adult would discipline a recalcitrant child).

Many of us have joined Combs and Nicholas to ask: 'Who or what drives education and language policies for minoritized populations? Majority policymakers at the state level? Or the policies they impose on other people's children?' (Combs & Nicholas, 2012: 115–116; see also Tiersma, 2012 for court cases in Arizona). Combs and Nicholas hope that at some future time there will be more reasonable policy makers. Unfortunately it does not seem that this is coming any time soon.

There are similar stories about how states and decision makers all over the world, acting irrationally and against solid research results, harm children, violate their human rights to education and their linguistic and cultural rights, and participate in genocide and crimes against humanity (e.g. Skutnabb-Kangas, 2009). And when the harm is done, and these children suffer as adults and this goes on to influence future generations (see, for example, Churchill, 1997; Reyhner, 2010; Reyhner & Singh, 2010a; Richardson, 1993), the decision makers have long since gone; it is impossible to hold them responsible for what they have done to 'other people's children' and, through that, to the future of everybody's children and grandchildren.

7.13.2 Can others learn from the Finnish experience?

Have the Finnish authorities, then, been more broad-minded, better informed or 'nicer' than the corresponding USA ones? After all, now Indigenous peoples in Finland *are* 'allowed' to organise language nests, classes and schools where their own languages are the main teaching languages. The Finnish Ministry's vision (see Info Box 10 Visions for Saami Revitalisation, Finland) is just what Native Americans in Arizona and elsewhere would hope for. How can this be explained? The Saami are, after all, only 0.03% of the population of Finland.

The first part of the explanation could be that the Saami in all four countries (Norway, Sweden, Finland, Russia) see themselves as one people, with 10 languages, and they act in solidarity, getting support for their demands from all the Saami on many issues (see, for example, the Saami Council at http://www.saamicouncil.net/?deptid = 1116). Many Indigenous peoples exist in one country only (even if there are exceptions, in Latin America, in India, Nepal, etc.) or they are not able to organise across borders due to political, neocolonial or other constraints.

Secondly, knowing that Indigenous peoples all over the world follow what happens with the Saami (who are really visible among the world's Indigenous peoples) may in the best case make the Nordic states somewhat more aware of their international responsibilities. On the other hand, even when electronic media make communication and sharing much easier now than even a decade ago, most atrocities that states, multinational corporations and large landowners commit against Indigenous peoples go largely unnoticed by the general public. In addition, some states (including the Nordic states) may be more sensitive to outside criticism – but many others do not care.

Thirdly, the attitudes of majority populations have consistently been somewhat more positive towards the right to mother tongue maintenance for immigrant minorities in Finland than in the other Nordic countries, especially Sweden (see Jaakkola, 1989, 1995, 1999, 2005, 2009 for Finland; Lange & Westin, 1981, 1993; Westin, 1984, 1988 for Sweden; Körmendi, 1986 for Denmark; Puntervold Bø, 1984; Kulbrandsdal, 2011 for Norway). Some Finns are still acutely aware of the fact that we have struggled to maintain our unique Finno-Ugric languages (to which Saami also belongs), though we are situated between two Indo-European speaking neighbours who have historically taken turns in colonising us (Sweden from around 1050–1809, Russia from 1809 until Finland's independence in 1917). This might make Finns more prone to support other similar struggles for mother tongue maintenance. Likewise, many Finns know about and sympathise with the recent struggles for Finnish-medium education for both Finnish migrant minorities and the autochthonous (Finnish) *Meänkieli* speakers in Sweden. This may also colour majority attitudes towards Saami in Finland favourably.

Another factor may be that the Saami are at or close to the top (together with Estonians) of the various ranking lists of people with whom Finns want to associate (marry, have as neighbours, etc.; see Jaakkola in the References). This is, however, not necessarily the case in northern Finland, where there has been and sometimes still is some tension between the Saami and some Finnish speakers. This tension might be due to the fact that reindeer herding is not restricted to the Saami in Finland, as opposed to Sweden and Norway where only the Saami are allowed to herd. Attitudes to the profession among Finnish speakers and the Saami seem to be very different indeed: herding is a mere business, or a way of life, respectively (Holmén, 2012). On the other hand, many of the basic decisions about Indigenous rights are taken centrally, i.e. the tensions in Northern Finland do not necessarily always influence them in a negative way.

A fourth factor in Finland's relative supportiveness may be that small groups, especially when they are not seen as a threat by the majority population, can be granted rights more easily than larger groups. On the other hand, as soon as they start demanding any kind of land rights, or compensation for past wrongs, or more self-determination, or maybe even autonomy or independence, they may be seen as a threat by the state (which may perceive this as a risk for disintegration), and the willingness to grant rights diminishes rapidly. There have so far been fairly few land right demands in Finland, even if the numbers are now growing. Finland's reluctance to ratify ILO 169 can partially be seen as a reflection of this kind of (unfounded) fear.

To shed some light on this issue, I (Tove) and Ulla Aikio-Puoskari, the Education Secretary of the Saami Parliament in Finland, compared in an article (Skutnabb-Kangas & Aikio-Puoskari, 2003) the results and strategies used by two linguistic minorities, the Saami and Signing Deaf. We wanted to see whether there are any systematic differences between situations where attempts to guarantee language rights to certain groups have been 'successful' or less successful, respectively (see also Aikio-Puoskari & Skutnabb-Kangas, 2007). After fairly detailed descriptions of each group and their rights, and their attempts to get more rights, we list some similarities and differences between the groups. We conclude that we still know too little about all the important factors that decide the outcomes; some possible predictors do not seem to work in the way theories assume, while others do.

7.13.3 Land rights or linguistic and cultural rights – or both?

It is necessary to add in one more factor: the goals that an Indigenous people has for its future, and to what extent the dominant population in a state shares these goals. In other publications (most recently in Skutnabb-Kangas, 2012), I have compared groups/peoples (such as the Saami on the Finnish side of the border), whose mobilisation started with linguistic and cultural demands, with groups where more material demands, e.g. around ownership to land and water, have taken precedence, i.e. demands for some aspects of structural incorporation. It seems that the first type of group may possibly be more successful in reaching both types of goal.

In many – but by no means all – Asian countries, cultural and linguistic pluralism have been much more widely accepted than in Europe and Europeanised monolingually oriented countries. In countries such as India and Nepal, for example, language rights have been codified in constitutions and other legal texts (even if implementation has been and is lacking; see articles in Skutnabb-Kangas *et al.*, 2009 and references in them). At the same time, Indigenous/tribal peoples and even many national linguistic minorities are excluded from social justice in these countries too, i.e. they are not structurally incorporated into the 'mainstream' economically, socially, educationally, politically or in other ways. These structural inequalities are often discussed either in addition to linguistic, ethnic and cultural characteristics or only in terms of class/caste hierarchies (which are, however, often language based, or coincide with ethnicity- and language-related characteristics).

Looking back at the history of small and large tribal protests and movements in India, one finds that, more often than not, the tribals (unlike the Saami) began their protest essentially for land. They did not want to lose their languages, but language was definitely not an issue, since they did not collectively perceive it as a resource or a marker of identity or, at least, did not consider it endangered, at risk. Their collective protests were organised sporadically in time and space, and in small groups. Only when these led to bigger movements (as in the case of Bodos and Santhalis) were these three bases of identity (land, language, culture/ethnicity) conceptually distinguished by the leaders. But for the common people they were one and the same. Because of the multilingual ethos and multiglossia, non-use of tribal languages in formal/official spaces like school was not construed by the speakers of those language as a process that might lead to the loss of their own language, and therefore at some point their culture and ethnicity. It does not seem unrealistic to generalise this to other parts of the world, for instance non-dominant ethnolinguistic groups in Africa and Latin America, whether or not they are numeric minorities. The right to one's land, after all, has been and is the basis for earning a living.

This is why the demand for mother tongue-based multilingual education (MLE) has often been relatively weak among ITM parents – at least until a few years ago. It seems, however, that many tribals in India and Nepal, where the formative foundations of social identity are their language, culture and ethnicity along with their land (often seen holistically as inseparable, as described above), are now striving for both structural incorporation and cultural and linguistic rights, especially in education, at the same time. They are often using innovative strategies (e.g. the Dalits in India; see Ilaiah, 2009a, 2009b). For example, in Indian states like Andhra Pradesh and Orissa, MLE has been implemented in hundreds of pilot schools because of decisions taken at the state bureaucratic level, not because the parents of the tribal children demanded it. However, one can say that many tribal parents in Orissa and Andhra have now started noticing the benefits of MLE for their children and have therefore started lending emotional and moral support to these initiatives. They have also started seeing language as a resource, a cultural capital. But still there are very few demands being made for any kind of cultural autonomy (Skutnabb-Kangas *et al.*, 2009). We are now beginning to get results showing that well-conducted MLE can reach *both* goals (structural incorporation and linguistic and cultural pluralism) (see some results on the website of the Indian National Multilingual Education Resource Consortium, directed by Professors Mohanty and Panda at http://www.nmrc-jnu.org/; see also Mohanty & Skutnabb-Kangas, 2010).

Thus in many contexts worldwide, ITMs live in societies that are organised to exclude them – both from structural incorporation that might lead to more just societies socially, economically and politically, and from the right to maintain and develop their mother tongues and cultures (in addition to having access to additional languages and cultures, including the dominant ones). We interpret this situation as reflecting the intentions of the dominant groups and the state, regardless of the extent to which the intention is overtly expressed (or even when the opposite is expressed in declarations and laws but implementation is lacking). What requires further analysis is the extent to which ITMs agree with these goals. One might safely assume that no Indigenous peoples agree with a goal of *not* having the right and opportunity to achieve full structural incorporation. But many of them still take their languages and cultures as self-evident, and do not see their loss as a possibility – yet. Tragically, the loss of languages and cultures is happening more and more rapidly – just as it historically happened to the Saami. Today's assimilationist formal education leads directly to the future need for linguistic and cultural revitalisation.

This leads to some important questions. To what extent do those ITMs who 'want' linguistic and cultural assimilation think that this is a necessary price to pay for structural incorporation, as some 'rational-choice' theorists try to make them believe? Do ITMs believe in the myth that they have to choose between the two goals? Are they made to believe that it is a zero-sum game? To what extent do they know what the long-term consequences of their choices are? And is there in reality any choice in these power games? Ahmed Kabel from Morocco (see also Kabel, 2012a, 2012b) calls rational-choice theory

> sacred liberal dogma. The fact of the matter is that parents 'make choices' with regard to languages under enormous structural constraints. Some of these constraints may be too flagrantly palpable to simply ignore: violence, dispossession, threat to life ... while others may be beyond the conscious awareness of the actors themselves. Also, given the overwhelming amount of indoctrination and propaganda as well the systemic violence that they are subjected to, parents can hardly be said to be meaningfully 'choosing'. (Kabel, 2010, private email; quoted in Skutnabb-Kangas, 2012: 100)

This also means that there cannot be any mono-causal or static pieces of 'advice' or 'recommendations'. But we can certainly compare notes, share experiences and learn from each other.

7.13.4 Who is responsible?

In case this sounds as if we do not have enough knowledge to act, it is important to state that this is a completely false conclusion. We do know both what kind of language strategies in education do not work (among them those that have ultimately led to situations where languages need to be revitalised) and which do 'work' (i.e. lead to high levels of bi- or multilingualism, successful school achievement, a sound bilingual bicultural identity and life chances where people have been able to develop their capabilities and have choices), although it is acknowledged that contextualisation is vital for these strategies to be applied appropriately. We have all the pedagogical and other arguments needed for MLE, including Indigenous revitalisation programmes (see, for example, Benson, 2008, 2009; Benson & Kosonen, 2012; Benson et al., 2012; Heugh & Skutnabb-Kangas, 2012).

Still, most education programmes for ITMs in the world contribute significantly to genocidal assimilation which, among other things, creates and recreates the need for future revitalisation efforts. Who is responsible for these irrational and cruel language-in-education policies? Combs and Nicholas (2012: 115) state that it is 'difficult to make the case that Arizona's

English Only language policies have produced any benefits other than to further the political agendas of their sponsors. The intended targets – English language learners –are not learning English more efficiently.' What is the role of researchers in this whole story of policy development? Official language policies and the ideologies underlying them today are, in Durrani's view (2012: 30), 'created by researchers, journalists and other public figures'.

But this (mostly Western) researcher knowledge informing the negative official policies is, like all knowledge, 'marked geo-historically, geo-politically and geo-culturally; it has a value, colour and a place of "origin"' (Walsh, 2004: 2; quoted in Pérez Jacobsen, 2009: 213). By classifying Indigenous knowledge

> as 'traditional' or 'local wisdom' it is fixed in time and space. At the same time, words like 'abstract', 'neutral', 'pure science' or 'universal knowledge' hide the fact that all knowledge is produced *by somebody, at a certain time in history and at a certain place in history.* By defining academic knowledge as time- and spaceless, Western scientists are trying to hide their own philosophical foundations. (Pérez Jacobsen, 2009: 213)

We could also add that *within* 'Western' science, similar issues about whose knowledge is seen as scientific and valid play a role in the paradigmatic debates (see, for example, Harding, 1986, 1998). In discourses on the medium of education, the ones who claim 'neutrality' and 'abstraction' are often the assimilationist researchers. These include both the more directly assimilation-defending researchers, and the mainly postmodern more indirect ones whose ideologies and theories also lead to assimilation even if they do not own this as their intention.

Some of the 'sponsors' of English Only in the USA, i.e. supporters of enforced linguistic assimilation, are researchers who are furthering their careers, as stated by Combs and Nicholas (2012: 115). Many are playing intellectual games, with no consideration vis-à-vis the children whose lives their actions may contribute toward destroying.

Ironically, those supporting exactly the programmes that have been shown to have positive results for ITM children, or researchers who support the maintenance of ITM languages in general, are also accused of furthering their careers. Laitin and Reich (2003: 94) call those of us who want small languages to survive 'linguistic entrepreneurs of minority groups'. They call minority parents who want mother tongue-medium education 'regional separatists' (2003: 97). Laitin and Reich 'want to empower states to constrain parents from so limiting their children's language repertoires' and 'demand that [minority] parents provide linguistic repertoires to their children that allow them a meaningful range of choices as adults' (2003: 98). All this coercion by researchers and the state is in their view only needed in relation to *minority* parents. *Dominant group* parents seem to have a self-evident right to have dominant language-medium education only (often with no foreign languages on the curriculum) for their children; these children are allowed to become and remain monolingual. One could ask where the 'meaningful range of choices as adults' is for them?

Other misconceptions that abound, even among solid research-based scholars, are that minority people are somehow reluctant ('unable or unwilling': Kymlicka & Patten, 2003: 12) to learn the majority/dominant language, and that they will 'become ghettoised' (Kymlicka & Patten, 2003: 12), so that 'even the second and third generations of immigrant groups will live and work predominantly in their ancestral language, with only minimal or non-existent command of the state language' (Patten & Kymlicka, 2003: 8; Kymlicka & Patten, 2003: 6). Obviously choosing to learn both an ITM language *and* a dominant language, as one does in all Indigenous revitalisation or other MLE programmes, has never crossed the minds of Laitin and Reich or others from the assimilationist side. These 'either/or' researchers seem to think that wanting to learn one's own (including one's ancestors') language really well, and wanting to have it as a main medium of education, somehow prevents one from learning the dominant language (e.g. Laitin & Reich, 2003). Brutt-Griffler's publications (e.g. Brutt-Griffler, 2002, 2004a, 2004b) are prominent examples of this kind of misconception.[4] Jan Blommaert (2004: 60), in an article criticising what he calls 'an LHRs approach', also presents the medium of education as a matter of either/or choices, where choosing L1 promotion is seen as preventing upward mobility:

> The choice for English/French rather than indigenous languages in education is at the grassroots level often motivated by means of discourses of 'getting out of here' and towards particular centres – metropolitan areas – where upward social mobility at least looks possible ... L1 promotion is thus seen as *an instrument preventing a way out of real marginalization and amounting to keeping people in their marginalized places.* (Blommaert, 2004: 60, emphasis added)

Researchers like Brutt-Griffler and Blommaert also claim that both youngsters and ITM parents *want* their children to be educated through the medium of a dominant language. It is clear that there are some ITM parents who make this claim, and 'vote with their feet' by placing their children in dominant-language medium programmes – e.g. Lopez in Latin America and Annamalai and Mohanty in India have reported this. This provides some background for why many immigrant minority parents in the USA, e.g. in Arizona or California, have voted for English-Only medium education. These parents have mostly been made to believe that they *have* to choose one or the other language for their children, instead of both languages plus others. Their consent to something that ultimately harms their children may have been manufactured (see Benson, 2008; Herman & Chomsky, 1988). 'Children do not fail in school; schools fail the children' was one of the conclusions in a five-day high-level *International Hearing on the Harm Done in Schools by the Suppression of the Mother Tongue* in Mauritius (see Ah-Vee *et al.*, 2009).

7.13.5 The economics of language maintenance and revitalisation: Markets in globalisation

Yet another misconception, this time about what revitalisation researchers stand for, is the idea that schools alone can do it, i.e. maintain or 'save' ITM languages. They cannot – even if, as Joshua Fishman has written many times, schools can easily kill ITM languages in a few generations, and do.

> More than most other authoritative specialists, the authorities of the educational system are deeply implicated in planned language shift. ... Education [is] a very useful and highly irreversible language shift mechanism.. ... The usual postmodern critique ... misses the boat completely. (Fishman, 2006: 320)

It is very clear that no-one who works with revitalisation – not parents, teachers, school authorities, researchers or others – thinks that language nests or schools *alone* can 'save' or even teach endangered languages, nor do they think that some kind of moral 'missionary' motivation to 'save' languages for their own sake is the only or even a way to go. Language is communication, communication needs communities, and these communities have to be viable, economically as well as socially.

Further, the right to revitalisation is not 'only' or even mainly a half-naïve moral question, even if human rights law is involved. In a moral discourse the question of what kinds of rights, if any, should be granted to speakers of ITM languages, and at what cost, seems to depend on how 'nice' states are. This is a shaky foundation for human rights, as human rights lawyer Fernand de Varennes rightly observes (1999: 117):

> Moral or political principles, even if they are sometimes described as 'human rights', are not necessarily part of international law. They are things that governments 'should' do, if they are 'nice', not something they 'must' do. Being nice is not a very convincing argument and is less persuasive than rights and freedoms that have the weight of the law behind them.

In contrast, language economist Francois Grin suggests that welfare-oriented economic discourse should be used because

> the emphasis of the welfare-based argument is not on whether something is morally 'good' or 'bad', but on whether resources are appropriately allocated. The test of an 'appropriate' allocation of resources is whether society is better off as a result of a policy. (Grin, 2003: 25)

In a welfare-oriented economic discourse one can calculate in much more 'hard-core' terms (often but not necessarily always involving cash) who the winners and losers are. Here 'the question is whether the winners, who stand to gain from a policy, can compensate the losers and still be better off [than without the policy]' (Grin, 2003: 25). This is an empirical question, not a moral question. We can look at it by asking how any human rights, including the linguistic right to maintain one's language, fare in corporate globalisation.

In an article entitled 'Justice for sale. International law favours market values', Mireille Delmas-Marty (2003) discusses the dangerous conflict between legal concepts based on the one hand on 'universal' market values, and on the other hand on genuinely universal *non-market values*. The latter include individual and collective human rights as a part of the universal common heritage of humanity.

The epistemology of the fields of human rights law and of philosophically oriented political science are now starting to accept that normative rights should be stipulated at least in relation to some parts of this universal common heritage (in their terminology, 'common public assets'). On the other hand, the legal protection of market values is still 'incommensurably stronger' than the protection of non-market values. Laws based on market values, which are promoted by organisations like the WTO (World Trade Organization) and WIPO (World Intellectual Property Organization), are being developed extremely rapidly, with harsh sanctions for violations.

Through his discussion of 'market failure', François Grin (2003: 35) offers excellent arguments for resisting market dominance for public or common assets/goods like cultural products, including (small) languages:

> Even mainstream economics acknowledges that there are some cases where the market is not enough. These cases are called 'market failure'. When there is 'market failure', the unregulated interplay of supply and demand results in an inappropriate level of production of some commodity.

In Grin's view (2003: 35), many public goods, including minority language protection, 'are typically under-supplied by market forces'. The level becomes inappropriately low. Therefore it is the duty of the state(s) to take extra measures to increase it.

Some researchers disagree, claiming that there is no such duty. Edwards, for instance, argues that, for minorities, the communicative and symbolic values of language 'are separable, and it is possible for the symbolic to remain in the absence of the communicative' (Edwards, 1984: 289). According to this view, even if minority group members no longer know their language and cannot communicate in it, they can still remain, and feel that they are, members of the group. Since the 'symbolic value of language is essentially a private ethnic marker' (Edwards, 1984: 289), governments should take no action to enable minorities to maintain their languages, 'on the grounds that matters of ethnicity are best left to those directly concerned' (Edwards, 1984: 299); and 'public institutions [like schools should not] promote private ethnicity' (Edwards, 1984: 300). In response, Grin's careful opinion is that 'this view is probably mistaken, and there are strong analytical reasons for state intervention – unless one were to argue that linguistic diversity is a bad thing in itself' (Grin, 2003: 34). Edwards neglects to say that schools strongly promote the 'private ethnicity' of the linguistic majority by using this majority's language as the teaching language.

Can states leave the responsibility for languages and linguistic diversity unconsidered (i.e. to the communities themselves), as Edwards suggests? States *can* be neutral in relation to religions, but *not* in relation to languages (see, for instance, Kymlicka & Grin, 2003: 10), because all states must function through the medium of *some* language or languages. A state or federation that does not actively support minority languages is in fact supporting (the dominance of) the official language(s) unjustly.

A European Parliament Resolution of 2003[5] exemplifies the attempt to build bridges between the market and cultural products, through a suggestion that cultural goods and services and education be exempted from market laws. Cultures, including languages and education, have a dual nature, as both economic and cultural goods, and 'must therefore be made subject to special conditions'. The market 'cannot be the measure of all things, and must guarantee in particular diversity of opinion and pluralism' (Article 16).

François Grin (2004) differentiates between *market and non-market values for private and social purposes*. Multilingualism has *social market value*, as many studies show. Even some English-dominant countries appreciate this, as an example from the UK demonstrates:

> English is not enough. We are fortunate to speak a global language but, in a smart and competitive world, exclusive reliance on English leaves the UK *vulnerable* and dependent on the linguistic competence and the goodwill of others [...] Young people from the UK are at a *growing disadvantage* in the recruitment market. (Nuffield Foundation, 2000, emphases added)

Another social market benefit flows from the relationship between creativity, innovation and investment, which can be a result of good mother tongue-based MLE, including an Indigenous language revitalisation programme. Creativity precedes innovation, also in commodity production, while investment follows creativity. High levels of multilingualism can enhance creativity, since high-level multilinguals as a group do better than corresponding monolinguals on tests measuring several aspects of 'intelligence' (a contested concept, of course), creativity, divergent thinking, cognitive flexibility and other aspects (Bialystok, 1991, 2009, 2010, 2011), and effective MLE mostly leads to high-level multilingualism. In knowledge societies, diverse knowledges and ideas (meaning the results of creativity) give access to markets and produce market value, whereas most kinds of homogenisation are a market handicap. Positive globalisation means context-sensitive localisation, as opposed to corporate McDonaldised one-size-fits-all homogenisation. A somewhat similar analysis grades European and some other countries in terms of their innovation and creativity potential (Florida & Tinagli, 2004). The sequence chain they present is as follows: tolerance entices diversity/difference, which entices creativity, which develops competitiveness, which brings money.

In a large-scale Swiss study, Grin concludes that, whereas each additional year of formal education adds an average 4.5% to net earnings, knowledge of an additional language generally adds more; additional earnings found in this study were between 4% and 20 + %, depending on a person's first language (L1), the second language (L2) considered, L2 skills levels, gender, type of job and some additional factors (Grin, 1999: 194; see also Grin & Sfreddo, 1997).

Many beautiful pronouncements about the historical, aesthetic, philosophical and other values of linguistic and cultural diversity for the whole of humankind, about languages as the libraries of humankind and other 'Unescoese' statements exemplify *social non-market values*. Social non-market-value arguments have often been labelled and rejected as romantic, non-realistic, elitist, moralistic, essentialising and the like (see Skutnabb-Kangas, 2009).

With the help of these economic distinctions, it is easier to classify and even weigh many positivistic and postmodernist arguments against the maintenance of linguistic diversity. It is relatively easy to discuss the *social* and even *private market* value of various languages, including the question of maintaining or not maintaining certain specified mother tongues. But it is difficult to apply economic rational choice theories to evaluate issues that represent private *non-market* values if they are seen by some discussants as non-values. Most of those who argue against diversity do not accept that using the mother tongue, or even having competence in several languages, can or should be given even private non-market value, let alone any market value, private or social. As long as a numerically small mother tongue does not give you a visibly better job with a higher salary than shifting to a numerically and politically more powerful language would, there are, according to this line of thought, few arguments for maintaining these mother tongues. Bilingualism is not often not considered as a real option; as mentioned above, the thinking here is 'either/or': either the ITM language *or* the dominant language (e.g. Kond-medium *or* English-medium schooling in India, not MLE with Kond, Oriya *and* English; see Mohanty *et al.*, 2009; Skutnabb-Kangas *et al.*, 2009).

In addition, many of the elites among native speakers of English or some other big dominant language, maybe especially English monolinguals but even multilinguals, need much more awareness of the (often emotional) *non-market value* of *their own*, often non-threatened and dominant mother tongues. They often lack awareness of what their own mother tongues mean for their identities, because these mother tongues have not been threatened or even questioned. Because these elites do not appreciate the non-market value of their *own* mother tongues, they often lack awareness of the non-market value of *other people's mother tongues*, and the fact that they themselves benefit unjustly from the market value of their own (dominant) languages.

It seems to be short-sighted to reject any of the (market or non-market, private or social) arguments for reasons why ITM languages *should* be supported: all of them are useful in various ways, as Grin has shown in many of his publications.

However, market logic and the rationality of economic theories are also being increasingly questioned (see, for example, the Dahlem paper 'Financial crisis and the systemic failure of academic economics' at http://ideas.repec.org/p/kie/kieliw/1489.html). The Institute for New Economic Thinking (INET) (http://ineteconomics.org) has in a very short time attracted over 10,000 researchers in economics who question both the validity and the appropriateness of the knowledge upon which economics is based, including growthism ideology. In April 2012, one of the Dahlem paper authors, Finnish professor Katarina Juselius, launched a new INET Center for Imperfect Knowledge Economics (http://www.econ.ku.dk/inet/) at Copenhagen University. These developments will hopefully strengthen the importance of those alternative values that many Indigenous peoples (and this book) stand for.

7.13.6 To conclude: Academic freedom to choose

It is tedious that similar debates and arguments have to be repeated over and over again. John Edwards (2012: 203), in a review of Nancy Hornberger's 2011 edited book *Can Schools Save Indigenous Languages?* has a snide and semantically interesting formulation:

> I don't doubt for a moment that all the authors in this book are well-meaning, and I would not like to think – as some have done – that many language efforts are most vigorously supported by those whose careers rest upon their continuation. The fact remains, however, that educational programmes of language revitalisation are the lamp-post in whose light we hope to recover things that were lost elsewhere.

Of course there are linguists who think of their careers *too* when describing endangered languages. This is obviously a fully legitimate undertaking. And for some of them, what Leanne Hinton (2009, n.p.) describes may be true:

> The implicit promise of support from academia for revitalising Indigenous languages turns out to be difficult to harness directly to the urgent needs of Native communities seeking to develop new fluent

speakers of their original languages. While linguists and community members can easily share a broad common goal of perpetuating Native languages, they operate out of surprisingly separate agendas. Many of the efforts from academia rely on long-standing strengths for producing lexicons and grammars, generally in the service of the demand for scholarly publications for career advancement. But for Native communities in the very late stages of language loss, with few resources and only handfuls of elderly speakers, much of the arcane academic output may be of little use in their hands-on, urgent struggle to pass their languages to the youngest generation.

CASLE reflected on these kinds of challenges, for instance when looking at how well or how badly the university courses in AS suited the needs of the community and the students. The students needed practical oral language for immediate revitalisation purposes, not language suited for future academics doing language research throughout a whole life career – even if what the students got was also a good preparation for that in the future, should any of them wish to pursue that career path. The fact that Marja-Liisa had worked with her own community for years, and that she worked well beyond the 'normal' workload of an academic and with great dedication, is evidence that she knew and was guided by the needs of the AS community. Regarding what Hinton describes, and what Edwards criticises, it is most often outsider linguists who may be 'unsuitable' for getting results that the communities need and want. Fortunately, revitalisation efforts can today count on both linguists who are members of the communities and outsiders who are activists as well as researchers, and many of those unjustly criticised by Edwards belong to one of these categories.

Joshua Fishman writes about his steps/stages in reversing language shift that '… Stage 6, consisting of home-family-neighborhood-community reinforcement … constitutes the heart of the entire intergenerational transmission pursuit' (Fishman, 1991: 398). He continues: '[I]f this stage is not satisfied, all else can amount to little more than biding time' (Fishman, 1991: 399). Leanne Hinton has suggested four pathways through which language revitalisation is reaching the home (Hinton, 2009, n.p.; for some of the results and reflections by participants, see Hinton, 2013):

(A) The teachers in the immersion school movement who have committed to using their language at home;
(B) Individual adult learning from elder speakers, either through one's own efforts, or through an organised program, mainly the Master–Apprentice approach;
(C) Learning from documentation;
(D) Organised programs that specifically target the home as the site of language revitalisation.

The CASLE programme has, with success, used the first three, pathways A, B and C. Many other features have been added, for instance encouraging CASLE graduates (i.e. not only teachers) to start using the language at home, or encouraging them to start discussions in their target language in the community at large instead of using the dominant language; Suvi, for instance, has done both. Many of us have also participated in organising and speaking at D-type activities, including various kinds of programmes for parents, grandparents and even children. We have discussed 'contracts' that language nests and schools could make with parents to the effect that parents commit to more revitalisation and use of the language at home, including parents learning the language themselves if they have lost it or have never known it. As the Fishman quotes attest, language revitalisers are aware of the various necessary and contributing factors. Most of us have cast our nets widely, and very few of us have relied on the schools alone.

CASLE's cooperation with employers, asking them to assess their needs and commit to employing CASLE students once they have learned the language, has also been vital for the economic viability of a small language (and motivation for learning it). It should be noted that at least nine new jobs were created as a direct result of CASLE, seven in language nests and two in primary schools. We can thus conclude that CASLE has created both private and social market and non-market value.

However, we should not forget the overarching human survival values encoded in Indigenous and local languages. As Terralingua states:

> As with biological species, languages and cultures naturally evolve and change over time. But just as with species, the world is now undergoing a massive human-made extinction crisis of languages and cultures. External forces are dispossessing traditional peoples of their lands, resources, and lifestyles; forcing them to [migrate or] subsist in highly degraded environments; crushing their cultural traditions or ability to maintain them; or coercing them into linguistic assimilation and abandonment of ancestral languages. People who lose their linguistic and cultural identity may lose an essential element in a social process that commonly teaches respect for nature and understanding of the natural environment and its processes. Forcing this cultural and linguistic conversion on [I]ndigenous and other traditional peoples not only violates their human rights, but also undermines the health of the world's ecosystems and the goals of nature conservation. (http://www.terralingua.org)

Many Indigenous and minority researchers have shown that, firstly, if granted a fair share of resources, Indigenous languages can perform many if not all of the same functions as dominant languages.

Secondly, there are many other functions that Indigenous people's mother tongues can perform, and not only for themselves. These languages might be able to perform, for the benefit of all humanity, functions that many dominant languages either have not been put to perform or that they in many cases cannot perform today. Indigenous and local languages may do this through sharing the traditional ecological, cognitive, spiritual and ideological knowledge encoded within them. This knowledge may be vital for saving the planet or at least for giving us the prerequisites for human existence on the planet. We do not think that it is necessary to discuss whether this is a private or social market or non-market value – it is all of them and goes far beyond.

Pierre Bourdieu, in his discussion on the practice of academic freedom, states that academics have three straight choices (Bourdieu, 1989: 486, translated and summarised here by Robert Phillipson). An academic can choose to be

- the expert serving societal needs as these are understood by the politically and economically powerful;
- the professor trapped in esoteric, erudite scholarly isolation;
- the scholar who intervenes in the political world in the name of the values and truths achieved in and through autonomy and academic freedom.

In work with Indigenous/tribal peoples, the first and second types often support (directly and indirectly, respectively) neoliberal, neocolonial, homogenising globalisation. We hope and believe that with this book we represent Bourdieu's third alternative.

The Education Secretary of the Saami Parliament, Ulla Aikio-Puoskari, once publicly said that the CASLE programme has been beneficial not only for the AS people themselves but for the whole Saami community. According to her, the reversal of language shift has affected people's dignity and the way they look at the future. From Aikio-Puoskari's point of view, language loss brings illness, shame and sorrow. She goes on to argue:

> When the language is brought back alive again; when it is heard, learned, sung, taught, written and used in new circumstances, it heals the whole community. At a personal level, the one who has lost his/her language becomes whole when reclaiming it.

I (Tove) would like to finish with something that Marja-Liisa wrote to Suvi and me (private email, 9 May 2012) when she was, as usual, in Aanaar:

> Yesterday I attended the 60th birthday party of one of the Masters. It was unbelievable to see old AS speakers with the status of Masters in discussion with each other – they did not shift to Finnish even when Finnish speakers were present. And the club started and run by one of

our students has worked wonders in the whole village – the village had stopped speaking AS, but now the language is getting new life.

The researcher's soul is also really moved when I see two language nest 'graduates' from the first generation of language nest children now, as young adults, working in a language nest.

Long-term work carries results. It is good to continue from here.

Indeed!

Notes

(1) The Skolt Saami are Orthodox, not Lutheran, which is why their language is not mentioned here.
(2) I have defined linguicism as 'ideologies, structures and practices which are used to legitimate, effectuate and reproduce an unequal division of power and (both material and non-material) resources between groups which are defined on the basis of language' (Skutnabb-Kangas, 1988: 13).
(3) See Durrani (2012) for a perceptive analysis of the workings of these ideologies and discourses in the educational system of Pakistan.
(4) See the whole Forum debate on this issue between Brutt-Griffler and Skutnabb-Kangas in the *Journal of Language, Identity and Education* 2004, 3 (2), with invited commentaries by Suresh Canagarajah, Alastair Pennycook and James W. Tollefson.
(5) The European Parliament Session document dated 15 December 2003 (A5-0477/2003) from the Committee on Culture, Youth, Education, the Media and Sport contains a 'Draft European Parliament Resolution on preserving and promoting cultural diversity: The role of the European regions and international organizations such as UNESCO and the Council of Europe' (2002/2269(INI)) and an explanatory statement. The text was adopted by the parliament.

Info Boxes

Info Box 1 Criticism of Sweden's Current Minority Policies and Practices

In February of 2012 the Swedish church published an official report, *Våga vara minoritet. En rapport om minoritetsrättigheter i Sverige* 2012 [*Dare to be Minority. A Report on Minority Rights in Sweden in 2012*] (Svenska Kyrkan, 2012) where they describe and criticise the Swedish policy toward minority groups, partly on the basis of the Council of Europe's monitoring reports. Here we quote a few of the educational points from their summary (translation by Tove Skutnabb-Kangas):

- **Children's legal minority rights are being violated**. The right to a pre-school education in Saami, Finnish and Meänkieli is not respected by many municipalities in the administrative areas [where these languages are called for]. Although a number of municipalities have not even investigated the need for such pre-schools, the parents' demands are being dismissed.
- **Swedish law violates the commitments made in the Council of Europe's minority conventions**. The stipulations in the Swedish Minority Act regarding the right to a pre-school education in Saami, Finnish and Meänkieli are too weak in relation to Sweden's commitments according to the European Language Charter. The provisions for mother tongue teaching in Sweden require learners to have fundamental knowledge in the minority language in order to participate in classes. Such requirements are not allowed according to the minority conventions.
- **Government funding for mother tongue teaching in national minority languages has not been used for national minority children**.

- **The legal regulations in the educational field are still weak and children's right to services in their minority language is not realised**. Bilingual education hardly exists. Many students are denied mother tongue teaching. There is no teacher training in national minority languages and this threatens the survival of the national minority languages, according to the Swedish National Agency for Higher Education. There is also a lack of teaching materials in several minority languages.
- **Ignorance is still a significant obstacle to respecting the needs and rights of national minorities.** The decisions currently made by authorities may even decrease access to current services in minority languages.

Info Box 2 Language Endangerment

In the UNESCO *Interactive Atlas of the World's Languages in Danger* (Moseley, 2010), a total of 2474 endangered languages are categorised into five categories: vulnerable (601 languages), definitely endangered (648), severely endangered (526), critically endangered (576) or extinct (231) (http://www.unesco.org/culture/languages-atlas/, accessed 10 February 2012). The most important criterion is intergenerational transmission, i.e. whether most speakers are elders or whether the languages are still learned by children (see http://www.unesco.org/new/en/culture/themes/cultural-diversity/languages-and-multilingualism/endangered-languages/faq-on-endangered-languages/ for details). UNESCO uses nine factors in assessing the vitality of languages (http://www.unesco.org/new/fileadmin/MULTIMEDIA/HQ/CI/CI/pdf/unesco_language_vitaly_and_endangerment_methodological_guideline.pdf).

Prognoses for the future vary. UNESCO uses an estimate stating that at the very least half, or even 90–95% (both estimates by Michael Krauss) of today's spoken languages will not be learned by children by the end of this century. UNESCO's webpage http://www.unesco.org/new/en/culture/themes/cultural-diversity/languages-and-multilingualism/endangered-languages/faq-on-endangered-languages/ contains many frequently asked questions about endangered languages, and replies to them.

Jonathan Loh and David Harmon's *ILD* (*The Index of Linguistic Diversity: Results from the First Quantitative Measure of Trends in the Status of the World's Languages*) covers the period from 1970 to 2005. Their conclusions are that, globally, linguistic diversity has declined by 20% over that period, whereas it has declined by 21% for the world's Indigenous languages. Of the world's six regions (Africa, the Americas, Asia, Australia, Europe and Oceania/Pacific), the sharpest declines by far in linguistic diversity have occurred in the Americas and Australia. The top 16 languages spoken worldwide increased their share of speakers among the world's population from 45% in 1970 to some 57% in 2005.

When the ILD global trend line is superimposed on that of the Living Planet Index (which uses species diversity as a proxy for biological diversity), the results are remarkably similar, leading Loh and Harmon to conclude that 'the world has lost 20–25% of its biocultural diversity over the period 1970 to 2005' (for *ILD*, see http://www.terralingua.org/linguistic-diversity/). 'Biocultural diversity' covers biological diversity, linguistic diversity and cultural diversity.

What is needed, then, is a complete reversal of the negative trends. Joseph Lo Bianco sees three kinds of activity needed for revival of a threatened language, depending on which phase of endangerment the language is in:

> Programmes of *language revitalisation* aim to extend the use of a threatened language among younger generations by drawing on the proficiency of the remaining speakers of a language; *language renewal* involves activity aiming to increase the usage and knowledge of a language no longer spoken in its full form, and *language reclamation* promotes the relearning of a language on the basis of historical documentation and archive materials. (Lo Bianco, 2012: 501)

Even if the CASLE project has concentrated on revitalisation, it has also exploited strategies used in the other two revival activities.

Info Box 3 The Situation of the World's Languages

The latest edition of the *Ethnologue* (16th edn, 2009), still the best list-ing of the world's languages, counted 6909 living languages with some 5960 billion speakers (http://www.ethnologue.com/ethno_docs/distri-bution.asp?by = area#1). Of these, 2110 (30.5%) are spoken in Africa, 993 (14.4%) in the Americas, 2322 (33.6%) in Asia, 234 (3.4%) in Europe and 1250 (18.1%) in the Pacific.

Just under 6% (389) of these living languages, with over one million first-language speakers each, are spoken by 94% of the world's popula-tion. The languages with the *largest* numbers of 'native' speakers are currently (Mandarin) Chinese, Spanish, English and Hindi, in that order (see also Skutnabb-Kangas *et al.*, 2003). It is the demographically *small* languages that are endangered. Currently, 1824 languages have between 10,000 and 99,999 speakers, 2014 have between 1000 and 9999 speakers, 1038 have between 100 and 999 speakers, and 133 have fewer than 10 speakers. Data are lacking for 277 languages (see Table IB3.1). Thus, almost half of the world's languages have fewer than 10,000 speakers. All Saami languages except North Saami are in this category, whereas the major languages that surround the Saami (Finnish, Norwegian, Russian and Swedish) are among the 132 largest languages of the world.

Table IB3.1 Distribution of languages by number of first-language speakers

Population range	Living languages			Number of speakers		
	Count	%	Cumulative	Count	%	Cumulative
100,000,000–999,999,999	8	0.1	0.1%	2,308,548,848	38.73721	38.73721%
10,000,000–99,999,999	77	1.1	1.2%	2,346,900,757	39.38076	78.11797%
1,000,000–9,999,999	304	4.4	5.6%	951,916,458	15.97306	94.09103%
100,000–999,999	895	13.0	18.6%	283,116,716	4.75067	98.84170%
10,000–99,999	1824	26.4	45.0%	60,780,797	1.01990	99.86160%
1000–9999	2014	29.2	74.1%	7,773,810	0.13044	99.99204%
100–999	1038	15.0	89.2%	461,250	0.00774	99.99978%
10–99	339	4.9	94.1%	12,560	0.00021	99.99999%
1–9	133	1.9	96.0%	521	0.00001	100.00000%
Unknown	277	4.0	100.0%			
Totals	6909	100.0		5,959,511,717	100.00000	

http://www.ethnologue.com/ethno_docs/distribution.asp?by = size.

Discussion and concern about the situation of the world's languages and their endangerment began among linguists in the journal *Language* in 1992, with Michael Krauss' article 'The world's languages in crisis'. He has continued the discussion (e.g. Krauss, 1996, 1997, 1998; Krauss *et al.*, 2004). This has resulted in many reports and actions by UNESCO to raise awareness (see Info Box 2 Language Endangerment), the founding of many organisations working to counteract language endangerment, and a number of research books and articles. There have also been opposing voices (mainly representing speakers of numerically large languages, e.g. English) claiming that it might be better for the world to have fewer languages and that nothing is lost by losing languages, or that, at least, it is inevitable even if it might be regrettable. We disagree. Scientific arguments against those claims are strong (see also Info Box 6 Indigenous Views).

Info Box 4 Linguistic and Cultural Genocide in Education

Can the education of Indigenous/tribal/minority/minoritised (ITM) children, historically and to a large extent also today, be seen as genocide if it is conducted through the medium of a dominant language in submersion (sink-or-swim) programmes, i.e. in a subtractive way where (some of) the teaching language is learned at the cost of the children's mother tongue? (See Skutnabb-Kangas & McCarty, 2008 for definitions).

The United Nations International Convention on the Prevention and Punishment of the Crime of Genocide (E793, 1948; http://www.hrweb.org/legal/genocide.html) has five definitions of genocide in its Article 2:

In the present Convention, genocide means any of the following acts committed with *intent to destroy*, in whole or in part, a national, ethnical, racial or religious group, as such:

(a) Killing members of the group;
(b) *Causing serious bodily or mental harm to members of the group;*
(c) Deliberately inflicting on the group conditions of life calculated to bring about its physical destruction in whole or in part;
(d) Imposing measures intended to prevent births within the group;
(e) *Forcibly transferring children of the group to another group* (emphases added).

All of the negative consequences of subtractive education, both practical and research based, are and have been well known for a long time, not only by the ITMs themselves but also by researchers, governments, NGOs, churches and international organisations. This is not new knowledge (as we show in Skutnabb-Kangas & Dunbar, 2010, the main source for this Info Box). Some of the main causes of educational failure in multilingual societies were correctly diagnosed centuries ago as linked to submersion in dominant languages. There are many indications that Indigenous peoples themselves knew this very early on. For instance, Handsome Lake, a Seneca from the USA born in 1735, knew the devastating results of submersion programmes, as quoted in Thomas (1994):

[Handsome Lake] 'created a code to strengthen his people against the effects of white society. The code helped to unify the Iroquoian community'. Chief Jacob Thomas's (1994) *Teachings from the Longhouse* contains 'The Code of Handsome Lake' ('The Good Message'). 'We feel that the white race will take away the culture, traditions, and language of the red race. *When your people's children become educated in the way of white people, they will no longer speak their own language and will not understand their own culture.* Your people will suffer great misery and not be able to understand their elders anymore. ... We feel that when they become educated, not a single child will come back and stand at your side because they will no longer speak your language or have any knowledge of their culture. ... Two children were selected from each tribe to receive the white race's education. The chiefs at the time believed that this education might benefit the native people. ... By following the Good Message, *the chiefs discovered that the education received from the white race robbed their children of their language and culture.* They realized the importance of educating their own children'. (Handsome Lake, in Thomas, 1994; emphases added)

Churches and educational authorities also knew that subtractive education was cruel and inhuman and had negative consequences (see, for example, Milloy, 1999 regarding Canada; there are many descriptions and references from the Nordic countries in, for example, Skutnabb-Kangas & Phillipson, 1989). The following describes attitudes in Canada according to Milloy:

In Canada, 'for most of the school system's life, though the truth was known to it', the Department of Indian Affairs, 'after nearly a century of contrary evidence in its own files', still 'maintained the fiction of care' and 'contended that the schools were "operated for the welfare and education of Indian children"' (Milloy, 1999: xiii–xiv). These schools represented 'a system of persistent neglect and debilitating abuse', 'violent in its intention to "kill the Indian" in the child for the sake of Christian civilization' (Milloy, 1999: xiv, xv). Finally closed down in 1986, the Department and the churches were 'fully aware of the fact' that the schools 'unfitted many children, abused or not, for life in either Aboriginal or non-Aboriginal communities. The schools produced thousands of individuals incapable of leading healthy lives or contributing positively to their communities' (Milloy, 1999: xvii). (Skutnabb-Kangas & Dunbar, 2010: 66)

State and educational authorities in the USA (including churches) also had knowledge about the negative results of subtractive teaching and the positive results of mother tongue-medium teaching, at least since the end of the 1800s:

The American Board of Indian Commissioners wrote [1880: 77]: '... first teaching the children to read and write in their own language enables them to master English with more ease when they take up that study ... a child beginning a four years' course with the study of Dakota would be further advanced in English at the end of the term than one who had not been instructed in Dakota. ... it is true that by beginning in the Indian tongue and then putting the students into English studies our missionaries say that after three or four years their English is better than it would have been if they had begun entirely with English.' (quoted from Francis & Reyhner, 2002: 45–6, 77, 98)

Colonial educational authorities (including churches) also had this knowledge, and some even suggested remedies consistent with today's research; however, these were not followed. A government resolution was formulated in (colonial British) India in 1904 when Lord Curzon was the Viceroy (Governor General). This resolution expressed serious dissatisfaction with the organisation of education in India, and blamed Macaulay for the neglect of Indian languages (see Phillipson, 1992b, 2009, 2012a, 2012b for background). The extract below shows its present-day relevance, and suggests that postcolonial education and most ITM education has failed to learn from earlier experience.

It is equally important that when the teaching of English has begun, it should not be prematurely employed as the medium of instruction in other subjects. Much of the practice, too prevalent in Indian schools, of committing to memory ill-understood phrases and extracts from text-books or notes, may be traced to the scholars' having received instruction through the medium of English before their knowledge of the language was sufficient for them to understand what they were taught. As a general rule the child should not be allowed to learn English as a language [i.e. as a subject] until he has made some progress in the primary stages of instruction and has received a thorough grounding in his mother-tongue. [...] The line of division between the use of the vernacular and of English as a medium of instruction should, broadly speaking, be drawn at a minimum age of 13. (Curzon, quoted from Evans, 2002: 277)

It is very clear that subtractive education through the medium of a dominant language at the cost of ITM mother tongues has 'caused serious mental harm' to children, and often also physical harm, for instance in boarding schools (e.g. Dunbar & Skutnabb-Kangas, 2008; Magga & Skutnabb-Kangas, 2001, 2003; Magga *et al.*, 2005). This form of education has also tried and often succeeded in 'transferring children of the group to another group', and this has happened forcibly, because the children did not have any alternative (e.g. mother tongue-medium education). Even when UNESCO's 1953 publication *The Use of the Vernacular Languages in Education* included firm recommendations, written by experts, on how multilingual education(MLE) could best be organised, these recommendations were not often followed. Similar informed consultations went into drafting UNESCO's education position paper in 2003, 'Education in a multilingual world'. There is very strong research evidence, and agreement among solid researchers, on how ITM education should be organised, and this has been clear among researchers at least since the 1970s (see, for example, Collier, 1989, all references to Cummins; Hornberger, 1996, 1998, 2003, 2006; May, 1999; Panda, 2012; Skutnabb-Kangas & Toukomaa, 1976; Thomas & Collier, 2002; Toukomaa & Skutnabb-Kangas, 1977). The remaining (fewer and fewer) counterarguments against strong models of mother tongue-based MLE are political/ideological, not scientific.

What about the requirement of 'intent' in Article 2 of the Genocide Convention? For obvious reasons, no state or educational authority today can be expected to *openly* express an intention to 'destroy' a group or even to 'seriously harm' it, even if some politicians in strongly assimilationist countries such as Denmark (see Example 20 in Skutnabb-Kangas & Dunbar, 2010) express what can be seen as a wish to forcibly 'transfer its members to another group'. However, the intention can be inferred in other ways, by analysing those structural and ideological factors and those practices which cause the destruction, harm or transfer. Skutnabb-Kangas and Dunbar (2010) have done this in several ways, comparing current situations with older, more overt ways of forced assimilation (which often used more 'sticks' and/ or 'carrots', in addition to 'ideas', than present-day more covert and structural methods). We can thus claim that, if state school authorities continue to pursue an educational policy which uses a dominant language as the main medium of education for ITM children, even though the negative results of this policy have long been known both through earlier concrete empirical feedback (as shown in the examples above from Canada, the USA and India) and through solid theoretical and empirical research evidence (as they have, at least since the early 1950s; see, for example, UNESCO, 1953), this refusal to change the policies constitutes, *from discourse-analytical, sociolinguistic, sociological, psychological, political science, and educational policy analysis perspectives*, strong evidence for an 'intention' as required in Article 2 above.

Structural and ideological factors have appeared also in some lawyers' interpretations of, for instance, the concept of discrimination in education (see Gynther, 2003 for a short summary of the development from more sociologically oriented discussions from Myrdal, via Carmichael & Hamilton, Knowles & Prewitt, Feagin & Feagin, Hill, Okin & Bacchi, as well as more legally oriented clarifications, mainly from the USA and Canada; see also Gynther, 2007). Gynther pleads for cooperation between lawyers, sociologists and educationists and for a broadened analytical framework in clarifying some of the basic concepts which are used when subjugated minorities are denied access to education. She traces a trend in academic discourses:

> from a concern with 'evil motive discrimination' (actions *intended* to have a harmful effect on minority group members) to 'effects' discrimination (actions have a harmful effect whatever their motivation) (Gynther, 2003: 48; emphasis added). However, she also points to 'a trend from the deconstructive social criticism of the 1960s and 1970s to a watering down of the conceptual framework of systemic discrimination towards the 1990s' (Gynther, 2003: 48). When discrimination and racism [including linguicism] 'permeates society not only at the individual but also at the institutional level, covertly and overtly ... racial control has become so

well institutionalized that the individual generally does not have to exercise a choice to operate in a racist manner. Individuals merely have to conform to the operating norms of the organization, and *the institution will do the discrimination for them.*' (Gynther, 2003: 47; emphasis added)

The Minority Ombud in Finland, Johanna Suurpää, states that Saami children's access to services through the medium of Saami, especially in daycare, is vital for the maintenance of Saami languages and culture (Suurpää, 2010: 115). In deciding whether children get the services that Finnish laws grant them (see Aikio-Puoskari, 2005, 2009; Aikio-Puoskari & Pentikäinen, 2001; Koivurova, 2010, 2011; Kokko, 2010, for some of these), she emphasises the relevance of structural discrimination. Suurpää (2010) relates several cases where decisions by the Commission on Discrimination have stated that Saami children have been discriminated against on the basis of their ethnicity because relevant Saami-medium daycare has not been made available. Reasons such as non-availability of Saami-speaking staff or municipal lack of financial resources are not acceptable in a legal discourse – the laws on children's rights to mother tongue-medium daycare have to be respected (Suurpää, 2010: 116). Thus even if the intention of the relevant municipalities has not been discriminatory, the structural organisation of the services has resulted in discrimination. These decisions will go to higher courts (Suurpää, 2010: 115). The same kind of reasoning needs to be tried in court in relation to the interpretation of 'intent' in the Genocide Convention.

Past genocide in education is the main reason why revitalisation and regenesis of languages are needed. Today in addition to education the public media also play an important role in killing ITM languages, as well as in reviving them. This is why CASLE was/is needed – the non-existence of working-age adult generations of AS is one reflection of this earlier linguistic and cultural genocide.

Info Box 5 Ethnic Identity and Language

Are there any Aanaar Saami? Is there an AS language? Is there a relationship between the Indigenous people (the ethnic group AS) and the AS language? Some research and debates that might highlight this kind of question are summarised in this Info Box.

Ethnicity has been proclaimed dead many times during the last and even the present century, especially after World War II. *Liberal researchers* have claimed that ethnic identity was a traditional, romantic characteristic, which would disappear with modernisation, urbanisation and global mobility, to be replaced by other loyalties and identities: professional, social, gender, interest-group, state-related, global, and so on. *Marxist researchers* claimed that class-related solidarities, crossing national borders, would replace ethnicity: an international proletariat would unite against world capitalism.

Many *postmodern researchers* now pronounce that we have (should have?) no lasting identities, only flexible temporary nomadic hybrid ones. In the same vein, some of them present claims about the relationship between forms and functions of language. They end up claiming that the 'object' of linguistic human rights, namely specific 'languages', do not exist as countable entities either, and thus neither do mother tongues.

Firstly some postmodernist claims are presented in some detail here; then some of them are countered.

All languages are changing all the time; therefore it is inevitable that efforts to demarcate the boundaries of a particular language are only able at best to provide a snapshot of the language at a particular time and place (Reagan, 2004: 44). A language is 'ultimately collections of idiolects [what individual speakers say] which have been determined to belong together for what are ultimately non- and extra-linguistic reasons' (Reagan, 2004: 46). A thorough recent argumentation about the non-existence of languages as objects of study, as countable nominal entities, is in Sinfree Makoni and Alastair Pennycook's, 2005 article 'Disinventing and (re)constituting languages', and in their 2007 edited book (see also Phillipson & Skutnabb-Kangas, 2012, an invited Commentary to a later Makoni article). They seem to overgeneralise to the whole world the fact that many 'languages' were in fact invented in Africa by missionaries from competing Christian groups, and also by European states dividing Africa between themselves in 1878–1890. At this time many dialects of the same languages started to be called 'languages' and the differences were exaggerated by missionaries; when the same language, spoken over a large area, was divided by Europeans into several 'states', speakers were also often told that they spoke different 'languages' (see, for example, Alexander, 1992). But claiming that most languages in the world were inventions of missionaries does not correspond to most realities outside the African continent.

Language names such as English, Swahili or Chinese belong, according to Jan Blommaert, 'to the realm of folk ideologies', and 'only every now and then are they salient as objects of sociolinguistic inquiry' (Blommaert, 2005: 390). Thus we who talk about languages or mother tongues are claimed to be reifying (i.e. making something abstract more concrete or real) something that by its nature is always changing and multifaceted.

We are also accused of romanticising the importance of languages and especially mother tongues and their importance for ITMs and their identities. Some postmodernists, especially political scientists, claim that language is not an important or even necessary feature in the construction of individual or collective identities (e.g. May, 2005; Patten & Kymlicka, 2003; but see also May, 2003, 2010, 2012 for some counterarguments). The existence of multiple linguistic identities and hybridity shows, according to them, that there is no link between language and identity. If there were a strong link, there would be no or little language shift. Stephen May summarises his own (older) views, referring to several other researchers and claims that there is

> ... widespread consensus in social and political theory, and increasingly in sociolinguistics and critical applied linguistics, that language is at most a contingent factor of one's identity. In other words, language does not define us, and may not be an important feature, or indeed even a necessary one, in the construction of our identities, whether at the individual or collective levels. (May, 2005: 327, referring to Bentahila & Davies, 1993; Coulmas, 1991; Eastman, 1984; J. Edwards, 1985, 1994; but see also May's classic 2001 book with different views, and his 2003, 2010, 2012)

The consequence of such a view is obvious. If language use were merely a surface feature of ethnic identity, adopting another language would only affect the language *use* aspect of our ethnic identity, not the identity itself. Thus the loss of a particular language is not the 'end of the world' for a particular ethnic identity – the latter simply adapts to the new language.

> ... there is no need to worry about preserving ethnic identity, so long as the only change being made is in what language we use. (Eastman, 1984: 275)

The fact that many people have more than one mother tongue is also seen as proof for the thesis that there is no link between language and identity. Hybrid people can have no roots, ethnically or linguistically. Rootedness is seen as essentialism.

How can these claims be countered? Firstly we can consider identities. *Of course* all of us have multiple identities. We may identify at the same time as, say, woman, socialist, ecological farmer, world citizen, mother, daughter, wife, researcher, Finnish, Scandinavian, European, witch, theosophist, and lover of music and plants. This can be done without these identities necessarily being in conflict with one another. Some identities will be more or less salient, focussed upon or emphasised than others at different times. New identities will emerge or be added, with others fading or being rejected over time.

Still, ethnic identities and in particular linguistically anchored ethnic identities seem to be remarkably resilient, as the literally tens of thousands of 'ethnic' organisations all over the world show. Lists of them? A Google search undertaken on 21 March 2012 on *ethnic organisations* gave over 84 million hits (up from four million around the same time in 2009) – a good starting point. Jim Cummins, who during the last two decades has also worked with students' 'identity investment' in schools, writes about

> the centrality of *identity enhancement* as a driving force fueling students' investment in learning ... unique minority languages [which] have little functional utility beyond their immediate territorial zone and are seldom even required within that zone because virtually everyone is fluent in the dominant language. [...] [He goes on to describe this enhancement of aspects of their identity as generating] the expanded sense of belonging that derives from linking one's identity to the community of speakers of the language. For those whose ethnic or national origin corresponds to the language, fluency solidifies the bond to previous generations and links the individual's emerging personal narrative to the collective history of the ethnic or national group. (Cummins, 2008: 1)

Most Indigenous and tribal languages are 'unique minority languages' in the sense described by Cummins; this concept comes from Cenoz and Gorter (2008). Both ethnicity and an attachment to one's language or mother tongue(s) as a central cultural core value (Smolicz, 1979, 1981) seem to draw on primordial, ascribed sources: you are 'born' into a specific ethnic group and this decides what your mother tongue (or mother tongues, if you have more than one, for instance growing up with parents/caretakers speaking different languages) will *initially* be. But what happens *later* to your ethnicity, your identity, and your language(s), and how they are shaped and actualised, is influenced by (achieved) economic/political concerns, by social circumstances and by later life. *Ethnicity, identity and mother tongues thus draw on primordial sources but are shaped by societal forces.*

These societal forces also influence the extent to which you are aware of the importance of your ethnicity and your mother tongue(s) and the connection between them. Often native speakers of dominant languages are not aware of this connection – they have not needed to be: their languages have never been threatened.

We do not agree with those researchers who see both ethnicity and mother tongues in an instrumentalist way as something you can choose to have or not have, to use or not use, according to your own whims and wishes. Because of the primordial sources reaching back into infancy and your personal history, neither ethnicity nor mother tongues, nor even identities can be treated as things, commodities, which you can choose at will or chuck out like an old coat. This book also testifies to this. Joshua Fishman's book, *In Praise of the Beloved Language. A Comparative View of Positive Ethnolinguistic Consciousness* (1997), is a collection of examples of the importance of the mother tongues to their speakers from all over the world. Human rights lawyers Mancini and de Witte (2008: 247) represent an opposite view to May's claim above (May, 2005: 327), saying '[L]anguage is at most a contingent factor of one's identity ... [It] is generally accepted that the use of a particular language not only serves as a means of functional communication, but also expresses that person's cultural identity as well as the cultural heritage developed by all previous speakers of that language'.

On the other hand, this does *not* mean that languages are unchangeable givens or impossible to influence or change. If languages are mainly studied as something that is being performed every minute, not as something that has been written down in grammar books and other texts to freeze as a snapshot (and in our view languages can be legitimately studied in *both* ways), we can compare ITM languages with what some Indigenous peoples' representatives say about change and Traditional Knowledge. This knowledge is in no way static either, as the Four Directions Council in Canada (1996, quoted from Posey, 1999: 4) describe it:

What is 'traditional' about traditional knowledge is not its antiquity, but *the way it is acquired and used*. In other words, the social process of learning and sharing knowledge, which is unique to each indigenous culture, lies at the very heart of its 'traditionality'. *Much of this knowledge is actually quite new,* but it has a social meaning, and legal character, entirely unlike the knowledge indigenous people acquire from settlers and industrialized societies. (Posey, 1999: 4, emphases added)

If those who are guardians of Traditional Knowledge still call it 'traditional', even if they know and accept that the 'body' of that knowledge is in constant flux in several ways, then it should be possible to see change as an *inherent* and necessary characteristic not only of knowledge or of languages but of everything living. And knowledge and languages are indeed 'living' in this sense, not any kind of static museal objects. Thus constant change (for instance taking in new technical vocabulary from other languages) does not in any way make the existence of 'a language' less real. Languages can be named. 'Mother tongues' are also 'languages' in this sense to those who claim them (regardless of whether they or others call them languages or dialects or variants or varieties). They have an existence. Mother tongues can thus be named too. As the ITM voices in thousands of books show, languages and mother tongues are not only 'real' for them; ITM views contradict strongly with views such as those seen by May as representing a 'widespread consensus in social and political theory, and increasingly in sociolinguistics and critical applied linguistics', views that claim that 'language does not define us, and may not be an important feature, or indeed even a necessary one, in the construction of our identities, whether at the individual or collective levels' (May, 2005: 327). As Jaffe (2011: 221–222) puts it:

Even though we can analytically deconstruct foundational myths and ideologies related to languages and identities as bounded, isomorphic entities, it does not mean that these ways of conceptualizing language are not meaningful to people as they go about constructing a minority identity in the contemporary world. It is also the case that these concepts of language are very widespread, and structure national and international language policy in ways that are consequential for minority and Indigenous language movements. In short, essentialism can be 'strategic' to the extent that it establishes sociolinguistic legitimacy, often a prerequisite for the mobilization of local or extralocal resources (material or attitudinal).

Further, as Skutnabb-Kangas and Heugh point out (2012):

We need to contextualise contemporary debates about the term 'mother tongue'. The extensive literature variously suggest that the term is reductionist, anachronistic, sexist, essentialist, obsolete, etc. These debates are mostly confined to philosophical lexical discussions amongst linguists and sociolinguists rather than the communities who use the term, not in a literal and necessarily monolingual sense, but in a figurative and often multilingual sense. Whether one is in a village in India or Nepal; in a small town in Tanzania, Malawi, Senegal, Cameroon, Mozambique or Eritrea; in the Republic of Mari-El in the Russian Federation; or in Northern China or Sri Lanka, ordinary people use the term 'mother tongue' in its broad figurative sense. Sometimes it is meant in a singular form, sometimes in relation to several varieties or a continuum. As Pattanayak (1992) puts it: 'Places are not geographical concepts; they exist in people's consciousness. So does the concept of "mother tongue". It is not a language in the general sense of the word, neither is it a dialect. It is an identity signifier waiting to be explained'. (Skutnabb-Kangas & Heugh, 2012: 14)

What is important to study, then, is not whether ethnic identities and languages 'exist', but under which circumstances ethnicities and languages of ITMs can become positive forces and strengths, sources of empowerment in people's lives.

But as usual in other matters important for Indigenous and Tribal peoples, their voices have been more or less completely absent in the debates (or, if they have been quoted, they have been ridiculed, not respected). They have had no right themselves to decide whether they have a named mother tongue or mother tongues; this has often been exo-defined, decided for them by researchers, bureaucrats or politicians. Often decisions and debates of the kind just referred to have been used not to promote ITM languages but to be complicit in or even actively support their destruction (see Skutnabb-Kangas, 2009). We fully agree with the Māori scholar Linda Tuhiwai Smith (2004) in her excellent discussion of the concepts of 'authenticity', 'essentialism' and 'spirituality', where she delineates Indigenous interpretations of these concepts and also posits them as strategic tools in the struggle for decolonisation of the mind. What she says about postcolonialism may apply with equal force to the postmodern discourses we have hinted at:

There is also, amongst indigenous academics, the sneaking suspicion that the fashion of post-colonialism has become a strategy for reinscribing or reauthorizing the privileges of non-indigenous academics because the field of 'post-colonial' discourse has been defined in ways which can still leave out indigenous peoples, our ways of knowing and our current concerns. (Tuhiwai Smith, 2004: 24)

Joris Luyendijk (2012), in his article 'Just doing their jobs. The world bankers inhabit has no sense of national solidarity', describes the new global elites whose solidarity 'is not geography-based or tied up with a state'. He continues:

This is where the left seems lost. It insists on solidarity across the nation, with higher tax rates for rich people to help their less fortunate countrymen. But this solidarity is predicated on a sense of national belonging, to which the left is allergic; national identity comes with chauvinism and nationalism, and creepy rightwing supremacists. *It's quite ironic how postmodernists and many contemporary social thinkers on the left will tell you that all sense of belonging is a construct, tradition is invented and nations are simply fantasies or imagined communities. Well, the global financial elite agrees.* (Luyendijk, 2012: 24, emphasis added)

The postmodernist deconstruction of both ethnicity and languages and the relationships between them thus seems to support the neoliberal global corporate agenda.

What is the relationship of the above to discussions about Saami languages? The official definitions of a Saami have mostly had a language component: either you yourself or one of your parents or grandparents must have had Saami as their first language. 'First language' can here be equated with 'mother tongue'. There are many Saami who define themselves as Saami but who do not know the ancestral mother tongue. Still, many of them see themselves as Saami – and this includes many of the Aanaar Saami. But if we define a mother tongue as in Info Box 9 Mother Tongue Definitions, AS can be their mother tongue even if they do not know it, provided they identify it as their mother tongue. This means that others with no Saami ancestry might be able to become members of the community linguistically and culturally, even if not legally, provided that they learn the language. Daniele Conversi (2012; see also Conversi, 1990, 1997) thinks that it is good to distinguish between ethnicity and culture (including language). In the context of Catalunya, according to him,

in principle membership in the moral community takes place voluntarily through the active practice of speaking Catalan, rather than depending on putative common descent. ... A thriving shared culture can provide a tool to avoid an excessive reliance on ethnicity, particularly when immigrants are willing or likely to learn, and integrate into, the regional culture. This can take place through language acquisition where language acts as a core value, or other cultural elements. (Conversi, 2012: 65)

Thus it is possible to see language as a core value, and a group as a tight-knit community, without needing to agree with the postmodern deconstructivism's negative aspects. People can belong to a group on the basis of language alone, ethnicity alone, or a combination. This position might also enable a people to maintain their language and culture without needing to exclude others.

Info Box 6 Indigenous Views

Here we give the reader a few examples of Indigenous (and a few other) individual and collective views on the importance of their languages. This Info Box could have filled the whole book.

Actions necessary to save the First Nation's languages from extinction

Our languages were given to us by the Creator and as such, they hold deep spiritual meaning describing our responsibilities and connecting us to all of creation.

(a) The right to educate our children in our languages is inalienable and an inherent Aboriginal and Treaty right.
(b) The denial of this right violates a growing body of international human rights standards and instruments, including the UN Convention on the Rights of the Child and the UN Declaration on the Rights of Indigenous Peoples.
(c) Our languages are integral to our civilizations, and the maintenance and revitalization of these languages are essential to the survival of First Nations as distinct societies in Canada.
(d) UNESCO reported in 1996 that the Indigenous languages of Canada were among the most endangered languages in the world,

and a state of emergency was declared in 1998 by the Assembly of First Nations regarding the drastic decline of Indigenous languages in Canada.

(e) This dire state of our languages is the direct consequence of deliberate state policies that were designed to eradicate our languages, most notoriously through residential schooling.

(f) The Federal Government's apology for residential schools has done nothing to bring restitution for the linguistic and cultural destruction wrought by these schools and the teaching of our Indigenous languages in core programs in schools have failed to produce new speakers.

(g) Immersion education is now recognized not only as the most effective means of creating new speakers, but also, for improving educational outcomes and increasing educational success rates that are key to building strong and thriving communities and to the full realization of self-determination.

(h) Legislation recognizing the importance of respecting and promoting Indigenous languages (as in Manitoba, the Yukon, and NWT) is important, but virtually useless without financial resources to support education in Indigenous languages.

(i) There is an urgent need for leadership and action to promote and protect Indigenous languages from extinction.

(From Draft Resolution 18/2010, AFN Special Chiefs Assembly, December 14–16, Gatineau, Quebec, Canada)

From National Congress of American Indians

Language encompasses and expresses a worldview shaped by centuries, in some cases tens of thousands of years, of experience, knowledge, practices, spiritual beliefs, and relationships between a people, its neighbors, and its environment, which cannot be replicated in any other tongue.

The survival of American Indian and Alaska Native languages is essential to the success of tribal communities and Native ways of life. However, without urgent and sustained intervention, far too many Native languages risk extinction within the coming decades.

NCAI is committed to ensuring that tribes have the tools and resources necessary to revitalize and sustain their Native languages for current and future generations.

(http://www.ncai.org/policy-issues/community-and-culture/
language, accessed 10 May 2012)

From a Recommendation by the United Nations Permanent Forum on Indigenous Issues, Session 7

The Permanent Forum calls on States to immediately support indigenous peoples' language revitalization efforts. This includes supporting the master apprentice programmes and assessment of language status, and the creation of increased links between formal schools and the family so that there is a continuous use of indigenous languages.

(http://esa.un.org/dspdEsa/unpfiidata/UNPFII_
Recommendations_Database_fulltext.asp?picfield=Full+Text&where=
+%5BUNPFII+Recommendations+Database%5D.%5BID%5D=1325,
accessed 10 May 2012)

Poems

(from Skutnabb-Kangas, 2000: 103–104)
The voice of the land is in our language.
(National First Nations Elders/Language Gathering, Mi'gmaq Nation, Canada)

It is easier to divest a nation of all its guns than it is to rob it of its language. Machine-guns will fall silent sooner than the loquacious mouths that raise so very different words up to the sky.
(Kosztolányi, 1987: 27)

It was not by chance that in Germany, the murderers in power were burning books (before burning in crematoriums the corpses of millions of victims). It was not by chance that the Francoists in Spain shot to death Lorca, who was poetry itself.
(Clancier, 1996: 28)

This tongue of mine I use to appreciate taste;
how can one taste with someone else's tongue?
(From a Wolof poem by Useyno Gey Cosaan; quoted in Fishman, 1997: 292)

What is thy sentence, then, but speechless death,

Which robs my tongue from breathing native breath?
(From William Shakespeare, *Richard II* 1.3; Mowbray when sentenced
to banishment from his country and language)

Remember what is good:
Your language.
Your tradition.
Your family, All the relations of the World.
We are not by ourselves,
We are in Unison, Watch …
(From a poem by Damon Clarke, Hualapai; quoted in Cantoni, 1996: 95)

Tzvetan Todorov, a neighbour from Paris, published a now-famous
book entitled 'Nous et les autres'. But 'Nous et nous', who will be writing this more complicated book?
The rest – as a classic says – is literature.
(Prelipceanu, 1996: 45)

In my warm, mild mother tongue foreign words intertwine.
Become a memory you trampled earth
where my tent stood and I played.
The sound of the bells hanging around the necks of my Father's
reindeer
has remained in the bottom of my soul.
Grown into my retina is our reindeer mark.
Everything I felt is part of my heart.
Remain in my memory; Father's staff,
lasso of sinew, loop in the edge of the sleigh,
the round-up and moving of the deer, the sled with the fare
Down by the river is the half load waiting for the baby.
Still moving up the valley,
remember the slender bow above the neck of the pack reindeer
Hold on to the land you inherited with all your heart!

But the right to the land, you have lost.
(Poem by Paulus Utsi; quoted in Marainen, 1988: 185; see also other
poems by Utsi in English in Gaski, 1997b)

The Nauruan language is the body into which in the past and present
have already been encoded.
(Barker, 2012: 31)

Yolnju language is our Power, our Foundation, our Root and everything that holds us together. Yolnju language gives us strength, language is our identity, who we are. Yolnju language gives us pride. Language is our Law and Justice. The importance of teaching our Indigenous language is to keep it alive and to nurture it, to preserve and to sustain our language.
(Indigenous teacher Yalmay Yunupingu, 2009; quoted in Ober & Bell, 2012: 68)

Ko te reo Māori te ha o te Māoritanga [*Māori* language gives meaning and life to being *Māori*].
(*Māori* proverbial saying; quoted in Smith & Rapatahana, 2012: 80)

The fluent use and knowledge of the *Māori* language is fundamentally essential to the preservation and vitality of *Māori* cultural knowledge systems. The language underpins the culture and helps to define it. The worldview and cosmology embedded in the language provide insights into aspects of *Māori* culture that are unique to the *tangata whenua* of this land. Arguably, the *Māori* language is the only appropriate means of transmitting *Māori* cultural knowledge.
(Williams, 2001: 124; quoted in Smith & Rapatahana, 2012: 83)

An oft-cited link between language and identity among Bruneians: '*Bahasa jiwa Bangsa*', literally 'Language is the soul of the people'.
(Quoted in Haji-Othman, 2012: 183)

Info Box 7 Language Nests

Language nests in their classical form are early childhood daycare/nursery/pre-school/kindergarten/crèche arrangements for children from birth to school age. They are used by Indigenous peoples to revive or revitalise their languages, cultures and values. They are based on total immersion in the community language, meaning that only the Indigenous language is spoken. Fluent elders support the staff, who are not necessarily highly proficient in the language; many of them are second-language speakers. Language nests can also be used (and are being used, e.g. in Catalunya and elsewhere) for non-Indigenous children who are later going to attend immersion programmes.

The concept of the language nest was developed by the Māori in Aotearoa/New Zealand. The background factors there were similar to Indigenous people's situations in many parts of the world; therefore a short summary is presented here.

When Europeans first went ashore on Aotearoa in the 18th century there were 220,000–250,000 Māori (Macdonald, 1985: 4). In 1840 the Europeans comprised less than 1% of the population. Twenty years later, the European and Māori populations were more or less equal. By 1896 the Māori population of New Zealand had declined from well over 100,000 people to 42,100. It seemed that the Māori would be completely eliminated due to genocide (Waitangi Tribunal, 1986: 12).

However, due to factors including improved health care, the Māori population started to increase again at the beginning of the 20th century. By 1981 the population had increased to 385,000 (Waitangi Tribunal, 1986: 13). In the 1991 census 10 years later, 12.9% of the population identified as Māori (Benton, 1996: 64); in the latest census taken in 2006, 14.6% (or 565,329 people) did so. The next census will be in March 2013.[1]

Despite the growing numbers of people identifying themselves as Māori, the Māori language has continued to decline. Earlier forms of education played a decisive part in this, including the practice of using corporal punishment when children spoke Māori, even in the playground (Benton, 1979, 1981; Waitangi Tribunal, 1986: 13). While in 1913 90% of Māori school children could speak Māori, by 1953 the figure had dropped to 26%, and by 1975 it was less than 5% (Waitangi Tribunal, 1986: 15). At that point most of the proficient speakers were elders. The survival of Māori was seen to depend on the existence of isolated rural communities and traditional villages, but according to Dr Richard Benton's testimony (Waitangi Tribunal, 1986: 16–17; see also Benton, 1986, 1996) it was 'apparent that the expectation that the language would survive because of those villages [was] not realistic'. Something else had to be done.

The shock of this realisation resulted in the creation of language nests. The first 50 Kōhanga Reo or language nests started up in December 1982. They used the Māori language as the teaching and learning medium, building on Māori culture. Elders were teaching both language and culture to staff and parents, who in most cases were L2 speakers. By March 1988 the number of nests had increased to 521, reaching 15% of Māori children under five. In 1993 there were 809 of these nests with 14,514 students (Benton, 1996: 79). Since then the numbers have declined (see Smith & Rapatahana, 2012 for an analysis).

As of July 2011, there were 463 language nests, 80–100% Māori-medium, with 9370 children (http://www.educationcounts.govt.nz/statistics/ece/66557); however, there are also other early childhood services with 12–80% Māori-medium instruction. It is estimated (King, 2001: 125) that children have become thoroughly bilingual in Māori and English, because of Kōhanga Reo; however, their individual language skills are strongly influenced by the time they spend in the language nest as well as by other exposure to Māori in the environment and beyond the early childhood level.

Today the language nests are funded by the state through the Te Kōhanga Reo National Trust; the amount given to each depends on the number and age of the children attending. Most nests also charge monthly fees to cover staff salaries and other costs, but these are usually lower than in other crèches. The smallest Māori language nests offer daycare for five children; the largest contain around 60. Each nest has a steering group consisting of teachers, parents, local elder language speakers and other language community members (King, 2001: 119, 121–124).

The language nest concept has since spread to many Indigenous peoples. There are language nests in other Pacific languages, e.g. in Fijian, Rarotongan, Samoan and Tongan. The concept has also been adopted by the Saami, following similar principles. Hawai'i started their Pūnana Leo nests only a few years after the Māori, and have developed them as a part of a comprehensive and thoroughly thought-through revitalisation plan which goes further than the plans that any other Indigenous peoples have – see Chapter 1 Introduction and Info Box 12 Advice From Revitalisation in Hawai'i.

Note

(1) http://www.stats.govt.nz/Census/2006CensusHomePage/QuickStats/quick-stats-about-a-subject/culture-and-identity/maori.aspx

Info Box 8 Immersion Programmes

Definitions of immersion programmes

There is still confusion about what is and what is not immersion. Therefore, fairly detailed definitions are needed.

Immersion programmes for dominant language speakers. Parents of linguistic majority children with a high-status mother tongue (e.g. Anglophones in Ontario, Canada) choose voluntarily to enrol their children in a programme in which instruction is conducted through the medium of a foreign/minority language. Most of the children in these classes are majority language children with the same mother tongue. Teachers in these programmes are bilingual so that children can initially use their own language and still be understood. These programmes are implemented in additive language learning contexts in which the children's mother tongue is not in danger of being replaced by the language of instruction. Although children enrolled in French immersion programmes in Canada initially represented a largely homogenous Anglophone population, increasingly, children whose mother tongue is neither English nor French are enrolling in these programs.

Immersion programmes for Indigenous peoples or minorities. Dominated-group children who have partially or completely lost their ancestral language choose voluntarily, among existing alternatives, to be instructed through the medium of the Indigenous/minority language, in classes with children with the same goal and target language, in which the teacher is bilingual so that children can initially use their dominant language, and in contexts in which that language is not in danger of being replaced by the Indigenous/minority language; an additive language learning context.

Two-way bilingual (dual language) programmes (sometimes erroneously called double or dual immersion in the US). Approximately 50% majority and 50% minority students (with the same mother tongue) choose voluntarily to be instructed by a bilingual teacher, initially mainly through a minority language (the 90%/10% model) or through both languages (the 50/50 model), with the dominant language taught as a subject (at the beginning separately to both groups, e.g. mother tongue English to native English-speakers and ESL to minority language speakers in the US).

The percentage of instruction in the dominant language increases in all 90/10 models, in some to 40%–60% by grade 6, whereas it stays the same in the 50/50 model. In cases where there is no follow-up through the medium of the minority language after grade 6 when many children move to another school, two-way models can be placed in the transitional model category when considering the child's full educational (K to 12) career. Two-way models thus combine in one classroom: a maintenance model for minorities (especially in the 90/10 model) and an immersion model for the majority, while maximizing peer-group contact in the other language for both groups. In some cases two-way immersion may include instruction in two minoritised languages (e.g. Navajo and Spanish in the US), coupled with ESL instruction for both groups. (Skutnabb-Kangas & McCarty, 2009: 6–7, 13–4)

The following short definitions are used in the United States Center for Applied Linguistics (CAL) directory:

Total immersion. Programs in which all or almost all subjects taught in the lower grades (K–2) are taught in the foreign language; instruction in English usually increases in the upper grades (3–6) to 20–50%, depending on the program.

Partial immersion. Programs in which up to 50% of subjects are taught in the foreign language; in some programs, the material taught in the foreign language is reinforced in English.

Two-way immersion. Programs that give equal emphasis to English and a non-English language and in which one- to two-thirds of the students are native speakers of the non-English language, with the remainder being native speakers of English (see CAL, 2011).

The new *Journal of Immersion and Content-Based Language Education* (edited by S. Björklund & D.J. Tedick, published by John Benjamin), to be published from 2013 onwards, uses the following definition:

Immersion programs are school-based, subject-matter driven programs that aim for academic achievement, additive bilingualism and biliteracy (multilingualism/multiliteracy) and cultural pluralism through increased intercultural competence. They incorporate high language intensity (i.e. at least 50% of subject matter instruction through the medium of the 'immersion' language).

Background, history and spread of immersion programmes

To be able to compare the principles used in and results from various types of immersion programmes, it is important to be acquainted with both the history of classical immersion and some of the new adaptations that Indigenous peoples have developed.

Immersion programmes were started by Wallace Lambert and his team at McGill University in Quebec, Canada in 1967, directly after Canada became officially bilingual in English and French. The English-speaking majority parents wanted their children to learn French well enough to be able to fulfil the job requirements of the now officially bilingual country, at the same time as they would develop their native English. Since then, hundreds of thousands of children have been through them. Some 7% of children in Canada are currently participating in immersion programmes. The results show that children in full immersion programmes develop good French competence, even if it is not in most cases fully comparable with native speakers. At the same time, their English develops at least to the same level as English speakers who are not in immersion programmes, and often somewhat higher. Initially, immersion programmes did not have formal mother-tongue literacy teaching; later this was deemed necessary, and even the results in French benefited (see Cummins, 1978, 1980a, 1980b, 1987a, 1987b, 1991, 1992, 1994a, 1994b, 1995, 2000, 2001, 2006, 2009; Cummins & Corson, 1997; Cummins & Skutnabb-Kangas, 1988; Cummins & Swain, 1986; Genesee, 1976, 1985, 1987, 1992, 1996, 2004, 2006; Genesee *et al.*, 2005, 2006; Lambert, 1975, 1977, 1978, 1984, 1987; Lambert & Taylor, 1982, 1996; Lambert & Tucker, 1972; Lindholm, 1990a, 1990b, 1991, 1992a, 1992b, 1992c, 1994; Lindholm & Aclan, 1991; Lindholm & Fairchild, 1989; Swain, 1984, 1997; Swain & Johnson, 1997; Swain & Lapkin, 1991, 2005).

In Canada there is a lively debate about whether Anglophone parents should choose for their children a 'regular' French-medium school or French immersion. There are 627 French language schools covering Kindergarten to grade 12 outside Quebec (FNCSF, 2010). According to Roger Paul, Executive Director of the *Fédération nationale des conseils scolaires francophones*, people do not quite realise that children who attend French-language schools as opposed to French immersion schools gain much more than a knowledge of French. They also develop a deeper understanding of their province's Francophone culture, while respecting their own identity (OCOL, 2011: 7 [translation]).

As already noted, immersion programmes have historically been associated with French-Canadian immersion for middle-class Anglophones (Cummins & Swain, 1986; Lambert & Tucker, 1972). The term was misleadingly appropriated by US policy makers and called 'structured immersion' to describe what are really submersion programmes, despite protests from the concept's originator (Lambert, 1984: 26–27; Skutnabb-Kangas & McCarty, 2008: 3).

Since their creation by Lambert, immersion programmes have spread from Canada to many parts of the world. In the USA in 2011, for example, there were 528 total or partial immersion programmes in 22 languages. Of these programmes, 239 (45.3%) were in Spanish, 114 in French, 71 in Mandarin, 34 in Hawaiian, 28 in Japanese, 13 in German. There were some in Indigenous/Native languages, in addition to Hawaiian: Ojiwbe (5), Diné (2), Yup'ik (2), Chinook (1), Dakota (1), Inupiaq (1) and Salish (1) (CAL, 2011). Also in the USA in October 2011 there were 398 two-way immersion programmes in 30 states, most of them (361) in Spanish/English. Other languages were Chinese (11), French (7), Korean (5), Japanese (4), German (1) (see http://www.cal.org/twi/directory/).[1] In Europe, Finland and Catalunya were the first to start immersion programmes, and there are now many, in different languages (do a Google search on immersion, Europe; there is no central information centre for them).

Immersion programmes for Indigenous peoples: The Māori as an example

The term immersion has recently taken on new meaning with programmes designed to revitalise endangered Indigenous languages (for some examples, see Bear Nicholas, 1996, 2003, 2005, 2007, 2009; Hinton, 1994, 2001, 2002; Hinton & Hale, 2001; Hinton et al., 2002; Holm, 2006; Holm & Holm, 1990, 1995; McCarty, 1997, 1998, 2002a, 2002b, 2005, 2008a, 2008b, 2009, 2011a, 2011b; McCarty & Wyman, 2009; McCarty et al., 2005, 2006a, 2006b, 2006c, 2007, 2009, 2011; Reyhner, 1995, 1996, 2008, 2010; Reyhner & Singh, 2010a, 2010b; Reyhner et al., 1999; Wilson, 1999; Wilson & Kamanā, 2001, 2009; Wilson et al., 2006). The ideological, historical, epistemological and empirical bases for these varied uses of 'immersion' are distinct, as are programme practices (Skutnabb-Kangas & McCarty, 2008: 3).

The first large-scale Indigenous immersion programmes started in Aotearoa with language nests to revitalise Māori. When the first Aotearoa language nest (Kōhanga Reo, see Info Box 7 Language nests) graduates started elementary schools in the late 1980s, the parents saw the earlier good work of the language nests – that is, children speaking everyday Māori fluently – being undermined by the English-saturated linguistic and cultural primary school environment. Māori-medium education thus started in elementary schools too. In 1993 there were a total of 74 schools (none of these secondary) with 3176 students, giving instruction 100% in Māori, and an additional 64 schools (among them six secondary schools) where 81–99% of instruction was in Māori (Benton, 1996: 81). Many Māori have wanted completely Māori-medium schools, where all subjects have been taught in Māori and English has been taught as a subject. These *kura kaupapa* Māori schools have rejected the type of bilingual education where Māori and English would have equal positions as classroom languages, and they clearly want Māori maintenance programmes (Benton, 1996, 79–80). There are thus many controversies regarding the extent to which English should be used as a medium in some subjects – or not. In 1993, only 10.3% of primary Māori students and 20% of non-Māori students did not have any Māori in their education; however, for secondary school students the corresponding figures were much higher: 50.5% and 88.6%, respectively (Benton, 1996: 80). Today (February 2012), Māori-medium education takes place in *kōhanga reo* in the early childhood sector, in other bilingual and immersion programmes in early childhood education centres, in *kura kaupapa Māori* (covering years 1–8) and *wharekura* (covering years 1–13), in immersion and bilingual programmes in mainstreams schools, and in *wānanga* in the tertiary sector (http://www.educationcounts.govt.nz/statistics/maori_education/schooling/6040, accessed 9 February 2012). In addition, Māori is taught as a subject. In July 2011, there were 20,131 students learning Te Reo Māori as a separate subject for three or more hours per week. Of these, 13,187 were Māori (http://www.educationcounts.govt.nz/statistics/maori_education/schooling/6040/mori-medium-education-as-at-1-july-2011).

Recent reports tell of a decrease in the numbers of students in Māori-medium education. Table IB8.1 shows that the decrease is mainly in those schools that have less than 50% of their teaching through the medium of Māori, whereas there is a slight increase in student numbers in programmes that use the language to a greater degree in the classroom. Knowing that students who are taught in the Māori language for 51–100% of class time are more likely to become fluent in Te Reo Māori' (Benton, 1996), and that enrolments increased by 75% at the secondary level between 2010 and 2011, this decrease does not seem threatening.

In the 1980s, the Māori Language Commission, headed by Professor Timoti Karetu, started to prepare all of New Zealand society to function bilingually. The Māori have learned that revitalisation efforts must be accompanied by an increase in the use of the Indigenous

Table IB8.1 Total number of students involved in Māori-medium education by highest level of learning

% of curriculum instruction undertaken in Māori	All students				Māori			
	2010	2011	Difference 2010–2011 No.	Difference 2010–2011 %	2010	2011	Difference 2010–2011 No.	Difference 2010–2011 %
Level 1: 81–100%	11,738	11,818	80	0.68%	11,565	11,710	145	1.25%
Level 2: 51–80%	4,587	4,729	142	3.10%	4,352	4,423	71	1.63%
Level 3: 31–50%	4,904	4,807	−97	−1.98%	4,372	4,308	−64	−1.46%
Level 4(a): 12–30%	6,303	5,640	−663	−10.52%	4,516	4,261	−255	−5.65%
Total	27,532	26,994	−538	−1.95%	24,805	24,702	−103	0.42%

Notes: Students are counted at their highest level of Māori-medium education.
Source: http://www.educationcounts.govt.nz/statistics/maori_education/schooling/6040/
   mori-medium-education-as-at-1-july-2011, accessed 9 February 2012.

language throughout society. Māori received official status in 1987 through the Māori Language Act (1987, No. 176).

Despite all these efforts, the revival of the Māori language has been slow. The Māori population is younger and has less formal education, lower incomes and worse housing and health than the rest of the New Zealand population, all concomitant to an oppressed situation. The Māori also claim that there is financial discrimination against the language nests (see, for example, http://www.nzherald.co.nz/nz/news/article.cfm?c_id = 1&objectid = 10740638). In the 2006 census, a total of 157,110 people reported being able to speak Māori (http://www.stats.govt.nz/Census/about-2006-census/2006-census-definitions-questionnaires/definitions/1.aspx#language-spoken, accessed 9 February 2012).

According to the 2006 census, 76.2% of the Māori reported speaking English only; 131,613 (23.7%) of Māori could hold a conversation about everyday things in Māori, a small increase of 1128 people since the 2001 census (http://www.stats.govt.nz/browse_for_stats/people_and_communities/maori/maori-language-week-2011.aspx). Just under half (48.7%) of Māori aged 65 and over, and more than one in six (35,148 people) aged under 15 could do this. The latest figures might be higher, but the planned Aotearoa 2011 census has been postponed until March 2013 because of the February 2011 Christchurch earthquake.

Many other Indigenous peoples have started immersion programmes in all parts of the world, and the literature about them is enormous.

The CASLE programme contains traits of all the immersion programmes defined and described above, either in its goals or in its methods (see Chapter 4).

Note

(1) For results, see references to Genesee, Lindholm and Lindholm & Leary.

Info Box 9 Mother Tongue Definitions

A starting point for definitions of mother tongues here is Skutnabb-Kangas (1984: 18):

Table IB9.1 Definitions of mother tongues

Criterion	Definition
Origin	The language one has learned first (the language in which one has established one's initial long-lasting verbal contacts).
Identification	
(a) Internal	(a) The language one identifies with as a native speaker.
(b) External	(b) The language one is identified as a native speaker of, by others.
Competence	The language one knows best.
Function	The language one uses most.

Source: Skutnabb-Kangas (1984).

The following are four theses about mother tongues:

(1) An individual can have at least two, possibly three mother tongues.
(2) A person's mother tongue can vary, depending on which definition is used.
(3) A person's mother tongue can change during her/his lifetime according to all definitions except the definition by origin. (The only exception is for the Deaf, as explained below.)
(4) Mother tongue definitions can be organised hierarchically in relation to how much they respect Linguistic Human Rights (LHRs).

For *linguistic majorities* (e.g. speakers of Nepali in Nepal, or Finnish in Finland) all of these definitions usually converge. They have learned Nepali/Finnish first, they identify with Nepali/Finnish, are identified by others as native speakers of Nepali/Finnish, know Nepali/Finnish best and use Nepali/Finnish most.

If *Indigenous/tribal peoples or linguistic minorities* live and work where the majority language dominates, the majority/dominant language mostly becomes their most used language in formal domains and even many informal ones. Therefore, from a language rights point of view, it is not fair to use the mother tongue definition based on function; people have not chosen freely to use the majority language more than their original language. In this case, the functional definition does not respect LHRs.

If linguistic minorities get their education in submersion programmes (through the medium of the majority language), the dominant language often becomes the language they know best in most formal domains. Therefore it is not fair to use the mother tongue definition based on competence.

Often a combination of mother tongue definitions by origin and by internal identification provides the best definition for linguistic minorities: the mother tongue/s is/are the language/s one has learned first and identifies with. But there are exceptions.

One exception must be made for the Deaf. It is estimated that 90–95% of Deaf children are born to hearing parents. If these children get a good education, they learn a Sign language early on, and get most of their formal education through a Sign language. In this case, the children and their parents do not have the same mother tongue. For most Deaf children the fairest mother tongue definition is: the language that they identify with. Often, at least later on in their lives, this can be used in combination with an external identification: the language that they are being identified as native speakers (=signers) of by others. For Deaf children, a Sign language is also the only language that they can express themselves fully in. They cannot do this in any spoken language, only in writing. This is also true for those Deaf children who have got cochlear implants – they do *not* become hearing children because of this, even if they can 'hear' to some extent in many situations. In this case we can add a modified definition by competence: the mother tongue is the language that they identify with and that they can express themselves fully in.

The other important exception to the combined definition of origin and internal identification as the best one is forcibly assimilated Indigenous/tribal or minority children or adults. If the forcible assimilation has happened already at the level of the parent or grand-parent generation, it is not fair to use a mother tongue definition by origin, because the parents have not spoken (or been able to speak) the mother tongue (e.g. Saami, Tharu or Maliseet) to their children. In this case a mother tongue definition by internal identification can be the only possible fair definition: the mother tongue/s is/are the language/s one identifies with.

Therefore, *a fifth thesis* must be added:

(5) It is possible to identify with a language that one does not know. It is possible to have a mother tongue in which one does not have (any or 'full') competence.

If this were to be accepted in international law (and it has not yet been tried in court), those few rights that exist regarding mother tongue-medium education and learning the mother tongue as a subject would also apply to Indigenous children in various revitalisation programmes.

There is an important conclusion in cases where forcible assimilation has led to a language being seriously endangered ('dying', 'moribund', in need of revival) or 'neglected' (endangered, in need of revitalisation). When demanding full LHRs for these individuals and collectivities, the strategy should be to use a mother tongue definition based on internal identification *only*, regardless of whether the individuals are receptive or productive users or non-users. At the same time, claims for compensation for mother tongue loss should be raised in courts.

There is a risk associated with using the identification definition on its own. If some people with no Indigenous/tribal background or family ties start claiming, e.g. for economic and/or political reasons, that an Indigenous language is their mother tongue (without knowing it or trying to learn it), this may lead to deep resentment by people who have experienced forced assimilation. This issue is really complex, and calls for sensitive discussion and analysis. Such questions have been relevant in many Saami contexts.

Info Box 10 Visions for Saami Revitalisation, Finland

This Info Box quotes extensively from *Toimenpideohjelma saamen kielen elvyttämiseksi* [Programme of action for revitalisation of the Saami languages] of the Finnish Ministry of Education and Culture, Section Education and research policy (OKM, 2012b, translation by Tove Skutnabb-Kangas and Robert Phillipson). After consultations, this programme will be revised and implemented, hopefully with strong economic resources attached.

A central observation in the programme is the link between the provision of daycare and primary education through the medium of Saami, and economic changes. The weak position of traditional Saami livelihoods has resulted in massive migration away from the Saami homeland areas:

One of the most central challenges in language revitalisation is guaranteeing sufficient Saami-medium daycare and school education and teaching of Saami as a subject. The migration of the Saami from their homeland area has reduced the environments where it is natural to use the Saami languages. Some 70% of Saami children and youth now live outside the homeland area. Rapid measures are needed to guarantee that also these children can enjoy their constitutionally guaranteed right to their own language and culture. Changes in the structure of the livelihoods, the language shift from Saami to Finnish, the weak profitability of the traditional livelihoods and the migration of the Saami away from their homeland threaten the maintenance of natural Saami language environments and the future of Saami languages. The connection between traditional Saami livelihoods, language, and traditional knowledge is weakened outside the Saami homeland. The very rich Saami terminology connected to traditional livelihoods, meaning reindeer herding, hunting, gathering, fishing and handicraft, risks falling into disuse or becoming obsolete. To revitalise and maintain the Saami languages and livelihoods-related Saami terminology it is vital to guarantee the economic profitability of Saami livelihoods and young Saami people's opportunities to practise traditional Saami occupations. The development of the administration, laws and regulations and support systems that guide Saami livelihoods is also decisive. (OKM, 2012b: 54)

The programme of action sets as its vision for 2025 that, at that point,

> there has been clear progress in the revitalisation of all three Saami languages by the year 2025. Aanaar and Skolt Saami will at that point no longer be seriously endangered languages. There are clearly more speakers than today. The Saami languages are visible and audible in the media, and they are used in a natural manner in public services. The use of the Saami languages is stimulated. Knowledge of Saami is considered an advantage and merit in many jobs. The Saami homeland functions as a centre for Saami languages and culture and its effects radiate to the whole country. Nordic cooperation supports the development of the languages and production of Saami-medium services.

When the goals in the vision have been reached (i.e. at the latest in 2025), the situation in relation to Saami language learning and revitalisation will be as follows:

- Children and young people who speak Saami as their mother tongue get day-care and education through the medium of Saami and have programmes in their own language in the media. Children and youngsters use their own language actively at home, in traditional livelihoods, with peers, in their interests/hobbies, and in school. Their parents and grandparents transfer their own languages and traditions to the children and grandchildren and receive knowledge and support in their parenting task. The Saami-speaking adult population knows how to read and write their own language.
- Speakers of Saami as a second language have developed their competence to mother tongue levels and they use the language actively at home, in their leisure activities, in school and in work. The language of children and youngsters who speak Saami as a second or foreign language is supported especially by Saami-medium nurseries, language nests and the schools.
- Permanent language revitalisation opportunities have been created for children of parents who have lost their Saami language. Saami nurseries, language nests and schools cooperate closely in supporting language learning and enabling the achievement of active bilingualism. The adult population, especially parents of school-age children, are actively revitalising their languages and supporting the language acquisition of their children.

The working group that prepared the action programme sees the following as the minimal prerequisites for this vision to be realised:

(I)   Language nest activities, which have proved to be efficient measures for revitalisation, have been stabilised and increased, and daycare is offered in accordance with the laws;

(II)   Saami education is being developed throughout the country and a system that supports Saami teaching through distance education is used throughout the country;

(III)   The educational system produces more professionals than today with more versatile Saami competence for various domains, especially to function in teaching and customer services;

(IV)   Special measures have been taken for the revitalisation of Skolt Saami, and there has been an increase in the use and study of the language;

(V)   The Saami language law works fully in the Saami homeland area, and authorities are actively promoting the use of Saami;

(VI)   Content in Saami-medium radio, TV and internet has been substantially increased;

(VII)   Saami language management, archiving and research have been developed, and research results and materials are easily available for [public] use;

(VIII) Support for Saami arts and culture has been increased;

(IX)   Cross-border cooperation supporting Saami languages and culture has stabilised and has created new strong Saami-using environments.

This action programme also presents concrete measures for the chosen priority areas. In addition there are suggestions for measures to be taken, including providing more information about bi- and multilingualism, and about activities following up on the action programme (OKM, 2012b: 55).

Info Box 11   Ann-Helén Laestadius: A Personal Example From Northern Sweden

During my whole school time I led a kind of double life. At home I was proud of my Saami family, I loved to hear the language, and *joik*, see my grandfather do handicrafts, and all the fine [Saami] clothes. But in school I denied everything that had to do with the Saami. I was afraid of being teased, or being called names, which was what many other children with Saami origins had to endure. Because my father is Swedish, I didn't have a Saami last name; therefore not many knew about my background, despite Kiruna being a small town.

The choice of not teaching Ann-Helén and her sister Saami was their mother Ellen's decision. Ellen grew up in a reindeer herder family, and while her parents took care of the reindeer herds and moved around with them in the mountains, the children had to attend a peripatetic [travelling] school.

In those times it was nasty to be a Saami; both the state and the church looked down on the Saami, and it was forbidden to speak Saami in school. If one did it, one got a beating. So, my mother wanted me to be spared the experiences that she had. There are many of us with Saami background born in the 1960s and 1970s who never learned the language.

For Ann-Helén there is great sadness involved in not being able to really speak with her maternal grandfather. Her maternal grandmother knew Swedish a bit better, so it was easier with her. As an adult, Ann-Helén has studied Saami, but she thinks it is difficult to really get started speaking it.

There is some kind of an emotional barrier that I cannot really explain, because actually I know quite a lot of words. But maybe it will be better now that William [her son, aged seven] is interested. He and my mother will get Skype so that they can talk to each other there. It is just wonderful, and it feels like one can take back something of what has been lost.

These extracts are taken from an article by Carina Nilsson (2012, translated from Swedish by Tove Skutnabb-Kangas) about Ann-Helén Laestadius, aged 40, an author with several books in Swedish. The first one, *SMS från Soppero*, is being made into a film.

Info Box 12 Advice From Revitalisation in Hawai'i

The description in this Info Box is mainly based on Wilson and Kamanā (2009).[1] Even if there are many revitalisation movements, it seems to us that the Hawaiian case is an excellent example of how to connect long-term plans for revitalisation to actions in everyday life. As background to this advice, it is useful to note that by the 1970s there were fewer than 50 child speakers of Hawaiian (Wilson *et al.*, 2006[2]). This almost total disappearance of Hawaiian happened in relatively few generations:

> Late 1800s: everyone spoke Hawaiian, but being monolingual in Hawaiian marked one as unsophisticated. Then Hawaiian medium schools were banned, resulting in young people speaking Hawaiian with adults and Hawai'i Creole English with peers. The next generation could understand, but not speak Hawaiian. Finally, the generation born in the 1940s through 1960s sometimes heard elders speaking Hawaiian but knew very little of it beyond a few words and phrases. Yet, today, as the result of a language revitalization movement that began in the 1970s and 1980s, many young people speak Hawaiian fluently. Increasing numbers are raising their children with Hawaiian as the first language of the home, as we ourselves did. (Wilson & Kamanā, 2009: 369)

The situation for the second to fourth generations above was diagnosed as *unhealthy linguistic diversity* (Wilson & Kamanā, 2006).

> In cases of unhealthy linguistic diversity, youth have widely variable fluency in the ancestral language and exhibit insecurity regarding their own abilities in it. While avoiding use of the ancestral language due to this insecurity, youth may also develop a resistance toward full mastery of the colonizing language used in schooling. The result is a distinctive nonstandard dialect marking the population as what Ogbu [see, for example, Ogbu 1978, 1983] calls 'a caste-like involuntary minority'. Among the characteristics of such a minority are poor academic performance as evidenced by the decline in Hawaiian academic achievement associated with the historical change from Hawaiian-medium to English-medium schooling. ... Unhealthy linguistic diversity is also characterized by class-based language differences. Peer-group use of the colonizing language characterizes the economically successful classes of the Indigenous community. Peer-group use of the ancestral language

characterizes the community's least successful, least progressive, and most unfashionable subgroups. ... A similar phenomenon once existed in Hawai'i. Today, however, a new high-status identity of Hawaiian has strengthened peer-group use of the language. (Wilson & Kamanā, 2009: 369–370)

What the revitalisers wanted instead was a 'linguistically healthy community', where the ancestral language is the regular means of community operation as well as the means of communication across inter-generational and peer-group boundaries. Fluency in other languages is individual and variable from person to person. They also wanted to overcome the 'two worlds philosophy' where one's life is divided between participation in both a 'culture-less' world of modernity and a 'culture-based' Indigenous world tied to elders who were raised in the past. Instead, they wanted a 'one world' philosophy of integrating new knowledge and activities into a community defined by the use of the Hawaiian language (Wilson & Kamanā, 2009: 369–370).

To achieve their goals, they used daycare and education through the medium of Hawaiian, starting with language nests, modelling their *Aha Pūnana Leo* on the Māori *Kōhanga Reo*, and continuing in the primary and secondary schools. They also noticed that young people are especially interested in using the ancestral language in subsistence activities (Wilson & Kamanā, 2009: 371). This can include growing taro in Hawai'i, which would be comparable to seal hunting in Yup'ik or reindeer herding among the Saami, for example.

The *Pūnana Leo* language nest curriculum includes many daily and annual school rituals, including student production of pre-Western feast foods. The focus, however, is not on preparing students to live in a subsistence economy, but on preparing them to make historical and metaphorical connections to it. These connections are crucial to a firm Hawaiian identity (Wilson & Kamanā, 2009: 371).

Successful Indigenous-language maintenance is, just as in most contexts, based on strong bonds between use of a language and a particular geographic location. Such bonds existed in all Indigenous communities in traditional times. The analogous contemporary situation is a political unit using a minority language particular to that unit (Wilson & Kamanā, 2009: 371). Some examples given by them are French in Canadian Quebec, Inuit in Danish Greenland, and Spanish in US Puerto Rico (see also http://www.terralingua.org for connections).

This bond between language and location has been and is still broken by one-way forced assimilation. Occupiers and colonisers do not learn the indigenous languages, not even when these achieve some official status:

> When a particular territory uses a language officially, there are mechanisms to teach that language to those who come to reside in the territory. In spite of federal legislation in both Mexico and the United States according the right to use Indigenous languages officially, Native American governing bodies and Mexican townships with Indigenous communities do not generally assimilate speakers of the colonial language to the Indigenous language. (Wilson & Kamanā, 2009: 371)

> Instead, they often treat Indigenous language speakers parallel to immigrants, providing 'accommodations' to assist them in participating in their own government and public functions carried out in English or Spanish. This is not true official use of Indigenous languages, but is instead transition to their replacement by dominant languages ... today young Hawaiians are campaigning for full equality in official use of Hawaiian and English in government. (Wilson & Kamanā, 2009: 371)

The Hawaiians, like many others, have identified schooling as the major cause of the elimination of Indigenous languages. They have analysed the various ways this happens, even the more sophisticated ones. For example, even if Indigenous language and culture are extensively included in the curriculum of a school, that school can still be a vehicle for language shift. 'Indigenous language teachers themselves can undermine their teaching by raising their own children in the colonial language and allowing community-internal denigration of a language to permeate Indigenous language schooling' (Wilson & Kamanā, 2009: 372).

The Hawaiian approach is explicitly pursuing a change from primary home use and peer-group use of English to primary use of the Indigenous language in one's peer group and the home. Some means used are the following (Wilson & Kamanā, 2009: 372):

- All instruction at all grades, preschool through 12, including the study of English, is through Hawaiian.
- A refusal of the teaching of English before grade 5 and all testing through English until grade 6.

This has resulted in a 100% high school graduation rate and an 80% college attendance rate.

Wilson and Kamanā (2009: 374) describe peer group use in this way: 'Upon entering [their] third year, students are expected to use Hawaiian exclusively as their peer-group language outside school. Fourth year students are expected to take a leadership role in triggering the use of Hawaiian among students [in classes under them].'

Many detailed suggestions regarding everyday practice are added, for instance about not speaking English to Hawaiian-speakers, and on mistakes in Hawaiian. While highly fluent and proper Hawaiian is admired in all contexts, speaking English rather than Hawaiian to other Hawaiian speakers is more likely to draw negative comments from others than are one's mistakes in Hawaiian. However, mistakes are corrected by teachers and advanced students – sometimes on the spot or in more discreet ways, such as by email or in a meeting with teachers (Wilson & Kamanā, 2009: 374).

Many revitalisers, including the Saami, are worried about peer-group language use by young adults. Here too the Hawaiians have good advice:

Peer-group use of Hawai'i Creole English and out-of-school-derived slang comes to signify intermediate students entering adolescence. However, Hawaiian skills continue to be developed through the total Hawaiian school curriculum. Students begin to move back to using Hawaiian with peers as they mature in high school. As students move back to using Hawaiian, they strengthen their repertoire of registers of Hawaiian appropriate for different situations. All students who graduate can therefore participate in use of Hawaiian as young adults. (Wilson & Kamanā, 2009: 374)

Finally, they identify who the central group in revitalisation is. They describe how total support for the use of Hawaiian by this group will positively influence the future of the language and culture:

The key demographic in reversing language shift is young people ages 12 to 30. For this demographic to ensure the survival of their language they must learn their ancestral language fluently, maintain fluency by daily peer-group use, pass the language on to their own children, protect and educate those children in strong Indigenous language medium schools, join with Indigenous language-speaking peers to expand use of the language into higher socioeconomic domains, and then live to see grandchildren repeat and strengthen the cycle. (Wilson & Kamanā, 2009: 374–375)

There is much to learn from this approach for all revitalising peoples.

Notes

(1) See also other references to Wilson *et al.*
(2) We thank the authors for their permission to quote extensively.

Info Box 13 Saami Media in Finland

In terms of reviving a language, the role of public media is undeniably significant. The media increase the use and the respect of language. They also transfer the language to subsequent generations, working in other words to preserve language. This Info Box concentrates on AS media in the larger context of the Saami media in Finland.

Radio and TV broadcasting

The total programme time of Saami radio in Finland is 35 hours weekly, seven hours per day (weekdays). Currently both Aanaar and Skolt Saami broadcasts are limited to one hour per week. The rest of the time is for North Saami broadcasts.

The obligation to broadcast programmes in Saami languages is written into the Finnish Broadcasting Act (1994) and falls under the responsibility of public services that are especially supposed to serve Saami speakers. They are also intended to support tolerance and multiculturalism, and to serve minority and special groups (http://www.finlex.fi/fi/laki/ajantasa/1993/1993138).

Saami radio has a long tradition of being part of the Saami revitalisation movement, and is one of the instruments of language revitalisation and maintenance (Sara, 2004). Regular broadcasts in North Saami began in Finland in 1947. Skolt Saami has been aired since 1973. AS was the last of Finland's Saami languages to arrive on radio waves (http://www.yle.fi/sapmi) with broadcasts starting in 1981. Ella Sarre, a Saami artisan from Njellim (see p. 25, Figure 3.2), was employed to plan and host AS broadcasts. The first AS programmes were mainly interviews and reports that were broadcast occasionally. In these programmes elders from the community looked back on how life was, for example during the evacuation of World War II, on how people used to make clothes and handicrafts, how they cooked, how the mail was delivered, how it was in the times of frost heave, etc. Even today, the most listened-to AS programmes are these 'oldies', replayed from the massive record collection at the office of *Yle Areena*.[1]

It was not until the 1990s that AS came to be heard regularly on the radio, first for half an hour and later, up to the present, for one hour per week. This one-hour programme is called *Anarâš saavah* [*AS Issues*]. The reporter is Anja Kaarret, who has worked part-time at the radio since 1985. Even though she is a native speaker and a radio journalist, she wanted to join CASLE as a part-time student because she could not write AS. As can be seen in this book, she acted in various roles in CASLE: as a Master, leader of the fishing courses, assistant teacher of the cooking course, supervisor of the practical training and team member of the study materials team (see Sections 5.3.1, 5.3.3, 5.4.2.2, 5.5.4 and 6.3.1.3).

According to Anja, the CASLE year brought a whole new set of content to AS broadcasting:

> *Anarâš saavah* had been a bit static. This was because I was the only journalist and the people I could interview were usually the few active ones in the community. The CASLE year changed that. Suddenly there were new speakers. *Anarâš saavah* were no longer *Matti Morottaja saavah* [Matti Morottaja's issues]. New AS music was composed by Koškepuško and Teija Linnanmäki. Of course, I wanted to participate in that year, at all the possible levels, and also professionally because there were new affairs to report on. (Suvi Kivelä's interview with Anja)

According to Juhani Nousuniemi, the Regional Manager of Saami Radio, *Anarâš saavah* has become a popular programme that has found its audience. It consists of news, interviews, current issues and AS music. The programme serves many purposes: it is a source of information, but for some people it is also one of the very few chances they have to hear the language regularly. The programme is also widely listened to by North Saami people. According to Nousuniemi, AS broadcasts have increased public knowledge of AS issues, culture and language in general. He recalls that, soon after the broadcasting in AS started, people began using their own language when communicating with North Saami people. In other words, the fact that their language was heard on the radio gave them the confidence to use it publicly. Every now and then one hears AS people saying: 'Why should we always speak North Saami? They can learn to understand us, just like we have learnt to understand them. After all, the languages do not differ that much from each other.'

In addition to the one hour of AS programming, AS is occasionally heard in the children's weekly radio programme *Binna Banna* [*Tiny Little One*] and the children's 15-minute TV programme *Unna Junná* [*Tiny J.*], both aired mainly in North Saami. Thus far Anja Kaarret has made a few children's programmes in AS for radio and TV in her free time. In addition, some of the weekly prayers are in AS.

- One regular (North) Saami TV programme is *Saami oddasat*, 15-min Saami news, broadcast daily (except for summer breaks) from Karasjok, Norway. This can be watched in Finland, Norway and Sweden. The reporters at Saami Radio in Aanaar attempt to edit one local story from the Finnish Saami area for each of these broadcasts.

Despite these efforts, it is a common wish among all Saami people to have more programme time and variety of programmes targeted to all age groups. For example, there is nothing broadcast for young people at this time. This is crucial from the viewpoint of the first language nest children, who are already young adults today. Most of them do not have the opportunity to use the language with their families or in other relationships. The media, especially electronic media, are present in every young person's life, so the media, possibly broadcast by the young people themselves, would work as the best possible preserver of AS.

The future of AS radio and TV broadcasting is unknown. The resources available for AS radio broadcasts were created at the beginning of the 1990s and have not been updated since. There should be more human and financial resources today because the community has expanded greatly since the time when the broadcasts began. New audiences and interviewees have developed. Unfortunately, YLE has not reacted to any recent demands – quite the opposite, as the company has suffered from financial difficulties for several years and has decreased personnel and programme time from the regions, concentrating services on Pasila (Helsinki), the headquarters of the company. All in all, the total programme time of Aanaar and Skolt Saami represents only a little more than 5% of the total broadcast time in a North Saami-dominating radio.

Aanaar Saami print media

The history of AS print media started the in same year that *Anarâškielâ servi* was founded, 1986 (see Info Box 17 Anarâškielâ servi

[Aanaar Saami Association]). One of the main targets of the AS association was to start publishing a communal magazine, *Anarâš* [*Aanaar Saami*]. This was initially done to strengthen written AS among community members. *Anarâš* is issued three to six times per year, including a calendar. It aims to offer interesting stories that are written in easy-to-read language. Its content and inspiration are drawn from the daily lives of ordinary readers (Morottaja, 2008). In *Anarâš* one can read articles about current issues, short stories, serial stories and children's and young people's writings. The magazine has had the same editor-in-chief since the beginning, Ilmari Mattus, who is a key figure in AS revitalisation. He has been characterised as a hard-working, humble, relentless man who is passionate about his own language and culture. *Anarâš* magazine has been his hobby for more than 20 years, work that he has done alongside his career as a border guard and many other book writing and translating projects. For language revitalisation, there is a great demand for people like him. *Anarâš*, which represents one of Ilmari's 'careers', is now the only Saami print media in Finland, since the discontinuation of the North Saami communal magazine *Sapmelaš* [*Saami*], issued in 1934–1993, followed by *Oḍḍa Sápmelaš* [*New Saami*], issued during 1994–2002. Table IB13.1 introduces *Anarâš* in a nutshell.

Between 2007 and 2011 an online weekly, *Kierâš* [*Black Woodpecker*], was also issued by *Anarâškielâ servi*. *Kierâš* offered news, announcements and current events in AS. Its news reports and bulletins concerned the AS

Table IB13.1 Facts about the communal magazine *Anarâš*

Number of copies printed	500
Distribution	Members of the AS Association (mainly in Finland, but also Sweden, Germany, The Netherlands, Japan, USA and Canada); some libraries and support members.
Total number of bound pages (as of May 2011)	2211
Team	Editor-in-chief and principal journalist Ilmari Mattus (born 1945); second journalist Petter Morottaja; layout Anssi Mattus (Ilmari's son)
Financial support for print costs	Saami Parliament; Finnish Ministry of Culture and Education
Annual budget	€13,000–20,000

community, and were written from the perspective of AS people. The editor-in-chief was Petter Morottaja. *Kieráš* was his hobby for many years but, due to his involvement in CASLE, including development of study materials and his own studies, *Kieráš* was forced to take a long break.

Saami print media are not protected by Acts like radio broadcasting is. The AS community has created alternative ways to find funding for print costs. *Anarâš* is a great example of that. The future of *Anarâš* is solid as long as Ilmari continues editing it. Ilmari does not believe that the magazine will be discontinued because of financial difficulties. The future of AS print media lies mainly in the hands of the small language community, but it also relies on external support. The situation of Saami print media in Norway is better than in Finland because magazines and papers get greater support from the government. In Finland, financial support for Saami newspapers has been available for a few years but apparently no-one has managed to establish one. Perhaps this is understandable; according to the government, the only reasonable way to get regular print media services in Saami languages is to start publishing Saami news as part of an existing newspaper. The government has therefore only recently changed the terms of support so that now any existing Finnish newspaper can apply for support to publish in Saami. The main newspaper in Lapland, *Lapin Kansa*, applied for that support in April 2011 and is now publishing news and reports in North Saami.

New and social media

Nettisaje (http://nettisaje.wikispaces.com/home) is an open Wiki, a community page on which contents are in AS only (see Section 7.12). The idea of this open interactive internet forum is to share information, to communicate and to make all possible materials like writings, pictures, musical lyrics, study materials, etc. available to everyone. A registered user can also edit pages and hence influence the content. There is also a calendar with dates of current events that anyone can update.

A Facebook group, *Anarâškielâ orroomviste* (*AS Living Room*; see Section 7.12) has become a popular daily forum for AS speakers and issues. Already one-third of the AS speakers are members of the open group where most of the inside information, news, stories, happenings and discussions on AS issues are being shared.

Note

(1) YLE Areena is the internet TV service (which is free of charge).

Info Box 14   Language Rights and Right to Education

Here we summarise some of the most important language rights in education stated in human rights documents. A much more thorough presentation can be read online in Chapter 2 of Skutnabb-Kangas and Dunbar (2010, at http://www.e-pages.dk/grusweb/55/), which is the main source of this Info Box. It is clear that ITM children who have been taught only in a dominant language which they do not (or initially did not) understand have *not* had access to education, even if it should have been their basic human right. The result of foreign language-medium education has in most cases been that children have not learned to read or write in their own languages; their competence in the dominant language has often not reached the level of dominant-language peers; their school achievement at least at a group level has been low, and many have become ashamed of their language and culture. This has convinced non-dominant language speakers that they should not teach their language to their own children, in the (wrong) belief that it will help their children if they are not 'burdened' with the language of their family. This vicious circle has in most cases been the main reason for the present need for revitalisation.

First in this Info Box the general right to education is presented; then the right to learn and be taught through the medium of one's mother tongue is summarised.

Paragraph 1 of Article 26 of the **Universal Declaration of Human Rights** (http://www.un.org/en/documents/udhr/, adopted on 10 December 1948 by the United Nations General Assembly), guarantees the right of everyone to education. Paragraph 2 provides that such education *shall be directed to the full development of the human personality*, and *shall promote understanding, tolerance and friendship among all nations, racial and religious groups*. In the **International Covenant on Economic, Social and Cultural Rights** (ICESCR) of 1966 (http://www2.ohchr.org/english/law/cescr.htm), paragraphs 1, 2 and 3 of Article 13 recognise the right of everyone to education, add a reference to the sense of dignity of the human personality, and add 'ethnic groups' to the list in the Universal Declaration of 1948 (just mentioned) among which understanding, tolerance and friendship shall be promoted. The Covenant also notes that education shall *enable all persons to participate effectively in a free society*. The 1960 **Convention Against Discrimination in Education** (http://www.unesco.org/education/pdf/DISCRI_E.PDF), Article 5, subparagraph 1 (a) provides that education shall be directed to, among other things, the full development of the human personality.

The United Nations' **Convention on the Rights of the Child**[1] of 1989 is important. The basic right to education is set out in Article 28, paragraph 1, in which the States party to the CRC recognise *the right of the child to education.* This paragraph also provides that States will take a range of steps with a view to achieving this right *progressively and on the basis of equal opportunity,* including, in subparagraph (e), *measures to encourage regular attendance at schools and the reduction of drop-out rates.* Article 29, subparagraph (a) stipulates that education shall be directed to the *development of the child's personality, talents and mental and physical abilities to their fullest potential.* Article 29, subparagraph (d) stipulates that education should be directed to the development of *respect for the child's parents, his or her own cultural identity, language and values.*

Moving to the rights in relation to the children's mother tongues/first languages, Article 30 of the CRC provides: *In those States in which ethnic, religious or linguistic minorities or persons of indigenous origin exist, a child belonging to such a minority or who is indigenous shall not be denied the right, in community with other members of his or her own group, to enjoy his or her own culture, to profess and practice his or her own religion, **or to use his or her own language*** (emphasis added). The **International Covenant on Civil and Political Rights** (ICCPR) of 1966 (http://www2.ohchr.org/english/law/ccpr.htm), Article 27, has the same famous 'minorities provision', except that the CRC has added 'or is indigenous' and 'he or she'.

The **ILO Convention No. 169 on Indigenous and Tribal Peoples** of 1989 (http://www.ilo.org/public/english/region/ampro/mdtsanjose/indigenous/derecho.htm), Article 28, paragraph 1, asks states to *implement indigenous children's right to be taught to read and write in their own indigenous language, wherever practicable, or in the language most commonly used by the group to which they belong, as well as the national language(s) of the country in which they live.*

The **United Nations Declaration on the Rights of Indigenous Peoples** (UNDRIP) (Resolution A/61/L.67, 13 September 2007; http://www.docip.org/declaration_last/finaladopted_UNDRIP.pdf) provides in Articles 13 and 14:

13.1.   Indigenous peoples have the right to revitalize, use, develop and transmit to future generations their histories, languages, oral traditions, philosophies, writing systems and literatures, and to designate and retain their own names for communities, places and persons.

13.2. States shall take effective measures to ensure that this right is protected and also to ensure that indigenous peoples can understand and be understood in political, legal and administrative proceedings, where necessary through the provision of interpretation or by other appropriate means.

14.1. Indigenous peoples have the right to establish and control their educational systems and institutions providing education in their own languages, in a manner appropriate to their cultural methods of teaching and learning.

14.2. Indigenous individuals, particularly children, have the right to all levels and forms of education of the State without discrimination.

14.3. States shall, in conjunction with indigenous peoples, take effective measures, in order for indigenous individuals, particularly children, including those living outside their communities, to have access, when possible, to an education in their own culture and provided in their own language.

The first two articles (13.1 and 13.2) imply that the child has the right to learn the mother tongue. Since most forms and levels of the *education of the State* (14.2) use the 'State' languages as a medium, the child cannot have access to this education without knowing the State language. These quotes, taken together, might imply that high levels of at least bilingualism must be a goal in the education of an Indigenous child. However, since state education through the medium of the dominant state language is 'free' (despite the fact that there are school fees even at the level of basic education in many countries where Indigenous peoples live), most Indigenous children are forced to 'choose' this 'State education'. Their parents are 'free' to establish and control their own educational systems, with their own languages as teaching languages – but at their own cost. How many Indigenous and tribal peoples can afford this? There is nothing about the State having to allocate public resources to Indigenous language-medium education.

The 'when possible' drawback in Article 14.3 also fits in all too well with similar modifications and conditions in the Council of Europe's **European Charter for Regional or Minority Languages** (the 'Minority Languages Charter' http://conventions.coe.int/Treaty/Commun/ListeTraites.asp?CM = 1&CL = ENG&NT = &NU = 148) and **Framework Convention for the Protection of National Minorities** (the 'Framework Convention', http://conventions.coe.

int/Treaty/Commun/QueVoulezVous.asp¿NT = 157&CM = 1&DF = 2/17/2007&CL = ENG; for news, see http://conventions.coe.int/Treaty/EN/v3News.asp); both came into force in 1998. Education Article 8 of the Minority Languages Charter includes a range of modifications, including *as far as possible; relevant; appropriate; where necessary; pupils who so wish in a number considered sufficient; if the number of users of a regional or minority language justifies it*; as well as a number of alternatives such as *to allow, encourage* or *provide teaching in* or *of the regional or minority language at all the appropriate stages of education* (emphases added). All of these caveats and drawbacks make it possible for education authorities to opt out of providing children with the basic language rights which they seem to guarantee by signing the conventions.

Article 8 in the Framework Convention, covering medium of education, is so heavily qualified that the minority is completely at the mercy of the state:

> In areas inhabited by persons belonging to national minorities traditionally or in *substantial* numbers, *if there is sufficient demand*, the parties shall *endeavour* to ensure, *as far as possible* and *within the framework of their education systems*, that persons belonging to those minorities have *adequate* opportunities for being taught in the minority language *or* for receiving instruction in this language. (Emphases added for modifications)

In sum, there are thus far very few binding and unconditional rights, with financial support, for mother tongue-medium education. The situation is even worse for language revitalisation programmes.

Note

(1) The CRC, http://www.hrweb.org/legal/child.html (see also http://www.unhchr.ch/tbs/doc.nsf/%28symbol%29/CRC.GC.2001.1.En¿OpenDocument): Article 17, paragraph 4; Article 28, paragraph 1; Article 29, paragraph 3; and Article 30, paragraph 2.

Info Box 15   Lost or Stolen Generations

In many mainly Western countries where primary education has been or is obligatory, even for Indigenous children, formal education is clearly responsible for the fact that most speakers of Indigenous languages are elderly – or where they are children, where revitalisation has started. The young adults and their parents' generation often do not speak the Indigenous languages. They are known as the *lost* or *stolen generations*. They are 'lost' from their own people because they do not know the culture or the language, or have not used the language or transferred it to the next generation even if they might know some of it. The term 'stolen' is used especially with reference to those who were taken away from their families, and brought to boarding schools or even orphanages (despite the fact that many had families), where they grew up without their communities, their languages and their cultures. Both groups were often punished if they tried to use or maintain their languages. This has happened, for instance, in Australia, Canada, Finland, Greenland, Norway, Sweden and the United States, to name only some. There are hundreds of thousands of individuals belonging to lost generations, and tens of thousands of belonging to the stolen ones.

Prevention of the learning and use of Indigenous (and minority) languages has been accomplished through many different means, overtly and directly through physical punishment or separation from one's group, but also through shaming and stigmatising the group and its language, culture, norms, traditions and ways of life, by calling group members uncivilised, barbaric, incapable of development, and so on. Today this continues through more covert and indirect means. It happens structurally, for instance by organising educational pro-grammes so that the learning of the language and culture is in fact prevented, either because the language is not the main teaching lan-guage or because teachers cannot speak it. Prevention of the learning and use of Indigenous languages also happens through ideological means, for example: by making the group invisible or stigmatising it; by making linguistic and cultural resources seem like handicaps, obso-lete or not useful; or by using false either/or arguments, e.g. claiming that ITMs have to choose between learning their own language and learning power languages. *Both/and* is not presented as the realistic pos-sibility that it is, of course.

The following are some examples of what has been described above (for many more, see Skutnabb-Kangas, 2000: 318–365). In Canada, com-pulsory attendance of all Indigenous children at school was secured as early as 1894, with the 'added provision for "the arrest and conveyance to school and detention there" of any children who might be prevented from attending by their parents or guardians (who, in such a case, would be liable to imprisonment)' (Richardson, 1993: 101). Children could be kept in the schools until they were 18 years old. Richardson heard many people describe how the priests in Mackenzie Valley would come down-river by barge, seizing Indian children in each village to take to school, and how parents would send the children to hide in the bush (Richardson, 1993: 101–102).

A combination of sticks and carrots (threats and benefits) was often used: 'Indian Affairs used to threaten people that if they didn't send their kids to school, they wouldn't get any welfare' (Buckley Petawabano, a Cree man from Mistissini reserve in northern Quebec; quoted in Richardson, 1993: 107). Parents who agreed to send their children away sometimes got small benefits.

Another example comes from Australia in the mid-1800s, where to enhance Aboriginal Kaurna children's 'irregular attendance ... children were "bribed" to attend the school with the provision of food, and blankets were distributed to adults whose children attended' (Amery, 2000: 153). Edwards and Read (1992) tell about the painful experience of Aboriginal children who were taken away from their parents and later tried to find their families again. There has been an official apology made by the government of Australia, and Canada has also apologised, but there has been no apology from Denmark regarding the 'stolen generations' of Greenlandic children taken to Denmark (see Bryld, 1998).

In Norway from 1851 until the 1920s, there were funds in the state budget specifically earmarked for Norwegianisation (carrots). Teachers could get a supplement to their salary from these funds if they could document good results in teaching Norwegian to Saami and Kven children. Children received grants if they showed good competence in Norwegian, and poor Kven and Saami parents could be given money for food and clothes if they showed a 'positive attitude' by sending their children to the Norwegian school (Eriksen & Niemi, 1981: 48, 53). In the 1938–1939 school year, in the northernmost county of Norway, Finnmark, where the Indigenous Saami, and the Kven (Finnish-speakers) lived, 3000 children, representing 36% of primary and lower secondary school-goers, were in boarding schools (Lind Meløy, 1980: 81). It was an officially stated goal of the boarding schools in Norway to Norwegianise minority children, reported by Lind Meløy, himself a former head of one of the schools. In the process of Norwegianisation it was the goal of many school administrators that the Saami languages should become extinct (e.g. Bernt Thomassen, Superintendent for schools 1902–1920; Lind Meløy, 1980: 98–99).

Also in Norway, radio licenses were cheaper in the Finnish- and Saami-speaking areas than in other parts of the country (Lind Meløy, 1980: 245) – a reward for listening to the radio programmes, which naturally were all in Norwegian), i.e. a reward for assimilation efforts (since the mother tongue was prevented from developing at the same time). Books, newspapers and journals in Norwegian were distributed free of charge, while there were severe restrictions on, for instance, books imported from Finland (and libraries in northern Sweden were forbidden to buy Finnish books so books could not be imported from Sweden either). People were suspected of lacking loyalty to Norway if they read such unpatriotic literature (Lind Meløy, 1980: 239). The same was true on the Swedish side of the border: books and journals in Swedish were distributed free of charge, while the library of Torneå was overtly explicitly forbidden to buy Finnish books until 1957 (Lind Meløy, 1980: 241). All of this positive reinforcement in favour of the dominant languages followed after a long period of negative reinforcement regarding the use of non-dominant languages, when, for example, the Swedish government insisted that civil servants should not use Saami or Finnish, on pain of losing their jobs (Lind Meløy, 1980: 252–253), or when neither Kven and nor Saami were allowed to buy land, etc. (Lind Meløy, 1980: 73–76).

In the USA, 'The Bureau of Indian Affairs operates 77 boarding schools, scattered throughout the nation ... Some 35,000 children are sent to boarding schools. ... In 1966, more than 16,000 Indian children of school age were not attending any school at all' (Cahn & Hearne, 1969: 28). The goals were the same as in the Nordic countries:

For nearly a hundred years the policy of the United States government was to acculturate the Navajo so that the Navajo could be assimilated into the White society. To effect this assimilation, Navajo children were taken from the shelter of the family and sent to boarding school. Almost every child who entered the boarding school spoke only Navajo, and most of the people employed at the boarding schools spoke only English. When a Navajo child spoke the language of his family at school, he was punished. (Platero, 1975: 57)

Indians (in the USA) were forced to try to live like 'white men'. Indian dances and Indian hand work was forbidden. A family's ration of food was cut off if anyone in the family was caught singing Indian songs or doing Indian hand craft. Children were physically beaten if they were caught speaking Indian languages. (Cahn & Hearne, 1969: 18)

During the last decade or two, many ITM adults have told horror stories about boarding schools and mission stations, stories of rape, severe beatings or being left without food or warm clothing. A Spanish-speaking teacher told me (TSK) in 1994 that she knew of several children who had frozen to death in her childhood in Arizona while trying to escape from boarding school – they did not have adequate clothing. Similar stories exist in all parts of the Pacific, Australia and New Zealand, among the Saami in the Nordic countries, the Welsh, Basques and Frisians, Finns in Sweden, and many groups in colonised Africa. Europe and Europeanised countries have shown extreme cruelty in these acts, Asia less so (see Skutnabb-Kangas, 1984, for more examples).

Forbidding the use of a language overtly, even if those who speak the language are not necessarily physically punished, is also part of direct prohibition. But embarrassment, shame, a feeling of doing something 'wrong' and at least doing something that is not 'good for one' – all of these rejections of the home language are inculcated through both overt and covert prohibitions. When a ban on speaking one's mother tongue is given as the first commandment, as in the next example, speaking it is equated with grave sins (i.e. you are a bad person if you do it, and God does not like you), or, in addition, it is turned into doing something uncivilised, like urinating where you are not supposed to. Norwegian boarding schools for Indigenous Saami and Finnish minority children used to have the same set of regulations on the wall to tell children what was forbidden:

(a) *Do not speak Saami or Finnish in your free time.*
(b) Do not go shopping or anywhere else without permission.
(c) No boys in the girls' room or girls in the boys' room after 8 o'clock in the evening.
(d) *Do not urinate on the stairs or along the walls of the building.* (Lind Meløy, 1980: 68, emphases added)

Speaking one's mother tongue was thus constructed as something as sinful, barbaric and shameful as running around pissing indiscriminately. This pattern of stigmatisation almost always combines the three strategies of *glorification, stigmatisation* and *rationalisation*. First, the dominant language and culture are constructed as superior, as the natural norm. Secondly, the dominated language (and culture) are constructed (erroneously, of course) as deficient. Thirdly, the 'deficiency' of the dominated language (and culture) is used as a rationalisation for imposing the glorified dominant language (and culture) at the cost of the dominated ones. The rationalisation claims that all of this is done 'for their own benefit'. Part of the rationalisation is also that if 'they' still do not succeed after receiving all this 'help' it is their own fault.

The following are just a few examples of what has been said of Indigenous peoples. 'Degeneration, a low cultural level and weak mental capacities, physical and mental stultification' (Saami, Norway); 'distinguished from beasts only by possessing the bodily human form' (Native Americans, California). A parish priest, Tandberg, wrote in 1904 in a letter to the Superintendent for Schools in Norway: 'The reason for the instruction not having much effect is, beside truancy, degeneration, a low cultural level and weak mental capacities, physical and mental stultification' (in Lind Meløy, 1980: 39–40). Another Superintendent, Christen Andreas Brygfjeld, wrote in 1923 of the Saami that 'those few individuals who still exist of the original Saami tribe are now so much degenerated that there is little hope of any change for the better for them. They are hopeless, are probably the most backward and most miserable group in Finnmark, and from them comes the largest contingent from this area to mental hospitals and schools for the mentally retarded . . . . The Saami people have no capacity to rise to a higher cultural level themselves without taking the road through the Norwegian language and Norwegian culture' (Lind Meløy, 1980: 103–104). Father Pedro Font wrote in his diary in 1775–1776 similar assessments about native Californians: they 'live like beasts without making use of reason or discourse, and being distinguished from beasts only by possessing the bodily human form, but not from their deeds'. They were 'among the most unhappy people in all the world. . . . In fine, they are so savage, wild and dirty, disheveled, ugly, small and timid that only because they have the human form is it possible to believe that they belong to mankind' (quoted in Lewis, 1987: 82, 83).

There are thousands of examples from all over the world, from both Indigenous and minority contexts, where the use of the children's language was either overtly or covertly forbidden. Language, culture, customs and traditions are not anything we are born with; they have to be lived and taught to be learned (see Skutnabb-Kangas, 2000: 91–97 for more Saami examples). If children are not surrounded by at least some elders from their own group who (are allowed to) teach them their languages, stories, customs, traditions and knowledges, these will not be learned proficiently. Not allowing children to learn their language and preventing them from using it through separation from proficient adult users means 'prohibiting the use of the language of the group in daily intercourse or in schools'. This was the definition of linguistic genocide in the final draft of what became the United Nations Genocide Convention (see Skutnabb-Kangas & Dunbar, 2010). Linguistic genocide was deleted from the final Convention, but the definition still stands.

A national inquiry in 1997 in Australia by the Human Rights and Equal Opportunity Commission, *Bringing Them Home: National Inquiry into the Separation of Aboriginal and Torres Strait Islander Children from Their Families*, found that 'the government policy of forced removal was a gross violation of human rights and technically an act of genocide because it had the intention of destroying Australia's indigenous culture by forced assimilation' (Sitka, 1998: 25).

The long-term consequences of many of the bans mentioned in this Info Box can still be seen today even in situations where the ban has been lifted long ago. The Royal Commission on the Northern Environment in Canada (1978: 207, quoted in Jordan, 1988: 193) heard evidence from one area:

> Within those 25 years (during which formal education had been available) the education system had produced in our area only two university graduates, countless elementary, secondary and post-secondary dropouts, a large absenteeism record and indifference to education as a whole by community members.

Skutnabb-Kangas and Dunbar (2010) give a detailed description of many of the extremely negative long-term consequences which can be seen today among many Indigenous peoples. The Saami are a people who, in comparison with many others, have to a large extent overcome some of the most horrendous consequences. But one of the consequences is today's age pyramid of speakers of those Saami languages which have speakers (see Section 3.1). This helps explain the need for the Aanaar Saami project: the stolen and lost generations must be regained. Without the assimilation and the ideological hangover of the stigmatisation of the Saami languages, a normal transfer of language and culture from parents and grandparents to children would have happened. It didn't – therefore CASLE was created.

Info Box 16 Third Language Learning

Many empirical studies show that students who are already bilingual or who have studied one foreign language in addition to their mother tongue learn a third language (L3) faster and more efficiently than those who are monolingual when they start studying a new language. Most of these studies concern school children and young adults. Several languages and countries have been involved (e.g. Catalan, Basque, Spanish, German, English, French; in Spain, Germany, Canada, Finland, and others – see, for example, Cenoz, 2008, 2009; Haenni Hoti *et al.*, 2011; Ringbom, 2007; Swain *et al.*, 1990; Valencia & Cenoz, 1992).

In addition, when two languages are used at home, children do better at learning an L3 than if they have only studied a foreign language in school. We also know (e.g. Cummins, 1981) that the better students know their mother tongue, both orally and in written form, the better the results in L3 (and of course in L2). Literacy in both/all languages helps because of additive bilingualism: language skills and proficiencies build on each other through cross-linguistic transfer (e.g. Bialystok, 2007).

Interestingly, even in subtractive contexts where the mother tongue of Indigenous or immigrant minority children does not get any support in school, knowing two languages already before starting to learn a third supports the development of metalinguistic awareness. Metalinguistic awareness, which involves being able to compare languages and knowing more about how languages function, is the main causal factor explaining why bilinguals are better language learners than monolinguals. Metalinguistic awareness is also responsible for many of the other benefits that high-level bilinguals as a group have when compared to monolinguals (see Mohanty, 1995). If the L3 is related to the mother tongue, learning is also faster.

The CASLE participants were thus in a very good position: their mother tongue, or their best known language, Finnish, had all the support schools can give – it had been their medium of instruction. All of them had studied at least two foreign languages in school (mainly Swedish and English, both Indo-European languages that are unrelated linguistically to Finnish) and most knew North Saami already. The Saami languages are related to Finnish even if the distance is fairly big. For all of these reasons, CASLE participants could be expected to be optimal AS language learners.

Info Box 17 *Anarâškielâ servi* [Aanaar Saami Association]

The operating principle of *Anarâškielâ servi* has been, and still is, to advance AS by engaging in language nest, newspaper and other publishing activities. The Association also provides information to the general public concerning AS and AS culture.

As of 2012, *Anarâškielâ servi* has three actively working language nests in Aanaar municipality: two in Aanaar (Inari) village and one in Avveel (Ivalo). The first language nest was set up in the Aanaar village in 1997 with a grant from the Finnish Cultural Foundation, which funded the language nest for the first five and a half years. Since this start-up period, the municipality has bought daycare facilities from *Anarâškielâ servi*, essentially funding the language nest on an ongoing basis. The enlargement of the language nest activities, i.e. establishing two more language nests, was made possible by the CASLE programme, which created enough human resources for two new language nests. Language nest activities were enlarged for two reasons: firstly, the number of speakers had to be stabilised, requiring more young speakers; and secondly, it was most efficient to set up two language nests for Aanaar, separating the younger children (0–3 years) from the older children (3–6 years). In this way, the caregivers have been able to spend more time on AS language transmission at the appropriate levels.

Anarâškielâ servi has issued a communal magazine known as *Anarâš* since 1997 and a weekly e-bulletin called *Kierâš* since 2007 (see Info Box 13 Saami media in Finland). It has also published AS literature, in total 10 books. These books are written mainly for children, but there is one anthology for adults. *Anarâškielâ servi* was the publisher of Marja-Liisa Olthuis's doctoral thesis *'Inarinsaamen lajinnimet'* [on AS species names] as well.

There is not much fiction written in AS; the total number of AS literary publications is approximately 40. Luckily the number is slowly increasing over time. A complete list of AS publications can be found at Nettisaje: http://nettisaje.wikispaces.com/almostum_kirjeh. The ongoing problem with new literature is that no-one can afford to become a full-time AS author, mainly because there are extremely low numbers of readers and thus small edition sizes. The costs of producing AS literature are still higher than the financial benefits. One proposed solution is to publish bilingually, for example in Finnish and AS. There is even a children's book in English and AS entitled *Forgetful Squirrel – Muštottes uárree*, which was written in English by Lee Rodgers and translated by Mervi Skopets and Petter Morottaja (2011). This book introduces the AS way of living in an enjoyable way through an AS boy named Sammeli, the main character of the book.

Because of the need for leisure time activities for children and youth, *Anarâškielâ servi* has recently organised creative expression classes for children and started evening activities for youth. This has been done with a grant from the Finnish Cultural Foundation. Unfortunately, there is still no long-term funding for these activities, which are clear attempts to create natural AS domains for younger language generations outside homes, language nests and schools. *Anarâškielâ servi* has also become one of the organisers of the AS evenings, which are designated for all AS speakers; funding for this activity can be applied for only year by year.

Among the activities of *Anarâškielâ servi* during the period of 2008–2012 was support for the planning and carrying out of the CASLE programme as a revitalisation project. The Association was able to constitute its own research group designed for the needs of CASLE.

Anarâškielâ servi is a lively association, full of ideas that are mainly realised as small or larger projects. Because of the expanded language nest activities, *Anarâškielâ servi* has become one of the most significant employers in the Aanaar municipality in recent years. Its annual budget is approximately €500,000.

Info Box 18 The Saami Language and Traditional Knowledge[1]

Jernsletten describes traditional professional Saami terminology for reindeer, salmon and snow. He states that the prerequisite for making a living from nature is for the hunter, fisherman/woman and reindeer herder to have an intimate knowledge of the landscape (Jernsletten, 1997: 90). Even if modern reindeer herding represents a relatively new development over the last 400 years (Jernsletten, 1997: 86), the reindeer herding culture has preserved a tradition thousands of years old of hunter-gatherers' ways of using the environment, because hunting, fishing, collecting berries, etc. have been important secondary modes of production that are well suited to the seasonal migratory life of a reindeer-herding family.

'*Traditional knowledge*' or '*Indigenous peoples' knowledge*' 'refers to that knowledge which is acquired and preserved through generations in an original or local society. This knowledge consists of experience in working to secure a subsistence from nature' (Jernsletten, 1997: 86).[2]

> In 'traditional knowledge', ... observations are tied to being able to understand phenomena and connections in nature, so that people will be able to use nature for sustenance. This knowledge can be said to be usage-oriented. The Saami language(s) has (have), for example, words for grasses and plants which have been used as foodstuffs, and which have been important in the grazing of live-stock, cattle and reindeer. But there are few terms for flowering plants which, though quite visible in the summer landscape, are nevertheless not useful. Likewise there are few names for small birds, and of these names many are compound words combining a modifier with *cizáš* (small bird, sparrow). At the same time there is a richer vocabulary having to do with sea and waterfowl, which have been useful as food sources. (Jernsletten, 1997: 87)

When a reindeer herd is lost, or when animals from different herds are to be separated from each other, one needs to have immensely sophis-ticated vocabulary in order to describe details about landscape and spe-cific animals[3] to others who must be able to identify them without the describer being present. The prerequisite for transmitting this knowl-edge to others when planning, solving problems and discussing hunt-ing, fishing, the movement of the reindeer across the countryside, etc., and for transmitting this information to subsequent generations is:

> that the language has exact expressions and precise terms for those concepts which are important for exploiting nature's possibilities to support life. Likewise a large vocabulary makes it possible to describe and remember landscapes and places in rivers and lakes when con-versing about hunting and fishing. (Jernsletten, 1997: 87, 90)

There are several ways that this intimate knowledge about the envi-ronment can disappear, whether it does so abruptly or gradually. *Abrupt disappearance* tends to be the result of outside forces, sometimes natural (e.g. earthquake) but most often human (e.g. invaders, war). *Gradual disappearance* may be the result of natural changes (e.g. a new Ice Age) or something that causes the group itself to change.

In the case of *gradual disappearance of knowledge* about the environ-ment, new ways of subsistence develop and some of the old ones disap-pear. If this development is really gradual (in human terms), taking millennia (as in Aboriginal Australia prior to the arrival of the colonisers) or at least centuries (like the transition from hunting wild reindeer – which ended in the Saami areas during the 1700s – to reindeer herding, with both coexisting for a long time), there is time for both people and nature to adjust.

> The close connection between people's activities and skills and the knowledge preserved in the form of terms and words is also evident when linguistic expressions and terminology disappear alongside the disappearance of the activity with which the knowledge is connected. (Jernsletten, 1997: 88)

Saami knowledge of wild reindeer hunting has indeed disappeared, even if some of the old words are still known and are present in dictionaries. When Peter Mühlhäusler (1998) says that 'it takes time to get to know a place', he is not talking about years or even decades but centuries (see also Diamond, 1992). Traditional knowledge about the environment is never instantaneous, McDonaldised knowledge. 'Knowing a place' in this sense is both a prerequisite for proper maintenance of the knowledge and for developing ways of talking about it. In turn, being able to talk about a place, in a language which has developed ways of talking about it and observing it in a detailed way, is a prerequisite for maintaining it, and for transferring knowledge about the place and its maintenance to future generations. Maintenance of the place and the knowledge, in turn, is a prerequisite for having a place to talk about in the first place – and this is true both locally and globally.

This is where education comes in. For youngsters to acquire traditional knowledge, they must partake in work alongside someone older who possesses the knowledge and experience (Jernsletten, 1997: 89). The teacher/master does not give theoretical introductions in advance; instead, the child learns through observing, experiencing, trying things out, developing skills, listening to stories, asking questions and making links to her/his own experience. The final step is systematising this learning into linguistic expressions, terms and professional jargon (Jernsletten, 1997: 89). Thus:

> the terms one learns are a rich mix of experiences and associations. As one begins to connect words and terms to one's observations and experiences, this knowledge is verbalized, systematized, committed to memory ... the terms are appropriated through an intensive and detailed education where the activity and *the learning of terminology through language* are closely connected. (Jernsletten, 1997: 88, 89, emphasis added)

When children accompanied their parents and others to work situations, taking part early on in adult tasks, they

> received a gradual introduction to professional knowledge together with training in professional skills. With personal experience in the work they could understand and participate in the conversations and stories of knowledgeable adults during free moments, and in this way they could *broaden their terminology and knowledge*. (Jernsletten, 1997: 98, emphasis added)

Jernsletten talks about a central concern of reindeer-herding Saami today:

> their children are taken away from work in reindeer-herding when they enter the Norwegian school system and thus are not exposed to an important introduction to the knowledge that is necessary for one who one day will become a reindeer owner or herder himself/herself ... [A]n important portion of the content of the Saami traditional knowledge is lost when the type of insight and understanding is taken away which is tied to a physical approach and experience together with *an introduction to and expansion of terminology*. (Jernsletten, 1997: 98–99, emphasis added)

Compared to modern physical sciences, where a good deal of learning takes place 'with demonstrations, exercises, and practice in laboratories and fieldwork out in nature' (Jernsletten, 1997: 99), without which learning is 'unimaginable', Jernsletten claims that

> the laboratories of the Saami and other small societies have been the landscape, the sea, rivers and lakes where the youth have practised and learned. Modern educational methods cannot fully replace this older manner of learning. If scholastic instruction is not supplemented with instruction in the environment where the knowledge belongs, that is, in nature itself, important aspects of that knowledge will be lost. In this sense 'Saami schools' are Saami in name only but European in content.

In Jernsletten's view (1997: 101, emphasis added):

> the use of modern media cannot replace learning combined with practice, and it is self-evident that the people who have grown up and lived with traditional modes of production and who have

learned from their parents in a traditional manner ... *must transmit their knowledge through their own language,* Saami.

All of Jernsletten's experience, shared not only with other Indigenous peoples but also with everybody who lives traditionally in contact with nature, strengthens our understanding of how the causal connections work. Research in the field of terminology and lifeways is only beginning, but it may prove vital for the future of Indigenous peoples and, indeed, of us all.

Notes

(1) Excerpted from Chapter 2 in Skutnabb-Kangas, 2000: 91–96).
(2) Reagan (1996) provides a useful discussion about the biases in Western education vis-à-vis traditional knowledge in general and educational knowledge of non-European cultures in particular. One of the 'broad common themes in the non-Western educational traditions concerned is that the Western tendency to conflate and confuse "formal schooling" with "education" is less common in non-Western societies; there is a continuum. Education has been more community-based and communal, a social responsibility shared by all adult members of the community, and with relatively little focus on identifying (and training) educational specialists' (Skutnabb-Kangas, 1999). Regrettably, one can even find examples of this conflation of formal schooling with education in the writings of some Indigenous scholars. For example, Asta Balto and Jon Todal write in their article on Sámi bilingual education: 'The history of Saami education begins in the 1700s with the Christian missions that sought to convert the Saamis' (Balto & Todal, 1997: 77). Balto, who is the former Chair of the Saami Education Council in Norway, is normally extremely aware of the need to free ourselves from the assimilationist thought patterns of colonial times.
(3) Harald Gaski has been involved in many debates about his language, which is Saami. Here is one of his points: 'Hi there, wait a minute! Didn't you tell us that our language is an inferior one? So what do you call a four-year-old male reindeer with a white spot on its leg, and with the antlers pointing forward? In one word, please' (Gaski, 1997a: 218)!

References

Ahola, A. (2010) *Suomi tuli Saamenmaahan [[When] Finland Came to the Saami Homeland]*, accessed 18 August 2012. http://ohjelmat.yle.fi/ykkosdokumentti/suomi_tuli_saamenmaahan

Aikio-Puoskari, U. (2005) *The Education of the Sámi in the Comprehensive Schooling of Three Nordic Countries: Norway, Finland and Sweden/Sámeoahpahusa sadji golmma Davviriikka vuođđoskuvlavuogadagas* (two separate publications, one in North Saami, one in English), Series Gáldu čála, February 2005. Guovdageaidnu, Norway: Resource Centre for the Rights of Indigenous Peoples (http://www.galdu.org).

Aikio-Puoskari, U. (2009) The ethnic revival, language and education of the Sámi, an Indigenous people, in three Nordic countries (Finland, Norway and Sweden). In T. Skutnabb-Kangas, R. Phillipson, A. Mohanty and M. Panda (eds) *Social Justice Through Multilingual Education* (pp. 238–262). Bristol: Multilingual Matters.

Aikio-Puoskari, U. and Pentikäinen, M. (2001) *The Language Rights of the Indigenous Saami in Finland Under Domestic and International Law.* Juridica Lapponica 26. Rovaniemi, Finland: Lapin yliopisto (University of Lapland/Northern Institute for Environmental and Minority Law).

Aikio-Puoskari, U. and Skutnabb-Kangas, T. (2007) When few under 50 speak the language as a first language: Linguistic (human) rights and linguistic challenges for endangered Saami languages. In *Revitalizing the Periphery* (Raporta/Report, January 2007) (pp. 9–63). Guovdageaidnu, Norway: Sámi Instituhtta.

Ah-Vee, A., Collen, L., Phillipson, R. and Skutnabb-Kangas, T. (2009) 'Children do not fail in school. School fails the children'. Triggering educational change in Mauritius? http://www.tove-skutnabb-kangas.org/pdf/Children_do_not_fail_in_school_School_fails_the_children_Triggering_educational_change_in_Mauritius_Alain_Ah_Vee_Lindsey_Collen_Robert_Phillipson_Tove_Skutnabb_Kangas.pdf

Alexander, N. (1992) South Africa: Harmonising Nguni and Sotho. In N. Crawhall (ed.) *Democratically Speaking: International Perspectives on Language Planning.* Cape Town: National Language Project.

Alidou, H., Boly, A., Brock-Utne, B., Diallo, Y.S., Heugh, K. and Wolff, H.E. (2006) Optimizing learning and education in Africa – the language factor. A stock-taking research on mother tongue and bilingual education in Sub-Saharan Africa. Working document prepared for ADEA 2006 Biennial Meeting, Libreville, Gabon, 27–31 March 2006. Association for the Development of Education in Africa (ADEA)/UNESCO Institute for Education/Deutsche Gesellschaft für Technische Zusammenarbeit.

Amery, R. (2000) *Warrabarna Kaurna! Reclaiming an Australian Language.* Multilingualism and Linguistic Diversity Series. Lisse, The Netherlands: Swets & Zeitlinger.

Andrýsek, O. (1989) Report on the definition of minorities. SIM Special Report No. 8. Utrecht: Netherlands Institute of Human Rights, Studie- en Informatiecentrum Mensenrechten.

Annamalai, E. (1998) Nativity of language. In R. Singh (ed.) *The Native Speaker: Multilingual Perspectives* (pp. 148–157). New Delhi/Thousand Oaks/London: Sage.

Arizona Revised Statutes. Title 15 (Education), Section 3.1: English language education for children in public schools, 751-756.01.

Baker, C. (2006) *Foundations of Bilingual Education and Bilingualism* (4th edn). Clevedon: Multilingual Matters.

Baker, C. (2007) *A Parents' and Teachers' Guide to Bilingualism* (3rd edn). Clevedon: Multilingual Matters.

Balto, A. and Todal, J. (1997) Saami Bilingual Education in Norway. In J. Cummins and D. Corson (eds) *Bilingual Education. Volume 5. Encyclopedia of Language and Education* (pp. 77–86). Boston & London: Kluwer Academic Publishers.

Barker, X. (2012) English language as bully. In V. Rapatahana and P. Bunce (eds) *English Language as Hydra* (pp. 18–36). Bristol: Multilingual Matters.

Bear Nicholas, A. (1996) Integrated education and the state of the Maliseet language: Revitalisation or linguicide? In W. Cichocki, A. Lister, M. Holder and A. House (eds) *Papers from the 20th Annual Meeting of the Atlantic Provinces Linguistic Association*. Fredericton: Graphic Services, University of New Brunswick, Legal Deposit National Library of Canada.

Bear Nicholas, A. (2003) Linguicide and historicide in Canada. Paper presented at Presence of the Past: The Third National Conference on Teaching, Learning and Communicating the History of Canada, accessed 6 August 2012. http://www.praxismedia.ca/transcripts/transcript_AndreaBearNicholas.pdf

Bear Nicholas, A. (2005) Education through the Medium of the Mother-Tongue: The Single Most Important Means for Saving Indigenous Languages. Rationales and Strategies for Establishing Immersion Programs, drawn from A Symposium on Immersion Education for First Nations sponsored by St. Thomas University and The Assembly of First Nations, Fredericton, N.B., Canada, accessed 3–6 October 2005. http://www.samediggi.fi/lausunnot/Andrea%20Revised%20Rationales%20for%20Immersion.htm

Bear Nicholas, A. (2007) The struggle of Indigenous peoples in Canada for linguistic rights and mother tongue schooling. Paper presented at the Seminar on Language Revitalisation, Language Rights and Indigenous Peoples, 6 February 2007. Elgå, Norway: Gáldu Resource Centre for the Rights of Indigenous Peoples (sponsors).

Bear Nicholas, A. (2009) Reversing language shift through a native language immersion teacher training program in Canada. In T. Skutnabb-Kangas, R. Phillipson, A. Mohanty and M. Panda (eds) *Social Justice through Multilingual Education* (pp. 220–237). Bristol: Multilingual Matters.

Benson, C. (2008) Language 'choice' in education. PRAESA Occasional Papers No. 30. Cape Town: University of Cape Town. http://www.praesa.org.za/files/2012/07/Paper30.pdf

Benson, C. (2009) Designing effective schooling in multilingual contexts: Going beyond bilingual 'models'. In T. Skutnabb-Kangas, R. Phillipson, A. Mohanty and M. Panda (eds) *Social Justice through Multilingual Education* (pp. 63–81). Bristol: Multilingual Matters.

Benson, C. and Kosonen, K. (2012) A critical comparison of language-in-education policy and practice in four southeast Asian countries and Ethiopia. In T. Skutnabb-Kangas and K. Heugh (eds) *Multilingual Education and Sustainable Diversity Work. From Periphery to Center* (pp. 111–137). New York: Routledge.

Benson, C., Heugh, K., Bogale, B. and Yohannes, M.A.G. (2012) Multilingual education in Ethiopian primary schools. In T. Skutnabb-Kangas and K. Heugh (eds) *Multilingual Education and Sustainable Diversity Work. From Periphery to Center* (pp. 32–61). New York: Routledge.

Bentahila, A. and Davies, E. (1993) Language revival: Restoration or transformation? *Journal of Multilingual and Multicultural Development* 14 (5), 355–373.

Benton, R.A. (1979) *The Legal Status of the Māori Language: Current Reality and Future Prospects.* Wellington: Maori Unit, New Zealand Council for Educational Research.

Benton, R.A. (1981) *The Flight of the Amokura: Oceanic Language and Formal Education in the South Pacific.* Wellington: New Zealand Council for Educational Research.

Benton, R.A. (1986) Schools as agents for language revival in Ireland and New Zealand. In B. Spolsky (ed.) *Language and Education in Multilingual Settings* (pp. 53–76). Clevedon: Multilingual Matters.

Benton, R.A. (1996) Language policy in New Zealand: Defining the ineffable. In M. Herriman and B. Burnaby (eds) *Language Policies in English-dominant Countries: Six Case Studies* (pp. 62–98). Clevedon: Multilingual Matters.

Bialystok, E. (ed.) (1991) *Language Processing in Bilingual Children.* Cambridge: Cambridge University Press.

Bialystok, E. (2007) Acquisition of literacy in bilingual children: A framework for research. *Language Learning* 57 (s1), 45–77.

Bialystok, E. (2009) Effects of bilingualism on cognitive and linguistic performance across the lifespan. In I. Gogolin and U. Neumann (eds) *Streitfall Zweisprachigkeit – The Bilingualism Controversy* (pp. 53–68). Wiesbaden: VS Verlag für Sozialwissenschaften.

Bialystok, E. (2010) Bilingualism. *Wiley Interdisciplinary Reviews: Cognitive Science* 1, 559–572.

Bialystok, E. (2011) Reshaping the mind: The benefits of bilingualism. *Canadian Journal of Experimental Psychology* 65, 229–235.

Blommaert, J. (2004) Rights in places. Comments on linguistic rights and wrongs. In J. Freeland and D. Patrick (eds) *Language Rights and Language Survival. Sociolinguistic and Sociocultural Perspectives* (pp. 55–65). Manchester, UK/Northampton, MA: St. Jerome Publishing.

Blommaert, J. (2005) Situating language rights: English and Swahili in Tanzania revisited. *Journal of Sociolinguistics* 9 (3), 390–417.

Board of Indian Commissioners (1880) *Report of the Board of Indian Commissioners* (11th Annual Report for 1879). Washington, DC: US Government Printing Office.

Bourdieu, P. (1989) *La noblesse d'État: grandes écoles et espirit de corps.* Paris: Minuit.

Brutt-Griffler, J. (2002) Class, ethnicity, and language rights: An analysis of British colonial policy in Lesotho and Sri Lanka and some implications for language policy. *Journal of Language, Identity and Education* 1 (3), 207–234.

Brutt-Griffler, J. (2004a) The sound of retreat: The linguistic imperialist camp in disarray. *Journal of Language, Identity and Education* 3 (2), 134–140.

Brutt-Griffler, J. (2004b) Concluding comments. The analysis of language, class, and language rights. *Journal of Language, Identity and Education* 3 (2), 155–157.

Bryld, T. (1998) *I den bedste mening [With the Best of Intentions].* Nuuk, Greenland: Atuakkiorfik.

Cahn, E.S. and Hearne, D.W. (eds) (1969) *Our Brother's Keeper: The Indian in White America.* New York: New Community Press.

CAL (Center for Applied Linguistics) (2011) *Directory of Foreign Language Immersion Programs in U.S. Schools,* accessed 9 February 2012. http://www.cal.org/resources/immersion/

Canagarajah, S. (2004) Language rights and postmodern conditions. Commentary. *Journal of Language, Identity and Education* 3 (2), 140–145.

Cantoni, G. (ed.) (1996) *Stabilizing Indigenous Languages.* Flagstaff, Arizona: Northern Arizona University, Center for Excellence in Education. [Download from http://jan.ucc.nau.edu/~jar/SIL/].

Carpelan, C., Kulonen, U-M., Pulkkinen, R., Seurujärvi-Kari, I., Porsanger, J., Korhonen, O., Svonni, M. and Beck, L.-D. (eds) (2003–2004) *The Encyclopaedia of Saami Culture,* accessed 5 August 2012. http://www.helsinki.fi/~ sugl_smi/senc/en/index.htm

CASLE students' feedback forms. Unpublished data.

Cenoz, J. (2008) Achievements and challenges in bilingual and multilingual education in the Basque Country. In J. Cenoz and D. Gorter (eds) *Multilingualism and Minority Languages: Achievements and Challenges in Education* (pp. 5–12). AILA Review, Vol. 21. Amsterdam: John Benjamins.

Cenoz, J. (2009) *Towards Multilingual Education. Basque Educational Research from an International Perspective*. Bristol: Multilingual Matters.

Cenoz, J. and Gorter, D. (eds) (2008) *Multilingualism and Minority Languages: Achievements and Challenges in Education*. AILA Review, Vol. 21. Amsterdam: John Benjamins.

Chief Jacob Thomas, cf. Thomas (1994).

Churchill, S. (1985) *The Education of Linguistic and Cultural Minorities in the OECD Countries*. Clevedon: Multilingual Matters.

Churchill, W. (1997) *A Little Matter of Genocide. Holocaust and the Denial in the Americas 1492 to the Present*. San Francisco, CA: City Lights Books.

Clancier, G.E. (1996) In the darkness: poetry as promise and hope. In É. Tóth and I. Földeák (eds) *Odi et Amo. Writers on the Love and Hate of Foreign Nations and Cultures* (pp. 27–32). Budapest: Hungarian P.E.N. Club.

Cobo, J.M. (1987) *Study of the Problem of Discrimination Against Indigenous Populations*. Final report submitted by the Special Rapporteur, Mr. José Martínez Cobo. New York: UNPFII (United Nations Permanent Forum on Indigenous Issues).

Collier, V.P. (1989) How long? A synthesis of research on academic achievement in a second language. *TESOL Quarterly* 23, 509–531.

Combs, M.C. and Nicholas, S.E. (2012) The effect of Arizona language policies on Arizona Indigenous students. *Language Policy* 11 (1), 101–118.

Combs, M.C. and Penfield, S.D. (2012) Language activism and language policy. In B. Spolsky (ed.) *The Cambridge Handbook of Language Policy* (pp. 461–474). Cambridge: Cambridge University Press.

Conversi, D. (1990) Language or race? The choice of core values in the development of Catalan and Basque nationalisms. *Ethnic and Racial Studies* 13 (1), 50–70.

Conversi, D. (1997) *The Basques, the Cataland, and Spain. Alternative Routes to Nationalist Mobilisation*. London: C. Hurst.

Conversi, D. (2012) Cultural autonomy, core values and Europe's legacy: A response to Joshua A. Fishman. In O. García and G. Schweid Fishman (eds) *Cultural Autonomy and Fishmanian Sociolinguistics*. Special issue of *International Journal of the Sociology of Language* 213, 63–70.

Cook, V. (1996) *Second Language Learning and Language Teaching* (2nd edn). London: Arnold.

Cook, V. (2006) Non-native language teachers: Perceptions, challenges and contributions to the profession. In E. Llurda (ed.) *Non-Native Language Teachers*. New York: Springer.

Coulmas, F. (ed.) (1981) *A Festschrift for Native Speaker*. The Hague: Mouton.

Coulmas, F. (1991) European integration and the idea of the national language. Ideological roots and economic consequences. In F. Coulmas (ed.) *A Language Policy for the European Community. Prospects and Quandaries* (pp. 1–43). Berlin/New York: Mouton de Gruyter.

Cummins, J. (1978) Immersion programs: The Irish experience. *International Review of Education* 24, 273–282.

Cummins, J. (1980a) The construct of language proficiency in bilingual education. In J.A. Alatis (ed.) *Current Issues in Bilingual Education* (pp. 81–103). Georgetown University Round Table on Languages and Linguistics. Washington, DC: Georgetown University Press.

Cummins, J. (1980b) The cross-lingual dimensions of language proficiency: Implications for bilingual education and the optimal age issue. *Tesol Quarterly* 14 (2), 175–187.

Cummins, J. (1981) The role of primary language development in promoting educational success for language minority students. In C.F. Leyba (ed.) *Schooling and Language*

Minority Students: A Theoretical Framework. Los Angeles, CA: California State University, Evaluation, Dissemination, and Assessment Center.

Cummins, J. (1987a) Bilingualism, language proficiency, and metalinguistic development. In P. Homel, M. Palij and D. Aaronson (eds) *Childhood Bilingualism: Aspects of Linguistic, Cognitive and Social Development* (pp. 57–73). Hillsdale, NJ: Lawrence Erlbaum.

Cummins, J. (1987b) Theory and policy in bilingual education. Centre for Educational Research and Innovation (eds) *Multicultural Education*. Paris: Organization for Economic Cooperation and Development.

Cummins, J. (1991) Conversational and academic language proficiency in bilingual contexts. In J.H. Hulstijn and J.F. Matter (eds) *Reading in Two Languages* (pp. 75–89). AILA Review, Vol. 8. Amsterdam: Free University Press.

Cummins, J. (1992) Interpretations of the Calgary RCSSD #1 Literacy Immersion Project Year 3 data. Report submitted to the Calgary Roman Catholic Separate School Division, September.

Cummins, J. (1994a) The discourse of disinformation: The debate on bilingual education and language rights in the United States. In T. Skutnabb-Kangas and R. Phillipson, in collaboration with M. Rannut (eds) *Linguistic Human Rights. Overcoming Linguistic Discrimination* (pp. 159–177). Berlin/New York: Mouton de Gruyter.

Cummins, J. (1994b) From coercive to collaborative relations of power in the teaching of literacy. In B. Ferdman, R. Weber and A.G. Ramirez (eds) *Literacy Across Languages and Cultures* (pp. 295–331). Albany, NJ: State University of New York Press.

Cummins, J. (1995) Reflections on the European Schools Model in relation to French Immersion Programs in Canada. In T. Skutnabb-Kangas (ed.) *Multilingualism for All* (pp. 159–168). Lisse, The Netherlands: Swets & Zeitlinger.

Cummins, J. (2000) *Language, Power, and Pedagogy: Bilingual Children in the Crossfire*. Clevedon: Multilingual Matters.

Cummins, J. (2001) *Negotiating Identities: Education for Empowerment in a Diverse Society* (2nd edn). Los Angeles, CA: California Association for Bilingual Education.

Cummins, J. (2006) Identity texts: The imaginative construction of self through multi-literacies pedagogy. In O. García, T. Skutnabb-Kangas and M. Torres-Guzmán (eds) *Imagining Multilingual Schools. Languages in Education and Glocalization* (pp. 51–68). Clevedon: Multilingual Matters.

Cummins, J. (2008) Foreword. In J. Cenoz and D. Gorter (eds) *Multilingualism and Minority Languages: Achievements and Challenges in Education* (pp. 1–2). AILA Review, Vol. 21. Amsterdam: John Benjamins.

Cummins, J. (2009) Fundamental psychological and sociological principles underlying educational success for linguistic minority students. In T. Skutnabb-Kangas, R. Phillipson, A. Mohanty and M. Panda (eds) *Social Justice through Multilingual Education* (pp. 19–35). Bristol: Multilingual Matters.

Cummins, J. and Corson, D. (eds) (1997) *Bilingual Education. Encyclopedia of Language and Education* (Vol. 5). Dordrecht/Boston/London: Kluwer Academic.

Cummins, J. and Skutnabb-Kangas, T. (1988) Introduction. In T. Skutnabb-Kangas and J. Cummins (eds) *Minority Education: From Shame to Struggle* (pp. 1–6). Clevedon: Multilingual Matters.

Cummins, J. and Swain, M. (1986) *Bilingualism in Education: Aspects of Theory, Research and Practice*. London/New York: Longman.

Danet, B. and Herring, S. C. (2007) Multilingualism on the internet. In M. Hellinger and A. Pauwels (eds) *Language and Communication: Diversity and Change*. Berlin: Mouton De Gruyter.

Dasgupta, P. (1998) The native speaker: A short history. In R. Singh (ed.) *The Native Speaker: Multilingual Perspectives* (pp. 182–192). New Delhi/Thousand Oaks/London: Sage.

Davies, A. (1991) *The Native Speaker in Applied Linguistics*. Edinburgh: Edinburgh University Press.

de Houwer, A. (2009) *Bilingual First Language Acquisition*. Bristol: Multilingual Matters.

Delmas-Marty, M. (2003) Justice for sale. International law favours market values. *Le Monde Diplomatique*, August (English edn).

de Varennes, F. (1999) The existing rights of minorities in international law. In M. Kontra, R. Phillipson, T. Skutnabb-Kangas and T. Várady (eds) *Language: A Right and a Resource. Approaching Linguistic Human Rights* (pp. 117–146). Budapest: Central European University Press.

Diamond, J. (1992) *The Rise and Fall of the Third Chimpanzee*. London: Vintage.

doCip (2012) Indigenous Peoples' Centre for Documentation, Research and Information (doCip) Update 101, May–June, accessed 6 August 2012. http://www.docip.org

Dunbar, R. and Skutnabb-Kangas, T. (2008) Forms of education of indigenous children as crimes against humanity? Expert Paper written for the United Nations Permanent Forum on Indigenous Issues. New York: PFII. [In PFII system: 'Presented by Lars-Anders Baer, in collaboration with Robert Dunbar, Tove Skutnabb-Kangas and Ole Henrik Magga'.]

Durrani, M. (2012) Banishing colonial specters: Language ideology and education policy in Pakistan. *Working Papers in Educational Linguistics* 27 (1), 29–49.

Eastman, C.M. (1984) Language, ethnic identity and change. In J. Edwards (ed.) *Linguistic Minorities. Policies and Pluralism* (pp. 259–276). London: Academic Press.

Edwards, C. and Read, P. (eds) (1992) *The Lost Children. Thirteen Australians Taken From Their Aboriginal Families Tell of the Struggle to Find Their Natural Parents*. Sydney/Auckland/New York/Toronto/London: Doubleday.

Edwards, J. (1984) Language, diversity and identity. In J. Edwards (ed.) *Linguistic Minorities. Policies and Pluralism* (pp. 277–310). London: Academic Press.

Edwards, J. (1985) *Language, Society and Identity*. Oxford: Blackwell.

Edwards, J. (1994) Ethnolinguistic pluralism and its discontents: A Canadian study, and some general observations. *International Journal of the Sociology of Language* 110, 5–85.

Edwards, J. (2012) Book review of: N. Hornberger (ed.) *Can Schools Save Indigenous Languages?* Language Policy 11 (2), 201–203.

Eriksen, K.E. and Niemi, E. (1981) *Den finske fare. Sikkerhetsproblemer og minoritetspolitikk i nord 1860–1940* [*The Finnish Danger. Security Problems and Minority Policy in the North 1860–1940*]. Oslo: Universitetsforlaget.

Esteva, G. (2010) Beyond education. In L. Meyer and B. Maldonado Alvarado (eds) *New World of Indigenous Resistance. Noam Chomsky and Voices from North, South and Central America* (pp. 115–131). San Francisco, CA: City Lights Books.

European Commission (2006) Summary. *Europeans and Their Languages. Eurobarometer Special* 243 (64.3). http://ec.europa.eu/languages/documents/2006-special-eurobarometer-survey-64.3-europeans-and-languages-summary_en.pdf

Evans, S. (2002) Macaulay's minute revisited: Colonial language policy in nineteenth-century India. *Journal of Multilingual and Multicultural Development* 23 (4), 260–281.

Faez, F. (2011) Reconceptualizing the native/nonnative speaker dichotomy. *Journal of Language, Identity, and Education* 10, 231–249.

Finlex (2003) Saamen kielilaki [The Saami Language Act] 15.12.2003/1086, accessed 5 August 2012. http://www.finlex.fi/sv/laki/ajantasa/2003/20031086

Fishman, J.A. (1991) *Reversing Language Shift. Theoretical and Empirical Foundations of Assistance to Threatened Languages*. Clevedon: Multilingual Matters.

Fishman, J.A. (1997) *In Praise of the Beloved Language. A Comparative view of Positive Ethnolinguistic Consciousness*. Berlin/New York: Mouton de Gruyter.

Fishman, J.A. (2006) Language policy and language shift. In T. Ricento (ed.) *An Introduction to Language Policy. Theory and Method* (pp. 311–328). Oxford: Blackwell.

Florida, R. and Tinagli, I. (2004) *Europe in the Creative Age*. http://www.demos.co.uk/files/EuropeintheCreativeAge2004.pdf?1240939425

FNCSF (Fédération nationale des conseils scolaires francophones) (2010) *Annuaire de l'éducation en français au Canada 2010–2011* (11th edn). Ottawa: GRICS.

Francis, N. and Reyhner, J. (2002) *Language and Literacy Teaching for Indigenous Education. A Bilingual Approach*. Clevedon: Multilingual Matters.

Gaski, H. (1997a) Voice in the margin: A suitable place for a minority literature? In H. Gaski (ed.) *Sami Culture in a New Era. The Norwegian Sami Experience* (pp. 199–220). Kárášjohka/Karasjok, Norway: Davvi Girji.

Gaski, H. (1997b) (ed.) *In the Shadow of the Midnight Sun. Contemporary Sami Prose and Poetry* (pp. 109–117). Kárášjohka, Norway: Davvi Girji.

Genesee, F. (1976) The suitability of immersion programs for all children. *Canadian Modern Language Review* 32 (5), 494–515.

Genesee, F. (1985) Second language learning through immersion: A review of U.S. programs. *Review of Educational Research* 55 (4), 541–561.

Genesee, F. (1987) *Learning Through Two Languages: Studies of Immersion and Bilingual Education*. Cambridge, MA: Newbury House.

Genesee, F. (ed.) (1992) *The Teaching of ESL*. New York: Newbury House.

Genesee, F. (1996) Second language immersion programs. In H. Goebl, P.H. Nelde, Z. Starý and W. Wölck (eds) *Kontaktlinguistik. Contact Linguistics. Linguistique de contact. Ein Internationales Handbuch zeitgenössiger Forschung. An International Handbook of Contemporary Research. Manuel international des recherches contemporaines* (Vol. 1) (pp. 493–501). Berlin/New York: Walter de Gruyter.

Genesee, F. (2004) What do we know about bilingual education for majority language students? In T.K. Bhatia and W. Ritchie (eds) *Handbook of Bilingualism and Multiculturalism* (pp. 547–576). Malden, MA: Blackwell.

Genesee, F. (2006) *The Suitability of French Immersion for Students Who Are at Risk: Students with Special Needs and Lower Academic Ability*. Ottawa: Canadian Parents for French.

Genesee, F., Lindholm-Leary, K., Saunders, W. and Christian, D. (2005) English language learners in U.S. schools: An overview of research findings. *Journal of Education for Students Placed at Risk* 10 (4), 363–385.

Genesee, F., Lindholm-Leary, K., Saunders, W.M. and Christian, D.C. (eds) (2006) *Educating English Language Learners: A Synthesis of Research Evidence*. New York: Cambridge University Press.

Gitlin, T. (2003) *Letters to a Young Activist*. New York: Basic Books.

Graddol, D. (2003) The decline of the native speaker. In G. Anderman and M. Rogers (eds) *Translation Today. Trends and Perspectives* (pp. 152–167). Clevedon: Multilingual Matters.

Grenoble, L.A. and Whaley, L.J. (2006) *Saving Languages. An Introduction to Language Revitalization*. Cambridge: Cambridge University Press.

Grin, F. (1999) *Compétences et récompenses: la valeur des langues en Suisse*. Fribourg: Editions Universitaires.

Grin, F. (2003) Language planning and economics. *Current Issues in Language Planning* 4 (11), 1–66.

Grin, F. (2004) On the costs of cultural diversity. In P. van Parijs (ed.) *Linguistic Diversity and Economic Solidarity* (pp. 189–202). Bruxelles: de Boeck-Université.

Grin, F. and Sfreddo, C. (1997) *Dépenses publiques pour l'enseignement des langues secondes en Suisse*. Geneva: CSRE-SKBF.

Gynther, P. (2003) On the doctrine of systemic discrimination and its usability in the field of education. *International Journal of Minority and Group Rights* 10, 45–54.

Gynther, P. (2007) *Beyond Systemic Discrimination: Educational Rights, Skills Acquisition and the Case of Roma*. Erik Castrén Institute Monographs on International Law and Human Rights Series. Helsinki: University of Helsinki.

Haenni Hoti, A.U., Heinzmann, S., Müller, M., Oliveira, M., Wicki, W. and Werlen, E. (2011) Introducing a second foreign language in Swiss primary schools: The effect of

L2 listening and reading skills on L3 acquisition. *International Journal of Multilingualism* 8 (2), 98–116.

Haji-Othman, N.A. (2012) It's not always English: 'Duelling aunties' in Brunei Darussalam. In V. Rapatahana and P. Bunce (eds) *English Language as Hydra* (pp. 175–190). Bristol: Multilingual Matters.

Harding, S. (1986) *The Science Question in Feminism*. Ithaca/London: Cornell University Press.

Harding, S. (1998) *Is Science Multicultural? Postcolonialisms, Feminisms, and Epistemologies*. Bloomington, IN: Indiana University Press.

Herman, E.S. and Chomsky, N. (1988) *Manufacturing Consent: The Political Economy of the Mass Media*. New York: Pantheon.

Hinton, L. (1994) *Flutes of Fire*. Berkeley, CA: Heyday.

Hinton, L. (2001) Language planning. In L. Hinton and K. Hale (eds) *The Green Book of Language Revitalisation in Practice* (pp. 51–59). San Diego, CA: Academic Press.

Hinton, L. (2002) Commentary: Internal and external language advocacy. *Journal of Linguistic Anthropology* 12, 150–156.

Hinton, L. (2009) Powerpoint presentation: Language revitalization at home. Honolulu: ICLDC.

Hinton, L. and Hale, K. (eds) (2001) *The Green Book of Language Revitalization in Practice*. San Diego, CA: Academic Press.

Hinton, L. (with M. Vera, N. Steel and the Advocates for Indigenous California Language Survival) (2002) *How to Keep Your Language Alive. A Commonsense Approach to One-on-One Language Learning*. Berkeley, CA: Heyday Books.

Hinton, L. (ed.) (2013) *Bringing Our Languages Home. Language Revitalization for Families*. Edited and with a How-to Guide for Parents by Leanne Hinton. Berkeley, CA: Heyday Books.

Holm, A. and Holm, W. (1990) Rock Point, a Navajo way to go to school: A valediction. *Annals of the American Academy of Philosophy and Social Science* 508, 170–184.

Holm, A. and Holm, W. (1995) Navajo language education: Retrospect and prospects. *Bilingual Research Journal* 19 (1), 141–167.

Holm, W. (2006) The 'goodness' of bilingual education for Native American children. In T.L. McCarty and O. Zepeda (eds) *One Voice, Many Voices – Recreating Indigenous Language Communities* (pp. 1–46). Tempe, AZ: Arizona State University Center for Indian Education.

Holmén, J. (2012) Push and pull among Finnish reindeer herders. *Fram Forum* 2012, 22–23.

Hornberger, N.H. (ed.) (1996) *Indigenous Literacies in the Americas: Language Planning From the Bottom Up*. Berlin: Mouton de Gruyter.

Hornberger, N.H. (1998) Language policy, language education, language rights. Indigenous, immigrant, and international perspectives. *Language in Society* 27, 439–458.

Hornberger, N.H. (ed.) (2003) *Continua of Biliteracy. An Ecological Framework for Educational Policy, Research, and Practice in Multilingual Settings*. Clevedon: Multilingual Matters.

Hornberger, N.H. (2006) Nichols to NCLB: Local and global perspectives on U.S. language education policy. In O. García, T. Skutnabb-Kangas and M. Torres-Guzmán (eds) *Imagining Multilingual Schools. Languages in Education and Glocalization* (pp. 223–237). Bristol: Multilingual Matters.

Hornberger, N.H. (ed.) (2011) *Can Schools Save Indigenous Languages?* New York: Palgrave Macmillan.

Hymes, D.H. (1972) On communicative competence. In J.B. Pride and J. Holmes (eds) *Sociolinguistics: Selected Readings* (pp. 269–293). Harmondsworth: Penguin.

Ilaiah, K. (2009a) [1996] *Why I Am Not a Hindu. A Sudra Critique of Hindutva Philosophy, Culture and Political Economy*. Calcutta: Samya.

Ilaiah, K. (2009b) [2007] *Turning the Pot, Tilling the Land. Dignity of Labour in Our Times.* New Delhi: Navayana Publishing.
Itkonen, E. (1986–1990) *Inarilappisches Wörterbuch. Unter Mitarbeit von Raija Bartens und Lea Laitinen [The Aanaar Saami Dictionary. With the assistance of Raija Bartens and Lea Laitinen].* Lecica societatis Fenno-ugricae XX, 1–3. Helsinki: Suomalais-Ugrilainen Seura.
Itkonen, E. (1992) *Inarinsaamelaisia kielennäytteitä – Aanaarkiela čájttuzeh* [Samples of AS]. Helsinki: Suomalais-Ugrilainen Seura.
Itkonen, T.I. (1984) *Suomen lappalaiset vuoteen 1945 I–II [The Finnish Lapps Until the Year 1945, I–II]* (2nd edn). Porvoo, Finland: WSOY.
Jaakkola, M. (1989) *Suomalaisten suhtautuminen ulkomaalaisiin ja ulkomaalaispolitiikkaan [Finnish Attitudes and Policies Towards Foreigners].* Työvoimaministeriö, Suunnitteluosasto, Siirtolaisuustutkimuksia 21. Helsinki: Valtion painatuskeskus.
Jaakkola, M. (1995) *Suomalaisten kiristyvät ulkomaalaisasenteet [Deteriorating Finnish Attitudes Towards Foreigners].* Työministeriö, Työpoliittinen tutkimus 101. Helsinki: Valtion painatuskeskus.
Jaakkola, M. (1999) *Maahanmuutto ja etniset asenteet. Suomalaisten suhtautuminen maahan-muuttajiin 1987–1999 [Immigration and Ethnic Attitudes. Finnish Attitudes Towards Immigrants 1987–1999].* Työministeriö, Työpoliittinen tutkimus 213. Helsinki: Edita.
Jaakkola, M. (2005) *Suomalaisten suhtautuminen maahanmuuttajiin vuosina 1987–2003 [Finnish Attitudes Towards Immigrants 1987–2003].* Työministeriö, Työpoliittinen tutki-mus 286. Helsinki: Työministeriö.
Jaakkola, M. (2009) *Maahanmuuttajat suomalaisten näkökumasta. Asennemuutokset 1987–2007 [Immigrants from a Finnish Point of View. Attitudinal Changes 1987–2007].* Helsinki: Helsingin kaupungin Tietokeskus. http://www.hel.fi/tietokeskus
Jaffe, A. (2011) Critical perspectives on language-in-education policy: The Corsican exam-ple. In T. McCarty (ed.) *Ethnography and Language Policy* (pp. 205–230). New York/ London: Routledge.
Jernsletten, N. (1997) Sami traditional terminology: Professional terms concerning salmon, reindeer and snow. In H. Gaski (ed.) *Sami Culture in a New Era. The Norwegian Sami Experience* (pp. 86–108). Kárášjohka/Karasjok: Davvi Girji.
Jordan, D. (1988) Rights and claims of indigenous people. Education and the reclaiming of identity: The case of the Canadian natives, the Sami and Australian Aborigines. In T. Skutnabb–Kangas and J. Cummins (eds) *Minority Education: From Shame to Struggle* (pp. 189–222). Clevedon: Multilingual Matters.
Jouste, M. (2011) *Tullâčalmaaš kirdâččij 'Tulisilmillä lenteli'. Inarinsaamelainen 1900-luvun alun musiikkikulttuuri paikallisen perinteen ja ympäröivien kulttuurien vuorovaikutuksessa [The One Who Flew With the Fire-eyes – Aanaar Sámi Music Culture as Interaction of the Local Tradition and Neighboring Cultures in the Beginning of the 20th Century].* Tampere, Finland: Tampereen yliopistopaino oy.
Kabel, A. (2012a) 'There is no such thing as "keeping out of politics"': Arabisation and Amazigh/Berber mother tongue education in Morocco. In T. Skutnabb-Kangas and K. Heugh (eds) *Multilingual Education and Sustainable Diversity Work. From Periphery to Center* (pp. 216–238). New York: Routledge.
Kabel, A. (2012b) 'The return of the represses': Scattered reflections on the state, liberal-ism, cultural autonomy, language rights and identity. In O. García and G. Schweid Fishman (eds) *Cultural Autonomy and Fishmanian Sociolinguistics.* Special issue of *International Journal of the Sociology of Language* 213, 71–85.
Kalla, A-M. (2010) Inarinsaamen kielen täydennyskoulutus 2009–2010. Kielimestareiden kokemukset kielimestarina toimimisesta [Aanaar Saami Complementary Education 2009–2010. Language Masters' experiences at work]. Unpublished.
Kandiah, T. (1998) Epiphanies of the deathless native user's manifold avatars: A post-colonial perspective on the native speaker. In R. Singh (ed.) *The Native Speaker: Multilingual Perspectives* (pp. 79–110). New Delhi/Thousand Oaks/London: Sage.

Kielitoimiston sanakirja [Dictionary of the Language Office] (2006) Helsinki: Kotimaisten kielten tutkimuskeskus.

King, J. (2001) Te kōhanga reo: Māori language revitalization. In L. Hinton and K. Hale (eds) *The Green Book of Language Revitalization in Practice* (pp. 119–128). San Diego, CA: Academic Press.

Kivelä, S. (2011) *Reborn*. Video (with English subtitles). http://www.youtube.com/watch?v=e0YcIkUoEhc&feature=youtu.be

Koivurova, T. (2010) Alkuperäiskansojen asema ja oikeudet kansainvälisessä oikeudessa [The position and rights of Indigenous peoples in international law]. In K.T. Kokko (ed.) *Kysymyksiä saamelaisten oikeusasemasta* [Issues Regarding the Legal Position of the Saami] (pp. 26–49). Sarja B No. 30. Rovaniemi, Finland: Lapin yliopiston oikeustieteellisiä julkaisuja.

Koivurova, T. (2011). Ihmisoikeustutkimus ja saamelaiset [Human rights research and the Saami]. In I. Seurujärvi-Kari, P. Halinen and R. Pulkkinen (eds) *Saamentutkimus tänään* [Saami research today] (pp. 393–417). Helsinki: Suomalaisen Kirjallisuuden Seura.

Kokko, K.T. (ed.) (2010) *Kysymyksiä saamelaisten oikeusasemasta* [Issues Regarding the Legal Position of the Saami]. Sarja B No. 30. Rovaniemi: Lapin yliopiston oikeustieteellisiä julkaisuja.

Körmendi, E. (1986) *Os og de andre. Danskernes holdninger til indvandrere og flygtninge* [Us and the Others. Danish Attitudes Towards Immigrants and Refugees]. Publikation No. 153. Copenhagen: Socialforsningsinstituttet.

Koškepuško (2010) http://www.casle.fi

Kosonen, K. (2009) Language-in-education policies in Southeast Asia: An overview. In K. Kosonen and C. Young (eds) *Mother Tongue as Bridge Language of Instruction: Policies and Experiences in Southeast Asia* (pp. 22–43). Bangkok: Southeast Asian Ministers of Education Organization.

Kosztolányi, D. (1987) [1939] The place of the Hungarian language on the earth. Open letter to Monsiour Anttoine Meillet, professor of the Collège de France. In É. Tóth (ed.) *Today. An Anthology of Contemporary Hungarian Literature* (pp. 21–37). Budapest: Corvina.

Krauss, M. (1992) The world's languages in crisis. *Language* 68 (1), 4–10.

Krauss, M. (1996) Status of Native American language endangerment. In G. Cantoni (ed.) *Stabilizing Indigenous Languages*. Flagstaff, AZ: Northern Arizona University. http://jan.ucc.nau.edu/~jar/SIL/

Krauss, M.E. (1997) The indigenous languages of the north: A report on their present state. In H. Shoji and J. Janhunen (eds) *Northern Minority Languages: Problems of Survival* (pp. 1–34). Senri Ethnological Studies, 44. Osaka: National Museum of Ethnology.

Krauss, M. (1998) The condition of Native North American languages: The need for realistic assessment and action. *International Journal of the Sociology of Language* 132, 9–21.

Krauss, M., Maffi, L. and Yamamoto, A. (2004) The world's languages in crisis: Questions, challenges, and a call for action. In O. Sakiyama, F. Endo, H. Watanabe and F. Sasama (eds) *Lectures on Endangered Languages 4* (pp. 23–27). Suita, Osaka: Endangered Languages of the Pacific Rim Project.

Kulbrandsdal, L.A. (2011) Attitudes to minority languages. Paper presented at the conference '4 or more languages for all', Tórshavn, Faroe Islands, 22–25 August.

Kulonen, U.-M., Seurujärvi-Kari, I. and Pulkkinen, R. (eds) (2005) *The Saami. A Cultural Encyclopaedia*. Helsinki: Suomalaisen Kirjallisuuden Seura.

Kuokkanen, R. (2008) Mitä on saamelaisten hyvinvointi? Tarkastelua kansainvälisessä alkuperäiskansojen kontekstissa. Puheenvuoro SámiSoster -seuran 10-vuotisjuhlaseminaarissa [What is the welfare of Saami? Analysis of the international context of Indigenous people. A statement made at the 10-year celebration seminar of the Saami Soster Association]. Inari, 21 April.

Kymlicka, W. and Grin, F. (2003) Assessing the politics of diversity in transition countries. In F. Daftary and F. Grin (eds) *Nation-building, Ethnicity and Language Politics in Transition Countries* (pp. 5–27). Budapest/Flensburg: Local Government and Public Service Reform Initiative, Open Society Institute/ECMI (European Centre for Minority Issues).

Kymlicka, W. and Patten, A. (2003) Language rights and political theory. *Annual Review of Applied Linguistics* 23, 3–21.

Kyrö, T. (2012) *Lohosierâ 1 [Counting game 1]*. (Translated from Okkonen-Sotka, P., Sihvo, T., Sintonen, A.-M. and Uus-Leponiemi, T. (2009) *Matikka*. Helsinki: WSOY Pro Oy.) Aanaar: Sämitigge.

Laitin, D.D. and Reich, R. (2003) A Liberal Democratic approach to language justice. In W. Kymlicka and A. Patten (eds) *Language Rights and Political Theory* (pp. 80–104). Oxford: Oxford University Press.

Laitinen, L. (1973) Keruukertomus 25.9.1973. Kotimaisten kielten tutkimuskeskuksen äänitearkiston käsikirjoitus [Collection of recitations, 25.9.1973. Manuscript of the Recording Archive]. Helsinki: Kotimaisten kielten tutkimuskeskus.

Laitinen, L. (1987) Inarinlapin sanakirja valmistumassa [The Aanaar Saami Dictionary will be completed]. In *Virittäjä* 2, 222–227. Helsinki: Kotikielen seura.

Laitinen, L. (2006) Elsa Valle 1924–2006. *Virittäjä* 3, 439–439. http://www.kotikielenseura. fi/virittaja/hakemistot/jutut/2006_438.pdf

Laitinen, L. (2009) Interviewed by Taarna Valtonen in December.

Laitinen, L. (2011) Interviewed by Marja-Liisa Olthuis in March.

Lambert, W.E. (1975) Culture and language as factors in learning and education. In A. Wolfgang (ed.) *Education of Immigrant Students* (pp. 55–83). Toronto: Ontario Institute for Studies in Education.

Lambert, W.E. (1977) The effects of bilingualism on the individual: Cognitive and socio-cultural consequences. In P.A. Hornby (ed.) *Bilingualism. Psychological, Social and Educational Implications* (pp. 15–27). New York: Academic Press.

Lambert, W.E. (1978) Some cognitive and sociocultural consequences of being bilingual. In J. Alatis (ed.) *International Dimensions of Bilingual Education* (pp. 214–229). Georgetown University Round Table on Languages and Linguistics. Washington, DC: Georgetown University Press.

Lambert, W.E. (1984) An overview of issues in immersion education. In *Studies on Immersion Education. A Collection for United States Educators* (pp. 8–30). Sacramento, CA: California State Department of Education.

Lambert, W.E. (1987) The effects of bilingual and bicultural experiences on children's attitudes and social perspectives. In P. Homel, M. Palij and D. Aaronson (eds) *Childhood Bilingualism: Aspects of Linguistic, Cognitive and Social Development* (pp. 197–221). Hillsdale, NJ: Lawrence Erlbaum.

Lambert, W.E. and Taylor, D.M. (1982) Language in the education of ethnic minority immigrants: Issues, problems and methods. Paper presented to Conference on Education of Ethnic Minority Immigrants, Miami, FL.

Lambert, W. and Taylor, D.M. (1996) Language in the lives of ethnic minorities: Cuban American families in Miami. *Applied Linguistics* 17 (4), 477–500.

Lambert, W.E. and Tucker, R.G. (1972) *Bilingual Education of Children. The St. Lambert Experiment*. Rowley, MA: Newbury House.

Lange, A. and Westin, C. (1981) *Etnisk diskriminering och social identitet. Forskningsöversikt och teoretisk analys*. Stockholm: Diskrimineringsutredningen.

Lange, A. and Westin, C. (1993) *Den mångtydiga toleransen [The Ambiguous Tolerance]*. Stockholm: CEIFO, Stockholm University.

Länsman, T. (2000) *Kaldoaivin erämaa-alueen asutus- ja elinkeinohistoria [The History of Colonisation and Livelihoods in the Kaldoaivi Wilderness]*. Helsinki: Metsähallitus.

Lassila, J. (2001) *Lapin koulutushistoria – kirkollinen alkuopetus, kansa-, perus- ja oppikoulut. I–II [The Educational History of Lapland – Basic Teaching as Organised by Churches,*

Elementary, Comprehensive and Secondary Schools]. Oulu, Finland: Kasvatustieteiden ja opettajankoulutuksen yksikkö.

Lehtola, T. (1996) *Lapinmaan vuosituhannet. Lapin ja saamelaisten historia kivikaudesta 1930-luvulle [Lapland over the Millennia. The History of Lapland and the Saami People from the Stone Age until the 1930s]*. Inari, Finland: Kustannus-Puntsi.

Lehtola, T. (1998) *Kolmen kuninkaan maa. Historian Inari [The Land of the Three Kings. Aanaar History]*. Inari, Finland: Kustannus-Puntsi.

Lehtola, V.-P. (1997) *Saamelaiset – Historia, yhteiskunta, taide [The Saami People – History, Society, Art]*. Inari, Finland: Kustannus-Puntsi.

Lehtola, V.-P. (2012) *Saamelaiset suomalaiset – Kohtaamisia 1896–1953 [The Saami Finns – Encounters 1896–1953]*. Helsinki: Suomalaisen Kirjallisuuden Seura.

Lewis, J.A. (1987) The natives as seen by the missionaries: Preconception and reality. In R. Costo and J.H. Costo (eds) *The Missions of California: A Legacy of Genocide* (pp. 81–98). San Francisco, CA: Indian Historian Press.

Li, D.C.S. (2009) Researching non-native speakers' views toward intelligibility and identity: Bridging the gap between moral high grounds and down-to-earth concerns. In F. Sharifian (ed.) *English as an International Language. Perspectives and Pedagogical Issues* (pp. 81–118). Bristol: Multilingual Matters.

Lind Meløy, L. (1980) *Internatliv i Finnmark. Skolepolitikk 1900–1940 [Boarding School Life in Finnmark. School Policy 1900–1940]*. Oslo: Det Norske Samlaget.

Lindholm, K.J. (1990a) Bilingual immersion education: Criteria for program development. In A.M. Padilla, H.H. Fairchild and C.M. Valadez (eds) *Bilingual Education: Issues and Strategies* (pp. 91–105). Newbury Park, CA: Sage.

Lindholm, K.J. (1990b) Bilingual immersion education: Educational equity for language-minority students. In A. Barona and E. Garcia (eds) *Children at Risk: Poverty, Minority Status and Other Issues in Educational Equity* (pp. 77–89). Washington, DC: National Association of School Psychologists.

Lindholm, K.J. (1991) Theoretical assumptions and empirical evidence for academic achievement in two languages. *Hispanic Journal of Behavioral Sciences* 13, 3–17.

Lindholm, K.J. (1992a) Two-way bilingual/immersion education: Theory, conceptual issues, and pedagogical implications. In R.V. Padilla and A.H. Benavides (eds) *Critical Perspectives on Bilingual Education Research* (pp. 195–220). Tempe, AZ: Bilingual Review Press/Editorial Bilingüe.

Lindholm, K.J. (1992b) Relationship between language proficiency, academic achievement and cognition: Outcomes from bilingual/immersion programs. Paper presented at the National Association for Bilingual Education Conference, Albuquerque, NM, January.

Lindholm, K.J. (1992c) The River Glen Elementary School Bilingual Immersion Program: Student progress after five years of implementation. Evaluation Report 1990–1991. River Glen Elementary School, San Jose, CA.

Lindholm, K.J. (1994) Promoting positive cross-cultural attitudes and perceived competence in culturally and linguistically diverse classrooms. In R.A. de Villar, C.J. Faltis and J.P. Cummins (eds) *Cultural Diversity in Schools: From Rhetoric to Practice* (pp. 189–206). Albany, NY: State University of New York Press.

Lindholm, K.J. (1997) Two-way bilingual education programs in the United States. In J. Cummins and D. Corson (eds) *Bilingual Education. Encyclopedia of Language and Education* (Vol. 5) (pp. 271–280). Dordrecht/Boston/London: Kluwer Academic Publishers.

Lindholm, K.J. and Aclan, Z. (1991) Bilingual proficiency as a bridge to academic achievement: Results from bilingual/immersion programs. *Journal of Education* 173 (2), 99–113.

Lindholm, K.J. and Fairchild, H.H. (1989) Evaluation of an 'exemplary' bilingual immersion program. Technical Report No. 13. Los Angeles, CA: UCLA Center for Language Education and Research.

Lindholm-Leary, K.J. (2001) *Dual Language Education*. Clevedon: Multilingual Matters.

Lindholm-Leary, K. and Borsato, G. (2006) Academic achievement. In F. Genesee, K. Lindholm-Leary, W. Saunders and D. Christian (eds) *Educating English Language Learners* (pp. 176–222). New York: Cambridge University Press.

Liu, J. (2006) Chinese graduate teaching assistants teaching freshman composition to native English speaking students. In E. Llurda (ed.) *Non-Native Language Teachers. Perceptions, Challenges and Contributions to the Profession* (pp. 155–177). New York: Springer.

Llurda, E. (ed.) (2006) *Non-Native Language Teachers*. New York: Springer.

Lo Bianco, J. (2012) National language revival movements: Reflections from India, Israel, Indonesia and Ireland. In B. Spolsky (ed.) *The Cambridge Handbook of Language Policy* (pp. 501–522). Cambridge: Cambridge University Press.

Luyendijk, J. (2012) Just doing their jobs. The world bankers inhabit has no sense of national solidarity. *Guardian Weekly* 24 February, 24.

Macdonald, R. (1985) The Maori of New Zealand. Report No. 70. London: Minority Rights Group.

Magga, O.H. and Skutnabb-Kangas, T. (2001) The Saami languages: The present and the future. In E. Quinn (ed.) Special issue on *Endangered Languages of Cultural Survival Quarterly* 25 (2), Summer.

Magga, O.H. and Skutnabb-Kangas, T. (2003) Life or death for languages and human beings – experiences from Saamiland. In L. Huss, A. Camilleri Grima and K. King (eds) *Transcending Monolingualism: Linguistic Revitalisation in Education* (pp. 35–52). Multilingualism and Linguistic Diversity Series. Lisse, The Netherlands: Swets & Zeitlinger.

Magga, O.H. and Skutnabb-Kangas, T. (2008) Some prerequisites for a life for Saami languages and the Saami people. In P. Huse (ed.) *Northern Imaginary* (Part 3) (pp. 109–122). Oslo: Delta Press.

Magga, O.H., Nicolaisen, I., Trask, M., Dunbar, R. and Skutnabb-Kangas, T. (2005) Indigenous children's education and indigenous languages. Expert Paper written for the United Nations Permanent Forum on Indigenous Issues. New York: United Nations.

Makoni, S. and Pennycook, A. (2005) Disinventing and (re)constituting languages. *Critical Inquiry in Language Studies: An International Journal* 2 (3), 137–156.

Makoni, S. and Pennycook, A. (eds) (2007) *Disinventing and Reconstituting Languages*. Clevedon: Multilingual Matters.

Maldonado Alvarado, B. (2010) *Comunalidad* and the education of Indigenous peoples. In L. Meyer and B. Maldonado Alvarado (eds) *New World of Indigenous Resistance. Noam Chomsky and Voices from North, South and Central America* (pp. 367–380). San Francisco, CA: City Lights Books.

Mancini, S. and de Witte, B. (2008) Language rights as cultural rights—a European perspective. In F. Francioni and M. Scheinin (eds) *Cultural Human Rights* (pp. 247–284). Leiden/Boston: Martinus Nijhoff Publishers.

Marainen, J. (1988) Returning to Sami identity. In T. Skutnabb-Kangas and J. Cummins (eds) *Minority Education. From Shame to Struggle* (pp. 179–185). Clevedon: Multilingual Matters.

May, S. (ed.) (1999) *Indigenous Community-based Education*. Clevedon: Multilingual Matters.

May, S. (2001) *Language and Minority Rights*. Harlow: Pearson Education.

May, S. (2003) Misconceiving minority language rights: Implications for Liberal political theory. In W. Kymlicka and A. Patten (eds) *Language Rights and Political Theory* (pp. 123–152). Oxford: Oxford University Press.

May, S. (2005) Language rights: Moving the debate forward. *Journal of Sociolinguistics* 9 (3), 319–347.

May, S. (2010) Book review of S. Makoni and A. Pennycook (eds) *Disinventing and Reconstituting Languages. Applied Linguistics* 31 (1), 159–163.

May, S. (2012) Contesting hegemonic and monolithic constructions of language rights 'discourse'. *Journal of Multicultural Discourses* 7 (1), 21–27.

McCarty, T.L. (1997) American Indian, Alaska Native, and Native Hawaiian bilingual education. In J. Cummins and D. Corson (eds) *Bilingual Education. Encyclopedia of Language and Education* (Vol. 5) (pp. 45–56). Dordrecht/Boston/London: Kluwer Academic Publishers.

McCarty, T.L. (1998) Schooling, resistance, and American Indian languages. *International Journal of the Sociology of Language.* 132, 27–41.

McCarty, T.L. (2002a) *A Place to be Navajo – Rough Rock and the Struggle for Self-Determination in Indigenous Schooling.* Mahwah, NJ: Lawrence Erlbaum.

McCarty, T.L. (2002b) Between possibility and constraint: Indigenous language education, planning, and policy in the United States. In J.W. Tollefson (ed.) *Language Policies in Education. Critical Issues* (pp. 285–307). Mahwah, NJ: Lawrence Erlbaum.

McCarty, T.L. (2003) Revitalising Indigenous languages in homogenising times. *Comparative Education* 39 (2), 147–163.

McCarty, T.L. (2005) The power within: Indigenous literacies and teacher empowerment. In T.L. McCarty (ed.) *Language, Literacy, and Power in Schooling* (pp. 47–66). Mahwah, NJ: Lawrence Erlbaum.

McCarty, T.L. (2008a) Native American languages as Heritage mother tongues. *Language, Culture and Curriculum* 21 (3), 201–225.

McCarty, T.L. (2008b) Schools as strategic tools for Indigenous language revitalization: Lessons from Native America. In N.H. Hornberger (ed.) *Can Schools Save Indigenous Languages? Policy and Practice on Four Continents* (pp. 161–179). New York: Palgrave Macmillan.

McCarty, T.L. (2009) Empowering Indigenous languages – what can be learned from Native American experiences? In T. Skutnabb-Kangas, R. Phillipson, A. Mohanty and M. Panda (eds) *Social Justice Through Multilingual Education* (pp. 125–139). Bristol: Multilingual Matters.

McCarty, T.L. (2011a) Language choice, education equity, and mother tongue schooling – comparing the cases of Ethiopia and Native America. In T. Skutnabb-Kangas and K. Heugh (eds) *Multilingual Education and Sustainable Diversity Work. From Periphery to Center* (pp. 62–84). New York: Routledge.

McCarty, T.L. (ed.) (2011b) *Ethnography and Language Policy.* New York/London: Routledge.

McCarty, T.L. (2012) Indigenous language planning and policy in the Americas. In B. Spolsky (ed.) *The Cambridge Handbook of Language Policy* (pp. 544–569). Cambridge: Cambridge University Press.

McCarty, T.L. and Wyman, L.T. (eds) (2009) Special issue on *Indigenous Youth and Bilingualism of Journal of Language, Identity, and Education* 8 (5).

McCarty, T. and Zepeda, O. (eds) (with V.H. Begay, Stephanie Charging Eagle, S.C. Moore, L. Warhole and T.M.K. Williams) (2006c) *One Voice, Many Voices. Recreating Indigenous Language Communities.* Tempe/Tucson, AZ: Arizona State University Center for Indian Education/University of Arizona American Indian Language Development Institute.

McCarty, T., Borgoiakova, T., Gilmore, P., Lomawaima, K.T. and Romero, M.E. (2005) Editors' introduction. Indigenous epistemologies and education – self-determination, anthropology and human rights. *Anthropology and Education Quarterly* 36 (1), 1–7.

McCarty, T.L., Romero-Little, M.E. and Zepeda, O. (2006a) Native American youth discourses on language shift and retention: Ideological cross-currents and their implications for language planning. *International Journal of Bilingual Education and Bilingualism* 9 (5), 659–677.

McCarty, T.L., Romero, M.E. and Zepeda, O. (2006b) Reimagining multilingual America: Lessons from Native American youth. In O. García, T. Skutnabb-Kangas and M. Torres-Guzmán (eds) *Imagining Multilingual Schools. Languages in Education and Glocalization* (pp. 91–110). Clevedon: Multilingual Matters.

McCarty, T.L., Skutnabb-Kangas, T. and Magga, O-H. (2007) Education for speakers of endangered languages. In B. Spolsky and F. Hult (eds) *The Handbook of Educational Linguistics* (pp. 297–312). Oxford: Blackwell.

McCarty, T.L., Romero-Little, M.E., Warhole, L. and Zepeda, O. (2009) Indigenous youth as language policy makers. In T.L. McCarty and W.T. Wyman (eds) Special issue on *Indigenous Youth and Bilingualism of Journal of Language, Identity, and Education* 8 (5), 291–306.

McCarty, T.L., Romero-Little, M.E., Warhole, L. and Zepeda, O. (2011) Critical ethnography and Indigenous language survival: Some new directions in language policy research and praxis. In T.L. McCarty (ed.) *Ethnography and Language Policy* (pp. 30–51). New York/London: Routledge.

Meyer, L. and Maldonado Alvarado, B. (eds) (2010) *New World of Indigenous Resistance. Noam Chomsky and Voices from North, South and Central America.* San Francisco, CA: City Lights Books.

Milloy, J.S. (1999) *'A National Crime': The Canadian Government and the Residential School System, 1879 to 1986.* Winnipeg: University of Manitoba Press.

Mohanty, A.K. (1995) *Bilingualism in a Multilingual Society. Psycho-social and Pedagogical Implications.* Mysore: Central Institute of Indian Languages.

Mohanty, A.K. (2009) 'Multilingual education – A Bridge Too Far?' In A. Mohanty, M. Panda, R. Phillipson and T. Skutnabb-Kangas (eds) *Multilingual Education for Social Justice: Globalising the Local* (pp. 5–19). New Delhi: Orient BlackSwan.

Mohanty, A.K. and Skutnabb-Kangas, T. (2010) MLE as an economic equaliser in India and Nepal: mother tongue based multilingual education fights poverty through capability development and identity support. In Henrard, K. (ed.) *Socio economic participation of minorities in relation to their right to (respect for) identity. Studies in International Minority and Group Rights, Volume 2.* Leiden and Boston: Brill/ Martinus Nijhoff Publishers.

Moseley, C. (ed.) (2010) *Atlas of the World's Languages in Danger* (3rd edn). Paris: UNESCO Publishing. Online at http://www.unesco.org/culture/en/endangeredlanguages/atlas

Morottaja, M. (2008) *Mii lostâ, tuu lostâ* [*Our communal magazine, your communal magazine*]. In *Anarâš*, juovlâmáánu [December]. Aanaar: Anarâškielâ servi, 2.

Morottaja, K. (2010) Language nest interview. Interviewed by Marja-Liisa Olthuis in December.

Morottaja, P., Kuuva, P. and Olthuis, M-L. (2012) *Kielâkyeimi 1* [*Language Fellow 1*]. Aanaar: Sämitigge.

Mühlhäusler, P. (1998) Landscape language. Interview with Pamela Lyon. *Adelaide University Newspaper*, January.

Nahkiaisoja, T. (2003a) Uudisasuttajien aika 1750–1876 [The Newcomer period 1750–1876]. In V-P. Lehtola (ed.) *Inari Aanaar. Inarin historia jääkaudesta nykypäivään* [*Inari Aanaar. The History of Aanaar from the Ice Age to the Present*] (pp. 166–184). Oulu, Finland: Painotalo Suomenmaa.

Nahkiaisoja, T. (2003b) Inarilaisyhteisön muutoksen aika 1877–1920 [The period of change in the Aanaar community 1877–1920]. In V.-P. Lehtola (ed.) *Inari Aanaar. Inarin historia jääkaudesta nykypäivään* [*Inari Aanaar. The History of Aanaar from the Ice Age to the Present*] (pp. 216–286). Oulu, Finland: Painotalo Suomenmaa.

Nettisaje (2012) http://nettisaje.wikispaces.com

Nettle, D. and Romaine, S. (2000) *Vanishing Voices. The Extinction of the World's Languages.* Oxford: Oxford University Press.

Nickul, E. (1968) Suomen saamelaiset vuonna 1962. Selostus Pohjoismaiden saamelaisneuvoston suorittamasta väestöntutkimuksesta [The Finnish Saami people in 1962. A report of the population exploration executed by the Saami Council]. Tilastotieteen pro gradu -tutkielma [Master's thesis in statistics]. Helsinki: University of Helsinki.

Nikula, P. and Kalla, A-M. (2011) *Vuosmuš tuhháát säännid anarâškiellân* [*The First Thousand Words in Aanaar Saami*]. (Translation from Amery, H. (2009) *The First Thousand Words in English*. London: Usborne Publishing.) Aanaar: Sämitigge.

Nilsson, C. (2012) Jag levde ett dubbelliv under hela skoltiden [I led a double life during all my school years]. *Allers* 4, 8–9.

Nuffield Foundation (2000) *Languages: The Next Generation. The Final Report and Recommendations of the Nuffield Languages Inquiry*. London: Nuffield Foundation.

Ober, R. and Bell, J. (2012) English Language as Juggernaut – Aboriginal English and Indigenous Languages in Australia. In V. Rapatahana and P. Bunce (eds) *English Language as Hydra* (pp. 60–75). Bristol: Multilingual Matters.

OCOL (2011) *Leadership, Action, Results. Annual Report 2010–2011*. Ottawa: Office of the Commissioner of Official Languages.

OECD (2010) *PISA 2009 Results: Executive Summary*, accessed 6 August 2012. http://www.oecd.org/pisa/

Ogbu, J.U. (1978) *Minority Education and Caste*. New York: Academic Press.

Ogbu, J.U. (1983) Minority status and schooling in plural societies, *Comparative Education Review* 27, 168–190.

OKM (Ministry of Education) (2012a) The Saami revitalisation report of the Ministry of Education and Culture. Helsinki: Ministry of Education and Culture.

OKM (Ministry of Education) (2012b) *Toimenpideohjelma saamen kielen elvyttämiseksi* [*Programme of Action for the Revitalisation of the Saami Languages*]. Opetus- ja kulttuuriministeriön työryhmämuistioita ja selvityksiä, July. Helsinki: Opetus- ja kulttuuriministeriö/Undervisnings- och kulturministeriet. Koulutus- ja tiedepolitiikan osasto/Utbildnings- och forskningspolitiska avdelningen/Ministry of Education and Culture, Section of Education and Research Policy. Online at http://www.minedu.fi/OPM/julkaisut

Olthuis, M-L. (2000) *Inarinsaamen kielioppi* [*Aanaar Saami Grammar*]. Aanaar: Sämitigge.

Olthuis, M-L. (2003) Uhanalaisen kielen elvytys: esimerkkinä inarinsaame [Revitalising an endangered language: The Aanaar Saami case]. In *Virittäjä* 4, 568–579. Helsinki: Kotikielen Seura.

Olthuis, M-L. (2007) *Inarinsaamen lajinnimet. Lintujen ja sienten kansannimitysten historiaa ja oppitekoisten uudisnimien muodostuksen metodiikkaa* [*Species Names in Inari Saami: A History of the Popular Names of Birds and Mushrooms and Methods for Creating New Names for Species*]. Avveel, Finland: Anarâškielâ servi ry.

Ouane, A. and Glanz, C. (eds) (2011) *Optimising Learning, Education and Publishing in Africa: The Language Factor. A Review and Analysis of Theory and Practice in Mother-Tongue and Bilingual Education in Sub-Saharan Africa*. Hamburg: UNESCO Institute for Lifelong Learning (UIL)/Association for the Development of Education in Africa (ADEA)/African Development Bank.

Paltto, K. (2010) Interviewed by Marja-Liisa Olthuis in December.

Panda, M. (2012) *'Bridging'* and *'exit'* as two metaphors of multilingual education: A constructionist analysis. *Psychological Studies* 57 (2), 1–22.

Pasanen, A. (2003) Kielipesä ja revitalisaatio. Karjalaisten ja inarinsaamelaisten kielipesätoiminta [Language nest and revitalisation. language nest activities of the Karelian and Aanaar Saami people]. Pro gradu -tutkielma [Master's thesis]. Helsinki: Suomalais-ugrilainen laitos , University of Helsinki.

Pasanen, A. (2005) Kielipesätoiminta osana karjalan ja inarinsaamen kielen revitalisaatiota [Language nest activities as part of the revitalisation of the Carelian and Aanaar Saami languages]. In P. Kokkonen (ed.) *Sukukansaohjelman arki. Suomalais-ugrilainen perintö ja arkipäivä* [*The Daily Life of the Kindred Nations Programme*] (pp. 67–81). Helsinki: Castreniaumin toimitteita 64.

Pasanen, A. (2006) Saami language: language nests and revitalization. Paper presented at Conference on Endangered and Minority Languages and Language Varieties: Defining, Documenting and Developing. Georgetown University Round Table on Languages and Linguistics, 5 March.

Pasanen, A. (2010a) Will language nests change the direction of language shifts? On the language nests of Inari Saamis and Karelians. In H. Sulkala and H. Mantila (eds) *Planning a New Standard Language. Finnic Minority Languages Meet the New Millennium* (pp. 95–118). Studia Fennica Linguistica. Helsinki: Finnish Literature Society.

Pasanen, A. (2010b) Loppuraportti täydennyskoulutuksen harjoitteluosuudesta. Kielimestariharjoittelu, työharjoittelu inarinsaamenkielisissä työkohteissa ja kulttuurikurssit [A final report of CASLE's practical parts. Master–Apprentice training, practical training at AS working places and culture courses]. Anarâškielâ servi's Annual Report 2010. Aanaar: Anarâškielâ servi.

Pattanayak, D.P. (1992) Mothertongue awareness. Lecture given at Cambridge University, UK, September. Unpublished manuscript. (In press, in a 7-vol. collection of Pattanayak's articles, Bhubaneswar, India.)

Patten, A. and Kymlicka, W. (2003) Introduction: Language rights and political theory: Context, issues, and approaches. In W. Kymlicka and A. Patten (eds) *Language Rights and Political Theory* (pp. 1–51). Oxford: Oxford University Press.

Pennycook, A. (2004) Beyond mother tongues and access to English. Commentary. *Journal of Language, Identity and Education* 3 (2), 145–150.

Pérez Jacobsen, S. (2009) The contribution of postcolonial theory to intercultural bilingual education in Peru: An indigenous teacher training programme. In T. Skutnabb-Kangas, R. Phillipson, A. Mohanty and M. Panda (eds) *Social Justice through Multilingual Education* (pp. 201–219). Bristol: Multilingual Matters.

Pérez Jacobsen, S., Rao, A.G. and Skutnabb-Kangas, T. (2010) Book review of L. Meyer and B. Maldonado Alvarado (eds) *New World of Indigenous Resistance. Noam Chomsky and Voices from North, South and Central America. Language Policy* 9, 371–374.

Prelipceanu, N. (1996) We in the mirror. In Tóth (ed.), 27–32.

Peura, M. and Skutnabb-Kangas, T. (eds) (1994) *'Man kan vara tvåländare också'. Den sverigefinska minoritetens väg från tystnad till kamp* ['You Can Be Binational Too.' The Road of the Sweden–Finnish Minority From Silence to Struggle]. Stockholm: Sverigefinländarnas Arkiv.

Phillipson, R. (1992a) ELT – the native speaker's burden? Special IATEFL 25th Anniversary issue of *ELT Journal* 46 (1), 12–18.

Phillipson, R. (1992b) *Linguistic Imperialism*. Oxford: Oxford University Press.

Phillipson, R. (2009) *Linguistic Imperialism Continued*. New York: Routledge/Taylor & Francis.

Phillipson, R. (2012a) Imperialism and colonialism. In B. Spolsky (ed.) *The Cambridge Handbook of Language Policy* (pp. 203–225). Cambridge: Cambridge University Press.

Phillipson, R. (2012b) Macaulay alive and kicking: How linguistic imperialism continues. In A.G. Rao (ed.) *Foreign Languages in India: Towards a Glocal World*. Hyderabad: Orient BlackSwan.

Phillipson, R. and Skutnabb-Kangas, T. (2012) Getting language rights right. A response to Makoni. *Journal of Multicultural Discourses* 7 (1), 29–35.

Platero, D. (1975) Bilingual education in the Navajo nation. In R.C. Troike and N. Modiano (eds) *Proceedings of the First Inter-American Conference on Bilingual Education* (pp. 54–61). Arlington, VA: Center for Applied Linguistics.

Posey, D.A. (1999) Introduction: Culture and nature – the inextricable link. In D. Posey (ed.) *Cultural and Spiritual Values of Biodiversity. A Complementary Contribution to the Global Biodiversity Assessment* (pp. 3–18). New York/Leiden: UNEP/Intermediate Technologies, Leiden University.

Puntervold Bø, B. (1984) Naboholdninger til innvandrere (Attitudes of neighbours towards immigrants). Nabolagsundersøkelsen, Delrapport III. Forskningsrapport no. 13. Oslo: Diakonhjemmets sosiale høgskole.

Rampton, M.B.H. (1990) Displacing the 'native speaker': Expertise, affiliation and inheritance. *ELT Journal* 44 (2), 97–101.

Rasmus, M. (2008) *Bággu vuolgit, bággu birget. Sámemánáid ceavzinstrategiijat Suoma álbmotskuvlla ásodagain 1950–1960-logus* [The Need to Leave, the Need to Survive. Survival Strategies of Saami Children in the Dormitories of Primary Schools in Finland]. Oulu, Finland: University of Oulu.

Reagan, T. (1996) *Non-western educational traditions: Alternative approaches to educational thought and practice* (second edition 2000). Mahwah, New Jersey: Lawrence Erlbaum Associates.

Reagan, T. (2004) Objectification, positivism and language studies: A reconsideration. *Critical Inquiry in Language Studies: An International Journal* 1 (1), 41–60.

Reyhner, J. (1995) American Indian languages and United States language policy. In W. Fase, K. Jaspert and S. Kroon (eds) *The State of Minority Languages* (pp. 229–248). European Studies on Multilingualism (Vol. 5). Lisse, The Netherlands: Swets & Zeitlinger.

Reyhner, J. (1996) Language activists panel summary. In G. Cantoni (ed.) *Stabilizing Indigenous Languages*. Flagstaff, AZ: Northern Arizona University. Online at http://jan.ucc.nau.edu/~jar/SIL/

Reyhner, J. (2008) Promoting human rights through Indigenous language revitalization. *Intercultural Human Rights Law Review* 3, 151–189.

Reyhner, J. (2010) Indigenous language immersion schools for strong Indigenous identities. *Heritage Language Journal* 7 (2), 138–152.

Reyhner, J. and Singh, N.K. (2010a) Cultural genocide in Australia, Canada, New Zealand, and the United States: The destruction and transformation of Indigenous cultures. *Indigenous Policy Journal* 21 (3).

Reyhner, J. and Singh, N.K. (2010b) Aligning language education policies to international human rights standards. *eJournal of Education Policy*, Spring.

Reyhner, J., Cantoni, G., St. Clair, R.N. and Parsons Yazzie, E. (eds) (1999) *Revitalizing Indigenous Languages*. Flagstaff, AZ: Northern Arizona University Center for Excellence in Education.

Richardson, B. (1993) *People of Terra nullius. Betrayal and Rebirth in Aboriginal Canada*. Vancouver/Toronto: Douglas & McIntyre.

Ringbom, H. (2007) *Cross-linguistic Similarity in Foreign Language Learning*. Clevedon: Multilingual Matters.

Rubagumya, C.M. (2009) Language in education in Africa: Can monolingual policies work in multilingual societies? In J.A. Kleifgen and G.C. Bond (eds) *The Languages of Africa and the Diaspora. Educating for Language Awareness* (pp. 48–63). Bristol: Multilingual Matters.

Salminen, T. (2009) *Uralic (Finno-Ugrian) Languages. Classification of the Uralic (Finno-Ugrian) Languages, With Present Numbers of Speakers and Areas of Distribution*. http://www.helsinki.fi/~tasalmin/fu.html

Sammallahti, P. (1998) *The Saami Languages. An Introduction*. Kárášjohka, Norway: Davvi Girji OS.

Sammallahti, P. (2011) Mennyttä ja tulevaa [The past and the future]. Speech given at the Saami National Day Seminar at Oulu University, 6 February.

Sara, I-A. (2004) *Saamelaisuutta vahvistamassa. Sámi Radion toimittajien käsitykset saamelaismedian tehtävistä*[Strengthening the Saami identity. Saami Radio reporters' views about the purpose of the Saami media.] Jyväskylä: University of Jyväskylä.

Sarivaara, E. (2012) *Statuksettomat saamelaiset: Paikantumisia saamelaisuuden rajoilla [Non-Status Sámi. Locations Within Sámi Borderlands]*. Dieđut 2. Guovdageaidnu: Sámi Instituhtta.

Sitka, C. (1998) A sorry business. *Guardian Weekly*, 7 June, 25.

Skutnabb-Kangas, T. (1981) *Tvåspråkighet.* Lund: Liber Läromedel, 369 p. (Bilingualism).

Skutnabb-Kangas, T. (1984) *Bilingualism or Not – the Education of Minorities.* Clevedon: Multilingual Matters. [Translation and revision of Skutnabb-Kangas, T. (1981) *Tvåspråkighet.* Lund, Sweden: Liber Läromedel. Also see *Bilingualism* (2007) South Asian edition, with Foreword by Ajit K. Mohanty. Delhi: Orient Longman.]

Skutnabb-Kangas, T. (1988) Multilingualism and the education of minority children. In T. Skutnabb-Kangas and J. Cummins (eds) *Minority Education: From Shame to Struggle* (pp. 9–44). Clevedon: Multilingual Matters.

Skutnabb-Kangas, T. (1990) *Language, Literacy and Minorities.* London: Minority Rights Group.

Skutnabb-Kangas, T. (1999) Review of T.G. Reagan (1996) *Non-Western Educational Traditions: Alternative Approaches to Educational Thought and Practice. News from the Nordic Africa Institute* 3 (October), 34–35.

Skutnabb-Kangas, T. (2000) *Linguistic Genocide in Education – or Worldwide Diversity and Human Rights?* Mahwah, NJ/London: Lawrence Erlbaum. [South Asian updated edition (2008) Delhi: Orient Longman.]

Skutnabb-Kangas, T. (2004a) 'Do not cut my tongue, let me live and die with my language'. A comment on English and other languages in relation to linguistic human rights. *Journal of Language, Identity and Education* 3 (2), 127–134.

Skutnabb-Kangas, T. (2004b) Needed – constructive scholarly dialogue. *Journal of Language, Identity, and Education* 3 (2), 157–160.

Skutnabb-Kangas, T. (2005) Multilingual universities and globalisation – promoting creativity and linguistic human rights? Or? Keynote presentation at Bi- and Multilingual Universities – Challenges and Future Prospects Conference, University of Helsinki, Finland, 1–3 September. http://www.palmenia.helsinki.fi/congress/bilingual2005/program.asp

Skutnabb-Kangas, T. (2008) MLE for global justice: Issues, approaches, opportunities. In T. Skutnabb-Kangas, R. Phillipson, A. Mohanty and M. Panda (eds) *Social Justice through Multilingual Education* (pp. 36–62). Bristol: Multilingual Matters.

Skutnabb-Kangas, T. (2012) Indigenousness, human rights, ethnicity, language, and power. In O. García and G. Schweid Fishman (eds) *Cultural Autonomy and Fishmanian Sociolinguistics.* Special issue of *International Journal of the Sociology of Language* 213, 87–104.

Skutnabb-Kangas, T. and Aikio-Puoskari, U. (2003) Exclusion or inclusion – linguistic human rights for a linguistic minority, the Deaf Sign language users, and an indigenous people, the Saami. In P. Lee (ed.) *Many Voices, One Vision: The Right to Communicate in Practice* (pp. 59–88). Penang/London: Southbound/WACC.

Skutnabb-Kangas, T. and Cummins, J. (eds) (1988) *Minority Education: From Shame to Struggle.* Clevedon: Multilingual Matters.

Skutnabb-Kangas, T. and Dunbar, R. (2010) Indigenous children's education as linguistic genocide and a crime against humanity? A global view. *Gáldu Čála. Journal of Indigenous Peoples' Rights* 1. Guovdageaidnu/Kautokeino, Norway: Galdu, Resource Centre for the Rights of Indigenous Peoples (http://www.galdu.org). Available online at http://www.e-pages.dk/grusweb/55/

Skutnabb-Kangas, T. and Heugh, K. (2012) Introduction: Reclaiming sustainable linguistic diversity and multilingual education. In T. Skutnabb-Kangas and K. Heugh (eds) *Multilingual Education and Sustainable Diversity Work. From Periphery to Center* (pp. 1–31). New York: Routledge.

Skutnabb-Kangas, T. and Heugh, K. (eds) (2012) *Multilingual Education and Sustainable Diversity Work: From Periphery to Center List of contents.* New York: Routledge.

Skutnabb-Kangas, T. and McCarty, T. (2008) Clarification, ideological/epistemological underpinnings and implications of some concepts in bilingual education.

In J. Cummins and N.H. Hornberger (eds) *Bilingual Education. Encyclopedia of Language and Education* (Vol. 5; 2nd edn) (pp. 3–17). New York: Springer.

Skutnabb-Kangas, T. and Phillipson, R. (1989) Wanted! Linguistic human rights. ROLIG-papir No. 44. Roskilde, Denmark: Roskilde University Centre. [Microfiche available from ERIC Clearinghouse on Languages and Linguistics, Center for Applied Linguistics, Washington, DC.]

Skutnabb-Kangas, T. and Toukomaa, P. (1976) Teaching migrant children's mother tongue and learning the language of the host country in the context of the sociocultural situation of the migrant family. UNESCO Research Report No. 15. Tampere, Finland: University of Tampere, Department of Sociology and Social Psychology.

Skutnabb-Kangas, T., Maffi, L. and Harmon, D. (2003) *Sharing a World of Difference. The Earth's Linguistic, Cultural, and Biological Diversity*. Paris: UNESCO Publishing for UNESCO, Terralingua and World Wide Fund for Nature. Available online at www.terralingua.org/RecPublications.htm

Skutnabb-Kangas, T., Phillipson, R., Mohanty, A. and Panda, M. (eds) (2009) *Social Justice through Multilingual Education*. Bristol: Multilingual Matters.

Smith, G.H. and Rapatahana, V. (2012) English language as nemesis for Māori. In V. Rapatahana and P. Bunce (eds) *English Language as Hydra* (pp. 76–103). Linguistic Diversity and Language Rights Series. Bristol: Multilingual Matters.

Smolicz, J.J. (1979) *Culture and Education in a Plural Society*. Canberra: Curriculum Development Centre.

Smolicz, J.J. (1981) Core values and cultural identity. *Ethnic and Racial Studies* 4 (1), 75–90.

Suurpää, J. (2010) Saamelaiset ja syrjintä [The Saami and discrimination]. In K.T. Kokko (ed.) *Kysymyksiä saamelaisten oikeusasemasta [Issues on the Legal Position of the Saami]* (pp. 111–118). Sarja B, No. 30. Rovaniemi, Finland: Lapin yliopiston oikeustieteellisiä julkaisuja.

Svenska Kyrkan (2012) Våga vara minoritet. En rapport om minoritetsrättigheter i Sverige 2012 [Dare to be a minority. A report on minority rights in Sweden 2012], accessed 27 March 2012. www.svenskakyrkan.se/default.aspx?id=867553

Swain, M. (1984) A review of immersion education in Canada: Research and evaluation studies. In California Department of Education (eds) *Studies on Immersion Education: A Collection for U.S. Educators* (pp. 87–112). Sacramento, CA: Bilingual Education Office.

Swain, M. (1997) French immersion programs in Canada. In J. Cummins and D. Corson (eds) *Bilingual Education. Encyclopedia of Language and Education* (Vol. 5) (pp. 261–270). Dordrecht/Boston/London: Kluwer Academic Publishers.

Swain, M. and Johnson, R.K. (1997) Immersion education: A category within bilingual education. In R.K. Johnson and M. Swain (eds) *Immersion Education: International Perspectives* (pp. 1–16). Cambridge: Cambridge University Press.

Swain, M. and Lapkin, S. (1991) Additive bilingualism and French immersion education: The roles of language proficiency and literacy. In A.G. Reynolds (ed.) *Bilingualism, Multiculturalism, and Second Language Learning: The McGill Conference in Honour of Wallace E. Lambert* (pp. 203–216). Hillsdale, NJ: Lawrence Erlbaum.

Swain, M. and Lapkin, S. (2005) The evolving socio-political context of immersion education in Canada: Some implications for program development. *International Journal of Applied Linguistics* 15, 169–186.

Swain, M., Lapkin, S., Rowen, N. and Hart, D. (1990) The role of mother tongue literacy in third language learning. *VOX, Journal of the Australian Advisory Council on Languages and Multicultural Education* 4, 111–121.

Tesol (2012) http://www.tesol.org

Thomas, Chief J. (1994) *Teachings from the Longhouse*. Toronto: Stoddart.

Thomas, W.P. and Collier, V.P. (2002) *A National Study of School Effectiveness for Language Minority Students' Long-term Academic Achievement*. Santa Cruz, CA: Center for

Research on Education, Diversity and Excellence, University of California, Santa Cruz. http://repositories.cdlib.org/crede/finalrpts/1_1_final or http://crede.berkeley.edu/research/crede/research/llaa/1.1_final.html

Tiersma, P.M. (2012) Language policy in the United States. In P.M. Tiersma and L.M. Solan (eds) *Oxford Handbook of Language and Law* (pp. 248–260). Oxford: Oxford University Press.

Tollefson, J.W. (2004) Theory and action in language policy and planning. Commentary. *Journal of Language, Identity and Education* 3 (2), 150–155.

Toukomaa, P. and Skutnabb-Kangas, T. (1977) The intensive teaching of the mother tongue to migrant children of pre-school age, UNESCO Research Report No. 26. Helsinki/Tampere: Finnish National Commission for UNESCO/Department of Sociology and Social Psychology, University of Tampere.

Tuhiwai Smith, L. (2004) [1999] *Deconstructing Methodologies: Research and Indigenous Peoples*. New York/Dunedin: Zed Books/University of Otago Press.

Turley, F. (2010) *The PRINCE2 Training Manual. A Common Sense Approach to Learning and Understanding PRINCE2*. http://www.mgmtplaza.com/elearn/files/The-PRINCE2-Training-Manual.pdf

UNESCO (1953) *The Use of the Vernacular Languages in Education*. Monographs on Fundamental Education No. VIII. Paris: UNESCO.

UNESCO (2003) Education in a multilingual world. UNESCO Education Position Paper. Paris: UNESCO. http://unesdoc.unesco.org/images/0012/001297/129728e.pdf

Valencia, J.F. and Cenoz, J. (1992) The role of bilingualism in foreign language acquisition: Learning English in the Basque country. *Journal of Multilingual and Multicultural Development* 13 (5), 433–449.

Waitangi Tribunal (1986) *Finding of the Waitangi Tribunal Relating to Te Reo Maori and a Claim Lodged by Huirangi Waikerepuru and Nga Kaiwhakapumau I Te Reo Incorporated Society*. Wellington: V.R. Ward, Government Printer.

Walsh, C. (2004) Geopolíticas del conocimiento, interculturalidad y descolonialización. *Boletín ICCI ARY Rimay* 6 (60). http://icci.nativeweb.org/boletin/60/walsh.html#N_1

Walter, S. and Benson, C. (2012) Language policy and medium of instruction in formal education. In B. Spolsky (ed.) *The Cambridge Handbook of Language Policy* (pp. 278–300). Cambridge: Cambridge University Press.

Warschauer, M. (1998) Technology and indigenous language revitalization: Analyzing the experience of Hawai'i. *Canadian Modern Language Review* 55 (1), 140–161.

Warschauer, M. (2003) *Technology and Social Inclusion. Rethinking the Digital Divide*. Cambridge, MA: MIT Press.

Westin, C. (1984) *Majoritet om minoritet. En studie i etnisk tolerans i 80-talets Sverige [The Majority Regarding the Minority. A Study of Ethnic Tolerance in 1980s Sweden]*. Stockholm: Liber.

Westin, C. (1988) Den toleranta opinionen. Inställningen till invandrare 1987 [The tolerant opinion. Attitudes towards immigrants in 1987]. DEIFO-rapport No. 8. Stockholm: DEIFO.

Winstead, T., Lawrence, A., Brantmeier, E.J. and Frey, C.J. (2008) Language, sovereignty, cultural contestation and American Indian schools: No child left behind and a Navajo test case. *Journal of American Indian Education* 47 (1), 46–64.

Wilson, W.H. (1999) The sociopolitical context of establishing Hawaiian-medium education. In S. May (ed.) *Indigenous Community-based Education* (pp. 95–108). Clevedon: Multilingual Matters.

Wilson, W.H. and Kamanā, K. (2001) 'Mai Loko Mai O Ka 'I'ini: Proceeding from a dream' – the 'Aha Punana Leo Connection in Hawaiian language revitalization. In L. Hinton and K. Hale (eds) *The Green Book of Language Revitalization in Practice* (pp. 147–176). San Diego, CA: Academic Press.

Wilson, W.H. and Kamanā, K. (2009) Indigenous youth bilingualism from a Hawaiian activist perspective. In T.L. McCarty and L.T. Wyman (eds) Special issue on *Indigenous Youth and Bilingualism* of *Journal of Language, Identity, and Education* 8 (5), 369–337.

Wilson, W.H., Kamanā, K. and Rawlins, N. (2006) Nāwahi Hawaiian Laboratory School. *Journal of American Indian Education* 45 (2), 42–44.

YLE News (2011) 21 November.